Jeffrey Weeks was born in 1945 in Rhondda, Wales, and educated at University College, London. He is currently a lecturer in Sociology at the University of Kent. He is the author of *Sex, Politics and Society* (1981) and the co-author (with Sheila Rowbotham) of *Socialism and the New Life* (1977).

D1394236

# Coming Out

Homosexual Politics in Britain, from the
Nineteenth Century to the Present

## Jeffrey Weeks

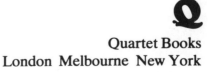

Quartet Books
London  Melbourne  New York

For Angus, with love

First published by Quartet Books Limited 1977
A member of the Namara Group
27/29 Goodge Street, London W1P 1FD

Reprinted 1983

Printed in Great Britain by Nene Litho
and bound by Woolnough Bookbinding
both of Wellingborough, Northants

ISBN 0 7043 3175 6

# Contents

## Preface and Acknowledgements

'Coming Out' is usually seen as a personal process, the acceptance, and public demonstration, of the validity of one's own homosexuality. But it can also be seen as a historic process, the gradual emergence and articulation of a homosexual identity and public presence. In this book I have attempted to trace the main features of this process in Britain over the past hundred years. Most books on the subject tell of hostility to homosexuality. Without avoiding this, I have tried to shift the emphasis towards the reaction of homosexuals themselves to hostile labelling, medical stigmatization, legal and social oppression. I have concentrated on the most coherent expression of homosexual resistance, in the reform groupings. The book tells, therefore, only a partial story, but one that has, nevertheless, been almost totally ignored.

This book would have been more incomplete than it is without the advice and encouragement of many friends and colleagues. For their helpful comments, references, sympathy, practical assistance or support I should like to thank Laurence Collinson, Chris Cook, Keith Hose, Ronald Hyam, Philip Jones, Jean L'Esperance, Mary McIntosh, Eileen Pattison, Ken Plummer, Sheila Rowbotham, Helen Rugen, Raphael Samuel, F. B. Smith, Jeremy Seabrook, Janet Scott, Peter Wells. For access to papers in his care I am especially grateful to Anthony Reid, and to him and his wife Betty for their kind hospitality. Sue Bruley, Bob Cant and Barry Davis read various chapters and gave me invaluable comments and encouragement, for which I am very grateful. My friends and comrades on the *Gay Left* collective gave me much stimulation during the writing of the book: Keith Birch, Gregg Blachford, Bob Cant, Derek Cohen, Emmanuel Cooper, Randal Kincaid, Nigel Young. For advice throughout the writing of the book I must thank William Miller of Quartet, and I am grateful to Peter Ford for his patience and care with the typescript. To Micky Burbidge I am deeply indebted for his warm encouragement, advice and ever-helpful comments. Angus Suttie has lived with the book (and with me) since its birth. His support has been especially vital, and the dedication is a small token of my thanks.

For permission to quote from copyright sources I have to thank: the Provost and Scholars of King's College, Cambridge, and Miss

Felicity Ashbee for extracts from the Ashbee Journals; Sheffield City Libraries for the Edward Carpenter collection; George Allen and Unwin for the published works of Edward Carpenter; The Society of Authors on behalf of the estate of Havelock Ellis; and the Society of Authors as the literary representative of the estate of A. E. Housman; Jonathan Cape Ltd, publishers of A. E. Housman's *Collected Poems*; Antony Grey for items from his essay on 'Homosexual Law Reform' in Brian Frost (ed.) *The Tactics of Pressure*; William Heinemann Ltd for items from H. Montgomery Hyde's *The Other Love*; Weidenfeld and Nicolson for quotations from Peter Wildeblood's *Against the Law*; Penguin Books Ltd for a quotation from Juliet Mitchell's *Psychoanalysis and Feminism*; George Allen and Unwin for quotations from Peter G. Richards's *Parliament and Conscience*; Lovat Dickson and the Radclyffe Hall Estate; Oxford University Press for Peter Gunn's *Vernon Lee (Violet Paget) 1856–1935*; Paul Elek Ltd for Dora Russell's *The Tamarisk Tree*; Longmans for quotations from Gordon Westwood's *Society and the Homosexual* and *A Minority*; Duckworth and Co. Ltd for quotations from Charlotte Wolff's *Love Between Women*; the Monthly Review Press for a quotation from Christopher Caudwell, *Studies and Further Studies in a Dying Culture*; *Gay News* for quotations from issues nos. 6 and 83–5; John Lauritsen and David Thorstad for quotations from their *The Early Homosexual Rights Movement*. I am further grateful to Jonathan Cape Ltd, who hold the copyright, for permission to quote from an unpublished letter of Laurence Housman. My apologies to other copyright holders who may have been inadvertently omitted.

# Introduction

*'The accomplished languages of Europe in the nineteenth century
supply no terms for this persistent feature of human psychology,
without importing some implication of disgust, disgrace, vitupera-
tion'* – J. A. Symonds, A Problem in Modern Ethics *(1891)*

Attitudes have changed since J. A. Symonds offered his bleak comments in the early 1890s. The English language now has a host of
words – good, bad and neutral – with which to contemplate homosexuality, while the gay liberation movement over the past decade
has provided an immense stimulus to homosexual self-expression,
and self-definition. But still, as Dennis Altman put it, 'to be a homosexual in our society is to be constantly aware that one bears a
stigma'. And while homosexuality is now a subject that is much
discussed, it is still apparently little understood, and in particular
little effort has been made to understand the homosexual consciousness. This book is intended as an exploration of a particular homosexual experience – that of the reform groupings – but in pursuing
this I hope to be able to offer some more general comments about the
nature of the changing homosexual situation in Britain over the past
hundred years.

The reform movements, though usually tiny in size and limited in
achievement, have reflected and crystallized the changing homosexual
consciousness during the past hundred years. They were not imposed
on barren ground but grew from soil that had been turned and cultivated over a long period. Two themes are therefore essentially linked.
First, there are the social and ideological circumstances from which
the reformers drew their stimulus, and against which they directed
their efforts. And secondly, there is the work of the reformers themselves – who were usually homosexual and often necessarily secretive.
Their labours were a basic but creative response to the culture which
defined and oppressed them.

Unfortunately our historical understanding of homosexuality is
still limited, and the framework for grasping the implications of
changing attitudes is immature. Most of the works that we have are
either anecdotal and gossipy in style, relying for evidence to a large
extent on famous homosexuals and notorious court cases, or products of special pleading. Part of the difficulty is that homosexuality

is usually seen as a separate 'problem', to be explored in isolation from other social phenomena. In fact a closer examination reveals that attitudes to homosexuality are inextricably linked to wider questions: of the function of the family, the evolution of gender roles, and of attitudes to sexuality generally. And far from being, in Professor François Lafitte's words, a 'very minor' facet of social history,[1] 'official' and popular responses to homosexuality and the homosexual can be taken as crucial indicators of wider notions of sexuality.

The late nineteenth century sees a deepening hostility towards homosexuality, alongside the emergence of new definitions of homosexuality and the homosexual. I believe these developments can only be properly understood as part of the restructuring of the family and sexual relations consequent upon the triumph of urbanization and industrial capitalism. The result of these changes was the emergence in a recognizably modern form of concepts and meanings which are now commonplaces of public discussion: for example, the notion of 'the housewife', 'the prostitute', 'the child'; and the concept of the 'homosexual'.

This is only surprising to generations brought up on the belief that certain social concepts are given, and correspond to eternal biological and historical truths. Fatherhood, motherhood, childhood, normality, abnormality, 'natural' sexuality, 'unnatural' sexuality: all are seen as being based on inherent and basic 'instincts', unchanging through history. But cross-cultural and historical studies have shown that there is a multitude of acceptable patterns, which vary widely from our own. Different societies define 'masculinity' and 'femininity' differently, stressing different qualities, interests, occupations as 'male' and 'female', while the social functions of 'fatherhood' and 'motherhood' and 'childhood' have been interpreted in many different ways. So has sexuality, which, as J. H. Gagnon and W. Simon put it, 'is subject to the socio-cultural moulding to a degree surpassed by few other forms of human behaviour'.[2] Seen in this light, sexuality appears less as a determinant of gender identity and more as the *vehicle* for expressing culturally determined social roles.

Homosexuality has existed throughout history, in all types of society, among all social classes and peoples, and it has survived qualified approval, indifference and the most vicious persecution. But what have varied enormously are the ways in which various societies have regarded homosexuality, the meanings they have attached to it, and how those who were engaged in homosexual activity viewed themselves. These are the crucial questions, for they raise the whole issue of consciousness. Christopher Caudwell warned that:

> The natural human failing is to suppose nothing changes, that ideas are eternal, and that what is denoted by a word is as changeless and invariant as the word. Wisdom consists chiefly in learning that these vague gestures towards part of reality, gestures we call concepts, not only cannot describe the things indicated, but cannot even point to the same thing.[3]

We tend to think now that the word 'homosexual' has an unvarying meaning, beyond time and history. In fact it is itself a product of history, a cultural artefact designed to express a particular concept. As Symonds indicated, few non-pejorative words existed before the late nineteenth century. The term 'homosexuality' was not even invented until 1869 (coined by the Swiss doctor Karoly Maria Benkert), and it did not enter English currency until the 1890s. Havelock Ellis, the pioneering sexologist, seems to have been the first to use the word widely in England. The other common term, 'inversion', did not become common until the same period, and it is only then that we find the gradual use of terms for the homosexual person which have in the twentieth century become general: words such as 'invert' and 'homosexual'. The shift in consciousness and awareness indicated by the general adoption in the contemporary homosexual world of the word 'gay' (which in the last century referred to 'loose women') parallels what occurred in the late nineteenth century in the use of these new words. They are not just new labels for old realities: they point to a changing reality, both in the ways a hostile society labelled homosexuality, and in the way those stigmatized saw themselves.

The focus of historical inquiry therefore has to be on the developing social attitudes, their origins and their rationale, for, without these, discussion of homosexuality becomes virtually incomprehensible. And as a starting-point we have to distinguish between homosexual behaviour, which is universal, and a homosexual identity, which is historically specific – and a comparatively recent phenomenon in Britain.

This is centrally related to the evolution of what Mary McIntosh has called a 'homosexual role': 'The creation of a specialised, despised and punished role of homosexual keeps the bulk of society pure in rather the same way that the similar treatment of some kinds of criminals helps keep the rest of society law abiding.'[4] This has two effects: it first helps to provide a clear-cut threshold between permissible and impermissible behaviour; and secondly, it helps to segregate those labelled as 'deviants' from others, and thus contains and limits their behaviour pattern.

Although there are signs of the emergence of this role from at least the seventeenth century in Britain, it crystallized into a modern form only in the late nineteenth century. This is the immediate context for the evolution of a homosexual identity and the related concepts of the 'exclusive homosexual' and of the 'homosexual condition' which still control our views of homosexuality.

Inevitably, the concepts which emerged from the nineteenth century carried with them a weight of ideological baggage, much of it stemming from the intertwined Hebraic and Christian traditions, in which the taboo against homosexual behaviour is deeply rooted. No one who has lived in the West, and particularly in Britain or North America, can deny the dreadful feelings of guilt and sin that our culture still produces. Attitudes to homosexuality, at least on a formal level, are still shot through with medieval hangovers, both in phraseology and attitudes, which suggest that sex outside rigidly defined areas is at best something to be tolerated, and at worst dirty and sinful.[5]

But ideologies do not survive by magic, or even by historical inertia. They go on because they serve a social function, in rationalizing and articulating certain material needs, and the material needs as defined by those who control society. To talk too freely about a single Judaeo-Christian tradition ignores the different circumstances in which the taboo has revealed itself and the variations and changes in Christian teachings in the last two millennia.

In the first place, it is not just homosexuality as such which is condemned in the Christian tradition, but all forms of sex which do not lead to procreation. This idea of 'purposive sex' was not new in Christianity: what was new in the Judaeo-Christian formulations was the claim that sex was *only* for procreation, and that all other cases were perversions. Authoritative theologians argued that acts of sodomy were the gravest of sins because, by definition, they could not result in pregnancy, whereas fornication, seduction, rape or incest could. These medieval attitudes persisted well into the nineteenth century.

The second aspect of Judaeo-Christian taboos is that they are directed chiefly against male sexuality. Lesbian acts are referred to in some of the medieval church penitentials, but these generally put lesbianism low on the list of sins. There appear to have been no provisions specifically against lesbian acts in any West European criminal code, apart from one statute of the Emperor Charles V in the sixteenth century, and this seems to have had little impact, either in practice or on local legislation in Germany. This is in line with the general ignoring of female sexuality in most criminal codes. A Dutch historian has traced this phenomenon to the idea that the procreative capacity lay exclusively in the male semen. There was no concept of the ovum, and so women were seen purely as passive receptacles. For this reason, women could not frustrate nature's procreative aims in the same way as men. It was not until the nineteenth century that sexual ideology attempted to deny female sexuality altogether, and then, as Havelock Ellis pointed out, this ideology was limited chiefly to certain countries, particularly Italy, Britain and the United States. But there was nevertheless a long earlier tradition of linking 'excessive' female sexuality with a challenge to nature, as in the association of witchcraft with sexual lasciviousness, which can be traced back at least to the fifteenth century.

The third element of continuity is linked with this: the association of 'deviant' sex with all forms of social unorthodoxy, and the use of this as a means of social control. Sex and its regulation is so basic to human society that breaches of the norms have invariably been equated with heresy and treason from the Ancient World to the present. The witch-hunting of reds and homosexuals that Senator Joseph McCarthy indulged in in the 1950s was a climax to a long tradition. It is this 'scapegoating' which is a major constituent of the homosexual role as it developed in the eighteenth and nineteenth centuries.

All the major elements of the medieval taboos are present in modern hostility towards homosexuality, but the contents of the kaleidoscope have been shaken and the pattern is different. And this is because, increasingly over the past hundred years, the reference point has not been 'religion' or 'sin', but 'family', and, in particular, the roles that men and women are expected to act out in the family. For it is within the specific context of the capitalist family that modern concepts of homosexuality have developed, though much of the language and terminology may have derived from pre-capitalist cultures.

Men are socialized in our society by being taught they are not women,[6] and it is significant that, as the legal penalties against homosexuality increased, it was essentially against men that they were directed. The male homosexual has been seen as a threat to the stability of roles enshrined in the family. The massive impact of industrialization and urbanization on family patterns, the gradual exclusion of women from the primary work force in the nineteenth century, the creation of a mass, propertyless working class, whose labour power was reproduced and serviced in the bosom of the family, had profound and still unexplored effects on the socially ascribed gender roles of men and women. What is apparent is that, as social roles became more clearly defined, and as sexuality was more closely harnessed ideologically to the reproduction of the population, so the social condemnation of male homosexuality increased.

This is clearly seen in the development of harsher legal penalties in the last decades of the nineteenth century, and is reflected ideologically in the evolution of new concepts of homosexuality as a derangement or a sickness. These set the parameters of the homosexual consciousness, but within their confines the possibilities existed for a creative response. Such a response can be traced from the nineteenth century on two levels: first, in a variegated sub-culture, where homosexuals met, developed a mode of social intercourse, and explored a network of ritualized sexual contacts; and secondly, in the reform groupings, which were themselves at first part of this sub-cultural response, but which in their urge to 'educate for reform' had to stretch beyond, develop a public front, adopt a 'respectable' face.

It was Germany that was to experience the most public manifestation of a homosexual consciousness: in a wide-ranging public debate, in relatively large-scale reform organization, in a mountain of books, and in the emergence of authorities able, and sometimes all too willing, to express their opinions. In Britain, not unexpectedly, the public manifestation was less fervent. The detritus from the humiliation of Oscar Wilde and others had its drear effect. Nevertheless, a small-scale but culturally significant reform movement had emerged by the early part of this century. Although influenced initially by men such as Havelock Ellis and Edward Carpenter, it developed a long and creative life of its own.

Four phases may be discerned. The first was essentially concerned with piecing together an identity, and laying the basis for future reforming efforts. For lesbians, this was an even more painful process than for homosexual men, and a separate section examines the lesbian milieu. Although rendered utopian by the social disasters of the inter-war years, a stretched line of continuity survived until the 1940s. The second phase was more narrowly directed: to obtaining limited, if fundamentally necessary, legal changes. Its choice of achievement dictated its methods: respectability, lobbying, deference. Although many homosexuals were involved, it was not concerned so much with the validity of homosexuality as with legal adjustments.

It achieved its apotheosis in the late 1960s, with the achievement of a limited reform, and limped on into the 1970s. But it was effectively transcended by a new type of movement, born of new social circumstances, as the 1970s proceeded. The gay liberation movement was itself a product of the breakdown of the rigid taboos about sex which had blighted lives for generations, but it went further to question not only modes of sexual behaviour but rigid gender divisions themselves. The result was immensely liberating, and its influence was profound, not only on homosexuals but among feminists and on the left generally. But its major achievement so far has been to give rise to a fourth type of reform movement which combines the methods of the third (militant, defiant, open) with the limited ambitions of the second. This looks set fair to dominate the scene for the rest of the decade.

The succeeding chapters will explore in detail these reform groupings, and the ways in which they were marked, and marred, by the circumstances of their birth. But this exploration will also amount to an implicit critique of the sexual liberalism which has dominated most reform efforts. There have been three central characteristics of this. First, there has been the implicit belief in the fixed characteristics of men and women, either genetically determined or socially and emotionally structured, which has sanctified the social differences between the sexes and defined homosexuality as a deviation. Secondly, because these differences were seen as inherent, there has been an overwhelming belief that reason, good sense and proper education are the only sensible roads to reform. If men and women of goodwill could only understand what nature had laid down, then surely the road to toleration was stretching towards infinity before us. Finally, there has been an absence of any real historical sense of the deeply rooted but changing nature of homosexual oppression.

Hostility towards homosexuality has usually been seen as an arbitrary figment of men's unreason, which would soon be thrown out on the junkyard of prehistory. All campaigners for homosexual rights until recently enjoyed an ambiguous dialogue with this tradition, and part of the fascination of the period lies in unravelling the tensions and conflicts that necessarily arose. A more radical view of homosexuality will have to take account of the varieties and diversity of sexual expression, of the arbitrariness of social labels, of the cultural moulding of gender and sexual identities: in short, of the historical creation of sexual beliefs and attitudes, and of the radical changes needed to transform them. These themes will emerge more clearly in the chapters ahead.

*Part One*

# DEFINITIONS AND SELF-DEFINITIONS

# 1
## From Sin to Crime

*'There is no worse crime than that with which the prisoners are charged' – Sir John Bridges (magistrate at the committal proceedings of Oscar Wilde, April 1895)*

Law does not create public opinion but it does shape and reinforce it. For close on a hundred years the male homosexual consciousness in Britain has been dominated by the legal situation. Between 1885 and 1967 all male homosexual acts, whether committed in public or private, were illegal. A series of dramatic court cases, countless minor convictions, the ever-present threat of blackmail and public disgrace, underlined the formal legal position and helped to perpetuate an oppressively hostile public opinion. Until 1967, therefore, the main ambition of reformers was to change the law. After 1967 the situation eased a little. The state partially removed itself from direct intervention in personal lives, and a free space was created for men in England and Wales, as long as they were aged over twenty-one, acted in private and worked outside the merchant navy and armed services. But it is also true that since 1967 the number of convictions for homosexual offences has actually increased, while police surveillance and harassment of homosexual meeting-places continues. At the beginning of the nineteenth century, the utilitarian philosopher Jeremy Bentham classed homosexuality as an 'imaginary offence', dependent on changing concepts of taste and morality. But in Britain in the 1970s the law has still not finally given up its function of being the 'guardian of the righteous'. In the social-morality debates of the 1880s which preceded the passing of the anti-homosexual Labouchère Amendment in 1885, one of the participants advocated making the fear of the consequences a deterrent. The deterrent legal situation has made the choice of a homosexual lifestyle more difficult. But, in the furnace fanned by the oppressive legal situation, a modern homosexual identity has been forged.

Before 1885 the only legislation which directly affected homosexual acts was that referring to sodomy or buggery. Even so, this 'sin against nature' evoked horrors enough. The classic position was summed up by the jurist, Sir William Blackstone, in 1811, who felt that its very mention was a 'disgrace to human nature'. But this defiance of nature's will was not a specifically homosexual offence.

The 1533 Act of Henry VIII, which first brought sodomy within the scope of statute law, superseding ecclesiastical law, adopted the same criterion as the Church: all acts of sodomy were equally condemned as being 'against nature', whether between man and woman, man and beast, or man and man. The penalty for the 'Abominable Vice of Buggery' was death. This keynote Act, re-enacted in 1563, was the basis for all homosexual convictions up to 1885.[1] The central point was that the law was directed against a series of sexual acts, not a particular type of person. There was no concept of the homosexual in law, and homosexuality was regarded not as a particular attribute of a certain type of person but as a potential in all sinful creatures. The law against sodomy was a central aspect of the taboo on all non-procreative sex. Lesbianism, as usual in criminal codes, was ignored.

There can be no doubt of the fear that the 'sin' often evoked in the public mind, including, it seems, the minds of those who practised it. One of the sailors court-martialled for buggery on H.M.S. *Africaine* in 1815, in a desperate attempt to clear his name, spoke of 'a crime which would to God t'were never more seen on earth from those shades of hellish darkness whence to the misery of Man its propensity has been vomited forth'. The man's hysteria may be pardonable when confronted with the yard arm, but the epithet 'sodomite' was certainly one to be feared well into the nineteenth century. There are occasional references to riots against sodomites, and intermittent purges on buggery certainly took place in schools, the navy, military establishments and the colonies.

Laws on the statute book, however, are fallible guides to behaviour and enforcement. There is no easy way of tracing popular attitudes, particularly as most of the evidence comes from trials which often served as theatrical events to both evoke and reinforce public opinion. Moreover, the actual enforcement of the law varied, as between different social classes and during different periods. There appears to have been a spate of convictions at the end of the seventeenth century, coinciding, significantly enough, with a morality crusade and the emergence of a distinctive male homosexual sub-culture.[2] But there was a decline in the number of convictions in the late eighteenth and early nineteenth centuries, owing to the need to prove both penetration and the emission of seed (following a legal decision of 1781); though the law was usually severe once emission had been proved. In 1810, for instance, four out of five convicted sodomists were hanged against only 63 out of 471 for other capital offences. And the law was particularly severe on members of the armed forces, where it was employed with particularly dramatic and exemplary results. In 1811 Ensign John Hepburn and drummer Thomas White were 'launched into eternity' before a 'vast concourse of spectators', including many notables and members of the Royal Family. And in February 1816, four members of the crew of the *Africaine* were hanged for buggery after a major naval scandal. The navy, in fact, was even more severe than civil society: buggery had been mentioned in the Articles of War since the seventeenth century, and was treated as seriously as desertion, mutiny or murder. The death penalty was ruthlessly applied – you were more likely to be hanged for buggery than for mutiny or desertion – and sentences of a thousand lashes were not uncommon.

The armed services, then as now, believed themselves to have special problems of order and discipline: sexual contact between men, and especially across ranks, threatened to tear asunder the carefully maintained hierarchy.[3] But then perhaps the ideological condemnation of the sin and vice of buggery, with its evocation of disaster and death, had a special impact on a machinery geared for war. Certainly, in the eighteenth and nineteenth centuries the numbers of buggery trials were directly related to whether or not Britain was at war or in a state of social turmoil.

As part of his consolidation of the English criminal law, Sir Robert Peel actually tightened up the law on sodomy in 1826. The need to prove emission of seed as well as penetration was removed, and the death penalty re-enacted. This was particularly striking at a period when the death penalty was abolished for over a hundred other crimes. The criminal reforms of the 1820s were a crucial stage in what has been termed a 'grappling for control', the process whereby the local, semi-amateur system of law enforcement of the eighteenth century was replaced during the nineteenth century by a network of professional police forces, responsible for the prevention of crime, the detection of offenders and, above all, the maintenance of order. This was an essential ruling-class response to the problems created by the spread of industrial capitalism and urbanization and the growth of a mass working class. It is startling, therefore, that the ancient taboos against sodomy should have been reinforced during this period. When Lord John Russell attempted to remove 'unnatural offences' from the list of capital crimes in 1841, he was forced to withdraw through lack of parliamentary support.[4]

But severe as the law was, it was not always obvious that its upholders knew what was actually meant by 'buggery'. As late as 1817 a man was sentenced to death under the buggery laws for oral sex with a boy (he was later pardoned), and the phrase with which Sir Robert Peel forbore to mention sodomy in Parliament, 'the crime *inter Christianos non nominandum*' (the crime not to be named among Christians), was widely used to cover all forms of non-procreative sex well into the nineteenth century. In 1854 Sir George Rickards, a political economist, used the same phrase in fulminating against birth control, and as late as 1868 the parliamentary candidature of Lord Amberley (Bertrand Russell's father) was marked by press attacks on him for advocating 'unnatural crimes' (meaning contraception).[5] 'Sodomy' was a portmanteau term for any forms of sex that did not have conception as their aim, from homosexual acts to birth control.

Nevertheless, indulgence in buggery was assumed to be the characteristic feature of what we would now call a homosexual. When two transvestites, Ernest Boulton and Frederick William Park, were arrested in 1870, they were immediately examined for anal penetration, though the medical evidence was confused and inconclusive.[6] And in 1895 Oscar Wilde was stirred into his disastrous libel case against the Marquess of Queensberry after being accused of 'posing as a somdomite [*sic*]'. Posing was enough! As Lord Sumner reaffirmed in 1918, sodomites were stamped with 'the hall-mark of a specialised and extraordinary class as much as if they had carried on their bodies some physical pecularities'.[7] It is therefore not surprising that many early reformers went out of their way to assert disingenuously that homosexual buggery was rare to the point of being exceptional. Better the lie that alleviates than the truth that kills.

The death penalty for buggery, tacitly abandoned after 1836, was finally abolished in England and Wales in 1861 (in Scotland in 1889) to be replaced by penal servitude of between ten years and life. It was to remain thus for homosexual activities until 1967. But this was a prelude not to a liberalization of the law but to a tightening of its grip. By section 11 (the 'Labouchère Amendment') of the 1885 Criminal Law Amendment Act, *all* male homosexual acts short of buggery, whether committed in public or private, were made illegal:

'Any male person who, in public or private, commits, or is a party to the commission of, or procures or attempts to procure the commission by any male person of any act of gross indecency with another male person, shall be guilty of a misdemeanour, and being convicted thereof shall be liable at the discretion of the court to be imprisoned for any term not exceeding two years, with or without hard labour.'

And thirteen years later, the Vagrancy Act of 1898 clamped down on homosexual 'soliciting'.[8] These two enactments represented a singular hardening of the legal situation and were a crucial factor in the determination of modern attitudes. Although products of traditional beliefs, their impact led to a significant shift in sexual meanings.

The Labouchère Amendment has usually been seen as an almost accidental event: passed late at night with few M.P.s present in the House of Commons, and even fewer aware of what they were about. Sir Travers Humphreys, who was junior counsel in the Wilde case, summed up this attitude: 'it is doubtful whether the House fully appreciated that the words in "public or private" in the new clause had completely altered the law'; while François Lafitte has spoken of 'a confusion, if not a deception, of Parliamentary thinking' in the passing of the Amendment.[9] The political significance of this is clear, for if an Act was passed so arbitrarily, and had no wider significance, then it could equally unilaterally be repealed. That was the rationale behind the single-issue campaigns in the 1960s to repeal the Labouchère Amendment. But the situation is actually more complex than this would suggest. Henry Labouchère, a demagogic radical M.P., may well have had a deep dislike of homosexuality, but the Amendment fitted in extremely well with other changes. The acting Speaker of the House overruled a challenge to the relevance of the motion, while the government accepted it, and even increased the penalty from one to two years. Labouchère had no doubt that the government was anxious to act on the issue, and clearly neither the House of Commons nor the government saw any total incompatibility between the various parts of the new Act.

The gross-indecency clause of the Criminal Law Amendment Act has to be seen against a background of a sharpening definition of and hostility towards homosexuality in the late nineteenth century, not only in Britain but in other European countries, especially Germany. The establishment of the German Empire after 1870 saw the imposition of the anti-homosexual measures of the Prussian penal code on all the German states (as Paragraph 175 of the German penal code). Under this, mutual masturbation between men was not illegal (unlike the situation in England and Wales after 1885), but all other male homosexual activities were. Even in countries like France and the Netherlands, which had, under the Napoleonic Code, removed homosexual offences from criminal sanctions, social hostility sharply increased towards the end of the century.[10]

Beyond this was a wider change in social roles and sexual attitudes which was to see in the next generation the reconceptualization of social attitudes to the family, the role of women in the home and in society, and the position of children and adolescents, among other changes. It is significant, therefore, that legislation on homosexuality should have been intimately tied in with changes in the law regarding prostitution and would remain so until the Wolfenden Report in 1957. Both the 1885 and the 1898 Acts were primarily concerned with prostitution. The Vagrancy Act set out to control soliciting for immoral purposes, while the original purpose of the Criminal Law Amendment Act was to 'make further provision for the protection of women and girls, the suppression of brothels and other purposes'. Its chief result, apart from its blighting effect on the lives of homosexuals, was to raise the age of sexual consent for girls from thirteen to sixteen. It was the culmination of some fifteen years of agitation concerning prostitution, and a concerted attack in the early 1880s on the 'white slave trade'. A combination of feminists and social-morality crusaders, with Josephine Butler as the most prominent figure, had campaigned vigorously against what they saw as the 'double standard of morality' – one law for women, another for men – enshrined in the Contagious Diseases Acts of the 1860s. Under these Acts, ostensibly designed to protect the armed forces from venereal disease, any woman could in a number of garrison towns in the South of England be picked up and medically examined on suspicion of prostitution. Men were exempt. This attack on the civil rights of (usually) working-class women aroused bitter opposition among sections of the working class, the women attacked and middle-class feminists with a social-purity bias. 'When a secret attack is made upon the liberty and virtue of our wives, daughters and sweethearts, there is a danger to our most secret instincts.'[11]

After the Acts were suspended in 1883 (to be finally repealed in 1886), the emphasis of the campaigns changed from rescuing the fallen prostitute to challenging what was seen as the root of the matter – the 'double standard' – with the aim of ensuring that 'the Law of Purity is equally binding on all men and women alike'. This became the representative moral tone of the moral-purity campaigners of the 1880s. And, in their mind, homosexuality was barely differentiated from prostitution. J. A. Symonds's doctor had advised him to take a prostitute or a wife to cure his homosexual longings. For the morality crusaders, however, both were part of the continuum of undifferentiated lust, products of men's sexual selfishness. Let one crack appear in the moral order and floods of lustfulness would sweep society away. In their minds the syndromes of schoolboy masturbation, public-school 'immorality' (meaning homosexuality)

and prostitution were closely intertwined. The progress of civilization, the Rev. J. M. Wilson, Headmaster of Clifton College, Bristol,
intoned, was in the direction of purity. This was threatened by 'sins
of the flesh', which threatened self and nation. He advised his students to 'strengthen your will by practice; subdue your flesh by hard
work and hard living; by temperance; by avoiding all luxury and
effeminacy, and all temptation'.[12]

Boys at school were the most vulnerable and the most susceptible
to earnest moralizing. From the 1860s the educational ideal of
'godliness and good learning' of the Arnold tradition was superseded in the public schools by the cult of games, manliness and
patriotic duty. Thomas Hughes's *Tom Brown's Schooldays* exalted
manliness in 1857; Samuel Smiles celebrated *Self-Help* in his book
of that title in 1859; and William Acton described the horrors of
masturbation in *The Functions and Disorders of the Reproductive
Organs*, again in 1857.[13]

The spectacular expansion of single-sex public schools (three times
as many had been founded between 1841 and 1870 as were founded
in the whole preceding century) produced a rich crop of sexual scandals, and in November 1881 the *Journal of Education* carried as a
supplement the Rev. J. M. Wilson's sermon, 'Morality in Public
Schools', which linked up all these issues and forecast dire personal
and imperial decay.

In the wider society beyond school, prostitution and homosexuality
were again linked, as products of upper-class lust and selfishness.
This had been dramatized by the trial and acquittal of Mrs Jeffries,
a notorious brothel-keeper, in 1884. *The Sentinel*, which campaigned
vigorously against the Contagious Diseases Acts, suggested strongly
that this was because of her friends in high places. And its reports
carried strong hints of decadence and effeminacy. The paper noticed
in the court 'eight or nine young men, whose fingers glistened with
diamond rings, and whose feet were covered with patent shoes'.[14]
Patent shoes, it seems, were in the 1880s what suède shoes were to
the more prurient papers of the 1960s. The trial was constantly
mentioned in the debates leading to the Criminal Law Amendment
Act.

The purity campaign was given a tremendous fillip by W. T. Stead,
editor of the *Pall Mall Gazette*, in the early summer of 1885. A
fervent Nonconformist, Stead believed that 'fallen women' were
produced by 'depraved men'. In a series of articles on the 'Maiden
Tribute of Modern Babylon', he described the ease with which
young girls could be purchased for sexual purposes. The resulting

uproar forced the government to rush through the Criminal Law Amendment Act while the articles were still appearing (though Stead, who in his zeal had not acquired the permission of the father for the girl he had 'bought' to illustrate his *exposés*, was sentenced to two months in prison). It was Stead, according to one story, who had suggested to Labouchère the need to change the law on homosexuality by sending him a report on the prevalence of male prostitution, though Stead himself opposed the famous Amendment.

A series of scandals in the early 1880s further served to link homosexuality with prostitution and sexual decadence, and in 1884 there was a full-scale homosexual scandal involving high officials in Dublin Castle. At a huge demonstration in Hyde Park on 22 August 1885, a speaker expressed the hope that 'our public men shall be pure'. The way to do this, it seemed, was to stamp out that breeding ground of both prostitution and homosexuality: male lust. What gave the social-purity campaign its peculiar significance was the way in which it fitted into the felt needs of the time. There had always been a strong puritan distaste for the 'double standard' of morality since the seventeenth century, and the emphasis on love in the Christian marriage had gone hand in hand with a peculiar distaste for homosexuality. By the 1880s the family had become the paradigm of a stable society. According to Josephine Butler, the institution of the family was in accordance with the law of God, and the claim that every person should live in accord with their instincts was a departure from the 'sternness of the moral law'. For the social-purity people, it was lust which threatened both the family and national decay: 'Rome fell; other nations are falling; and if England falls it will be this sin, and her unbelief in God, that will have been her ruin.'[15]

The year 1885 was one in which imperialism and national decline were on everybody's mind. The issue of Home Rule for Ireland and the threat of a break-up of the United Kingdom were looming. And early 1885 saw the fall of Khartoum and the death of the imperial hero, General Gordon. The press turned on floods of emotion, 'ready made from the great vats in Fleet Street and Printing House Square', as a Socialist League manifesto on the Sudan War put it. The 1880s also saw the first stirring of socialist propaganda after a generation, and this again seemed to pose a threat to bourgeois hegemony. The puritan emphasis on the family offered an antidote: 'In all countries the purity of the family must be the surest strength of a nation; and virtue from above is mighty in its power over the homes below.'[16]

The emphasis on national decline had a long resonance. Sidney and

Beatrice Webb, the epitome of 'national efficiency' ideologies in the early 1900s, made very clear associations between national decay and homosexuality. Its open practice in China was proof, for them, of the degeneracy of the Chinese. Beatrice Webb visited numerous 'boys' homes' for male prostitutes while in China in 1911, and commented in her diary in typical fashion: 'It is the rottenness of physical and moral character that makes one despair of China – their constitution seems devastated by drugs and abnormal sexual indulgence. They are essentially an unclean race.'[17] Such moralisms became commonplaces of twentieth-century culture.

By the 1890s all these pressures seem to have had their due impact at government level. The Cleveland Street scandal of 1889–90, involving prominent aristocrats, a homosexual brothel, telegraph boys and a hint of royal involvement in the person of Prince Albert Victor, son of the Prince of Wales, had brought heavy criticism on the government for attempting a cover-up. Henry Labouchère complained that, in trying to cover up the affair, the government had only aggravated it. So during the Oscar Wilde trials the Solicitor-General felt obliged to go ahead with the prosecution *because* prominent people, such as Lord Rosebery, and his own wife's nephew, had been named: 'it would be said, both in England and abroad, that owing to the names mentioned . . . we were forced to abandon it'.[18] By the 1890s new responses to homosexuality were clearly emergent.

The sexual respectability enshrined in the lower middle class was a natural social base for the anti-homosexual ideology, but there are signs, too, that new patterns of culture and life-style among sections of the working class were developing a sex-role pattern antipathetic to homosexuality. Gareth Stedman Jones, for instance, has traced the emergence in London of a distinctive working-class culture, staunchly impervious to middle-class attempts at 'colonization', but nevertheless politically indifferent and socially conservative, orientated distinctly towards family and home, with a socially structured and approved division of labour between men and women.[19] In such a context, a homosexual life-style would have little resonance, and though a distinctive male camaraderie with sub-sexual horseplay persisted, the developing working-class culture almost certainly provided a real base for entrenched sexual attitudes hostile to homosexuality.

Other changes in the late nineteenth century both encouraged and paralleled changes in attitudes towards homosexuality. Concepts of childhood are one such area. Childhood lengthened in the nineteenth century, and there was an increasing emphasis on the need to protect the innocence of children. Acts of Parliament sought to remove them from the contagious adult world of drink and crime, while state-sponsored voluntary organizations such as the Boy Scouts – formed to prevent the growth of luxury and idleness and to stop the British Empire following that of Rome – were explicitly designed to distract or rechannel youthful sexual energies.[20] Childhood sexuality became an important political issue. The 1885 Act had succeeded in raising the age of consent for girls to sixteen, and Labouchère at least claimed that his most famous Amendment was directed at preventing the corruption of youth. The theme of the corruption of youth is constant, and the public-school controversy kept it on the boil. Working-class boys were involved in all the major scandals. Messenger boys featured prominently in the Cleveland Street scandal, as did various working-class youths in the Wilde case. And all the prejudices can be seen in an *Evening News* comment on the day of Wilde's conviction: 'We venture to hope that the conviction of Wilde for these abominable vices, which were the natural outcome of his diseased intellectual condition, will be a salutary warning *to the unhealthy boys who posed as sharers of his culture.*' [author's italics]

These changes had long-term implications, some of which have only recently become apparent. But for prostitution and homosexuality the implications were broadly similar; both became increasingly differentiated into 'deviant' sub-cultures, with a visible increase of the gap between them and the 'moral' society they safeguarded. For instance, the late nineteenth century saw a sharper definition of the social role of prostitution. It was not, needless to say, driven completely underground, but after a quarter of a century of evangelical fervour the easy upper middle-class acceptance of it was challenged and it was channelled into more regular patterns. In particular, as Judith and Daniel Walkowitz have pointed out, we can trace an accentuation of the tendency towards the professionalization of prostitution in the 1880s under the impact of such social-purity legislation as that of 1885. The position of working-class prostitutes who came under the purview of the Contagious Diseases Acts in the 1860s did not seem to differ significantly from the rest of the poor in their own districts, whereas, by the late nineteenth century, 'prostitutes were on their way to becoming the professional class of women, isolated from the general lower-class community, that exists in contemporary society'.[21] Whatever its intention, the social-morality emphasis produced a new tone of disapproval of prostitution, expressed in the 1898 Vagrancy Act, which classified prostitutes with vagabonds and beggars, as well as in a motley of legislation up to the present.

A similar evolution can be traced in the homosexual situation. Wainwright Churchill, in *Homosexual Behaviour Among Males*, has suggested that, in attempting to suppress homosexuality completely, our society actually gives rise to a greater incidence of exclusively homosexual individuals than other societies which make some provision in their mores for homosexual tendencies. This was certainly the effect of changes in the nineteenth century. The tightening of the law was dramatized and reinforced by a series of well-publicized trials and scandals, whose every twist and turn was broadcast by a developing popular press: from Boulton and Park in 1870, to the Dublin Castle scandal of 1884, the Cleveland Street scandal of 1889–90, and culminating in the most sensational of all, the three trials of Oscar Wilde in 1895. The Wilde trials were not only the most dramatic, but also the most significant events, for they created a public image for the homosexual, and a terrifying moral tale of the dangers that trailed closely behind deviant behaviour. They were labelling processes of the most explicit kind, drawing an impassable border between acceptable and abhorrent behaviour. As Wilde himself put it, he had made his name a 'synonym for folly', 'a low byword among low people'. But his humiliation did more than this: it helped to give a name to his predilection. When Maurice, the hero of E. M. Forster's novel, confessed his homosexuality to his doctor, he said, with closed eyes and clenched fists, 'I'm an unspeakable of the Oscar Wilde sort.' Certain non-homosexual men recognized the significance of this even in the 1890s. W. T. Stead, who had been largely responsible for the 1885 Act but disapproved of its gross indecency clause, commented to Edward Carpenter: 'A few more cases like Oscar Wilde's and we should find the freedom of comradeship now possible to men seriously impaired to the permanent detriment of the race.'[22]

By making homosexuality explicit, the labelling process threatened to undermine traditional male camaraderie. But for those whose predilections were homosexual, the effect was disastrous: not only was there the threat of public disgrace, but the road was opened to other evils. There is evidence from at least the eighteenth century of men being blackmailed for homosexual activities, but, as Edward Carpenter indicated, the new situation 'opened wider than ever before the door to a real, most serious social evil and crime – that of blackmailing'.[23]

The 1885 Act was traditionally called the 'Blackmailers' Charter' and it earned its label. The direct applications of the law itself ground down countless lives in the decades that followed. Yet the new situation had its positive side. It made many people, perhaps for the first time, aware of their identity. As Havelock Ellis said of the Oscar Wilde trial, it 'appears to have generally contributed to give definiteness and self-consciousness to the manifestations of homosexuality, and have aroused inverts to take up a definite stand'.[24] The tightening grip of the law, and the force of public disapproval which it stimulated, was beginning to create a community of knowledge, if not of life and feeling, among male homosexuals. The 'definite stand' that Ellis described was not a political stand: it presented a sense of self rather than of oppression. But it was an essential step in the evolution of a modern homosexual consciousness.

# 2
## 'The Medical Model'

*'Suddenly, in the middle of the eighteenth century, a fear arose –
a fear formulated in medical terms but animated basically by
a moral truth. People were in dread of a mysterious disease that
spread, it was said, from the houses of confinement, and would
soon threaten the cities'* – Michel Foucault, Madness and
Civilisation (*1967*)

By the late nineteenth century, as J. A. Symonds among others
recognized, medicine was replacing the Church as the moulder of
public opinion. The identity that was emerging as a response to the
harsh legal situation was defined in terms of new sanctions: of madness, moral insanity, sickness and disease. And increasingly in the
twentieth century the 'medical model' of the homosexual has cast
an enveloping shadow over homosexual consciousness.

Images of disease and sin have always been inextricably linked in
the popular imagination, and often in the legal mind. In the most
notorious case involving homosexuality in the early seventeenth
century, the trial of the Earl of Castlehaven for the rape of his wife
and sodomy, the Attorney-General claimed the crimes to be of that
'pestiferous and pestilential nature that if they be not punished
they will draw from Heaven heavy judgements upon the Kingdom'.
The threat of divine retribution was accompanied by dire threats of
plague and disease. A pamphlet published in London in 1787 directed
its wrath against 'emasculated foreign singers', for their moral
degeneracy and effeminacy were 'contagious like the pestilence'.
The threat of moral contagion has been a potent one in keeping
people in line, and the medieval imagery has not entirely disappeared,
even today. As the *Gloucester Journal* put it in a lead article in 1967:
'This is perhaps the most revolting human perversion ever known . . .
a horrible sin . . . a disease more dangerous than diphtheria.'[1] But
from the eighteenth century we can trace that gradual differentiation
of religious and disease models which was to have a major impact on
modern notions of homosexuality.

For most of the next hundred years or so homosexuality was
intimately linked to ideas about masturbation. Just as homosexuality
was not legally differentiated from sodomy, so medically it was seen
as a continuation of onanism or masturbation, which developed a

remarkable reputation from the early eighteenth century as the gateway to all types of hell. As a recent historian E. H. Hare has put it, 'the masturbatory hypothesis was like Pascal's religious hypothesis. One doubted it at one's peril or at the peril of one's race.' It is not entirely clear why the harmless pleasures of masturbation should have evoked such sudden horror in the eighteenth century, but it is likely that the new attitude developed closely in step with changing attitudes to children. A new recognition of the separateness of childhood by the eighteenth century went hand in hand with a socially felt need to preserve children's purity and innocence. They became a form of property, to be admired and coddled, to be cared for and, above all, protected. 'They were to stay firmly in Eden with their hands off the apples and deaf to the serpents.'[2] It is through masturbation that children begin to explore their sexuality, and through fantasy to initiate themselves into adult patterns. By its nature a generally private and individual experience, masturbation is peculiarly difficult to prevent and thus, if it is to be tabooed, calls for the severest sanctions, ideological and physical.

The taboos against masturbation became an effective way of inducting the child into acceptable adult modes of behaviour, economic and social as well as moral. The Swiss physician Tissot, who did much to publicize the horrors of masturbation in the eighteenth century, made the connections clear by arguing that loss of semen weakened the body while the expenditure of nervous energy enfeebled the brain.

The ideology went through many refinements, but the links with an economic model of society were reaffirmed in the social-morality debates of the 1880s. The Rev. Richard Armstrong warned that this 'unwholesome indulgence' led to a situation where 'the average life-value of young men at twenty-five – as tested by the infallible test of the insurance tables – is only half the average life-value of the boy of fourteen'.[3] Such fantasies were given credence by the invention in the nineteenth century of a specific form of masturbatory insanity. David Skae, a Scottish physician, was the first to claim that a specific type of madness was the result of masturbation, while Henry Maudsley followed this in the 1860s by defining the insanity as characterized by 'intense self-feeling and conceit, extreme perversion of feeling and corresponding derangement of thought, and later by failure of intelligence, nocturnal hallucinations, and suicidal and homicidal propensities'.

Havelock Ellis was to describe graphically in his autobiography the terrors of the unknown opened up by his nocturnal emissions, and this must have been the experience of thousands with regard to the more conscious effort of masturbation. But if ideological sanctions failed, physical measures might succeed. J. L. Milton, who popularized a completely spurious disease called 'spermatorrhea', the consequence of which he described in grotesque black eloquence as leading to physical decay, madness and death, also advocated the use for males of locked chastity belts by day and spiked or toothed rings by night. For girls, clitoridectomy was popularized after 1858 by Dr Isaac Baker Brown, a London surgeon. Fortunately, the use of the latter seems to have been limited,[4] but as late as the 1920s even sexual liberals like Havelock Ellis and Sigmund Freud were still speculating about the merits of physical prevention.

The most horrific disease that masturbation opened up for the nineteenth-century pessimist was homosexuality. Both in the United States and Britain there was a frequent linking of masturbation, 'the secret sin', with homosexuality: 'The secret sin which has been learned at a private school, imported to a public school, and there taught to the youngest boys, will inevitably produce the more fashionable vices of the larger society.'[5] Masturbation opened up the temptation to all forms of corruption, so that 'if solitary vice could be stamped out, dual vice would be almost unknown'. Masturbation was the narrow gate through which nameless dangers could pour, and for that reason, as manifestation and cause, it was to be absorbed into the medical model as it developed. Richard von Krafft-Ebing noted primly that, 'The sexual functions of men exercise a very marked influence upon the development and preservation of character. Manliness and self-reliance are not the qualities which adorn the impotent onanist.'[6]

From the mid nineteenth century the medical profession began to break down the formerly universally execrated forms of non-procreative sex into a number of 'perversions and deviations', so that, for the succeeding generations, the prime task of theory seemed to be the classification of new forms, the listing of their manifestations, the discussions of their causes. Most of the pioneering works, such as Krafft-Ebing's *Psychopathia Sexualis*, appear as tentative mappings of new countries, recently discovered. But in this process homosexuality gradually emerges as a separate category.

Several factors contributed to this, but undoubtedly the main impetus to the medical labelling of homosexuality came from the demands of the new criminal codes. The most commonly quoted European writers on homosexuality in the mid nineteenth century were Drs Casper and Tardieu, the leading medico-legal experts of

Germany and France respectively. Both, as Arno Karlen put it, 'were chiefly concerned with whether the disgusting breed of perverts could be physically identified for courts, and whether they should be held legally responsible for their acts'.[7] That there was felt to be an urgent need for this can be seen in the court cases, even in Britain, where the availability of medico-forensic works was limited. Many of the 1,000 or so works on homosexuality which, according to Magnus Hirschfeld, appeared between 1898 and 1908 were directed specifically at the legal profession, so even J. A. Symonds's privately printed *A Problem in Modern Ethics* declared itself to be addressed 'especially to medical psychologists and jurists'.

But how was this new category to be classified? Between 1852 and 1863 Casper developed the distinction between 'innate' and 'acquired' characteristics which were to be the poles of the debate for generations. In terms of social significance, the split was between what the American psychologist William Lee Howard called 'true sexual perversion' and 'illegal vice'.[8] For if homosexuality was congenital, was it justified to punish it? And if it was acquired, how could one best legally control it? (As a famous question in the 1950s posed it: would you lock an alcoholic up in a brewery?) The 'acquired' school, which was the logical continuation of traditional moralistic views, had vigorous defenders, particularly in Germany and France. The key transitional figure at the end of the nineteenth century is Richard von Krafft-Ebing, Professor of Psychiatry at Vienna, whose *Psychopathia Sexualis* went through numerous editions, including two English translations. The various editions of this work do, in fact, illustrate very clearly the changing concepts. Krafft-Ebing at first tended to view homosexuality as a functional sign of 'degeneration', a part of a pathological state manifested throughout the person. He modified his position in the twelfth edition of his book, where he appeared more willing to accept the primacy of congenital influences, and thereafter combined curious elements of both the acquired and the congenital arguments: 'With tainted individuals the . . . latent perverse sexuality is developed under the influence of neurasthenia induced by masturbation, abstinence and otherwise.'[9]

The significance of congenital arguments was that they proffered an argument for the removal of legal penalties. Many of the early pioneers of these views were themselves homosexual. Karl Heinrich Ulrichs, a German lawyer and writer, and himself homosexual, pioneered congenital theories in Germany from the 1860s. Between 1862 and his death in 1895 he poured out numerous books and pamphlets explaining and defending homosexuality, first under the pseudonym 'Numa Numantius', then under his own name. Ulrichs argued that the homosexual could be regarded neither as criminal nor insane. He was the product of the anomalous development of the originally undifferentiated human embryo. In the homosexual, though the genitals develop male or female characteristics, differentiation fails to take place in the part of the brain that determines the sex drives. The result was an *anima muliebris virile corpore inclusa*, a female mind in a male body. This theory, though largely metaphysical in style and content, was to have real importance for many homosexual apologists. The theories of an 'intermediate sex' that flourished in the early twentieth century were logical extensions of Ulrichs's ideas.

However, for most of the biological school, homosexuality appeared less as a harmless trait and more as a symptom of 'degeneration' in the individual development. In this, post-Darwinian ideas, which apparently offered a scientific explanation for sexual evolution, were to play a significant part. Dr Karl Westphal described a 'contrary sexual feeling' and argued that homosexuality resulted from moral insanity resulting from 'congenital reversal of sexual feeling'. The French writer Paul Moreau (1887) classed 'paederasts, sodomites, saphists' and others as members of 'a mixed class, constituting a real link of union between reason and madness, the nature and existence of which are most frequently to be explained only by one word: Heredity'. Veniamin Tarnovsky, the leading pre-revolutionary Russian sexologist, found that born homosexuals could not help themselves. Their condition came from damage to their parents' genes, resulting from hysteria, epilepsy, alcoholism, anaemia, typhus, debauchery, soil, climate or altitude. The work of the Italian criminologist Cesare Lombroso perhaps summed this tendency up by seeing homosexuals, like criminals, as throwbacks to earlier stages of civilization. These born criminals or perverts were 'insane' and should be treated not in prison but in asylums.

Although dangerously simplistic to modern eyes, these arguments were highly significant at the time. Lombroso's in particular were influential because they directed attention away from general moral explanations towards causation rooted in the individual's make-up. Havelock Ellis's book *The Criminal* (1889) was deeply influenced by Lombroso's theories, and J. A. Symonds saw the reform of laws relating to sexual offences between men in Italy in 1889 as being the result of Lombroso's arguments.[10] And it was indeed true that many of the early writers on homosexuality gave support to law-reform efforts. Krafft-Ebing, among others, supported the campaign against Paragraph 175 in Germany.

The British medical profession, however, proved more cautious than the European. When the occasional homosexual case appeared in the medical press, it was treated with wonder and awe, as if a new type of human being had been discovered. An eminent doctor, Sir George Savage, described in the *Journal of Mental Science* in October 1884 a young man of twenty-eight, 'anaemic and emotional', and a female patient, with a 'powerful lust towards those of her own sex', and wondered if 'this perversion is as rare as it appears'. Havelock Ellis was to claim that he was the first to record any homosexual cases unconnected with prison or asylums.

To classify a social phenomenon as a disease is immediately to put validation into the hands of doctors, and here their class role, their relationship to their patients and their middle-class assumptions become central. One of the factors making for a sharper definition of homosexuality must have been the perception of many doctors that otherwise perfectly ordinary people were subject to this mysterious phenomenon. Sir Alexander Morison, consultant to the Bethlem Hospital ('Bedlam'), found it a consolation in 1838 'to know that it is sometimes a consequence of insanity'.[11] It gradually dawned that it was absurd to classify otherwise ordinary middle-class people as morally depraved or degenerate. An individual quirk of madness offered a better explanation. When Harry Park (brother of the Frederick Park of the 1870 case involving two transvestites) was arrested, his defence rested precisely on the grounds of 'moral imbecility'.

> Many persons were of the opinion that the perpetuation of such offences, in itself showed something wanting in mind and feeling that indicated that the offender was not in full possession of his faculties, and that such cases would be far better treated in a lunatic asylum than in a court of justice.[12]

Madness was the only explanation which did not undermine the middle-class norm. Steven Marcus in *The Other Victorians* has described the work of William Acton, the most notorious ideologist of the 'double standard' in the mid nineteenth century, as being directed at an audience composed of the urban middle class: only here could the right combination of circumstances, living conditions, ideology and ignorance fit the tone of his work. Similarly, most of the early medical speculations on homosexuality have the flavour of a distinctive middle-class morality. Many of the doctors must have had an intimate acquaintance with homosexuality. J. A. Symonds's father was an eminent physician, while the son of Dr Hack Tuke, whom Symonds described as 'unscientifically prejudiced' to a high degree, was a boy-loving artist who liked to 'capture the truth and beauty of flesh in sunlight by the sea'. Doctors confronted not only their own class but also their own families, and it was often important to demonstrate that homosexuals were not entirely corrupt: sickness in this light was preferable to wickedness.

Not surprisingly, the reaction of doctors was often confused. J. A. Symonds recorded his doctor's advice in his Memoirs. One doctor, Sir Spencer Wells, suggested cohabitation or marriage. Another cauterized him through the urethra. Sir George Savage's advice was less radical. He advised his patient 'to follow his occupation with energy, to seek mixed society, to go to places of amusement in cities, and to pursue his musical tastes'. But, judging from the mixed public and medical reactions to the books on homosexuality that began to appear from the 1890s, most advice consisted of admonition for men to harden their will, tighten their muscles and resist temptation. A good example of the general attitudes can be seen in the influential Home University Library book by Patrick Geddes and J. A. Thompson on *Sex* (1914). The authors follow Krafft-Ebing's wedding of heredity and environment:

It appears that sexual perversions usually develop (under appropriate stimulus) in those who are unhappily born with a taint, such as lack of control; or who acquire or are led into bad habits in the earliest childhood; or who have their will power and their sense of self-respect weakened by other vice.

But, after a while, the subject obviously gets too much for them, and they conclude a brief and rather opaque discussion by agreeing with 'Sancho Panza the Wise', who liked a man to be a man and a woman a woman.[13]

Even more telling is the attitude of the medical reviews. Krafft-Ebing's were the approved models, with the case-studies delicately breaking into Latin when they were relating their sexual exploits. Havelock Ellis's work on *Sexual Inversion* evoked some surprise that it was written in such a popular way, and Dr Hack Tuke commented that there were 'always the compositors' who might be shocked.[14] The official organs of the medical profession did not reveal any great sympathy or insight, as their treatment of Edward Carpenter's works illustrate. The *Medical Times* (27 February 1909) gave a moderate review to Carpenter's *The Intermediate Sex*, but the

*British Medical Journal* (26 June 1909) dismissed it sneeringly. The review began with a verse called 'The Uranian' ('Uranian' being Carpenter's term for the German *Urning*):

'If to abnormal practices,
We publicly adhere
Do you suppose', the Urning sighed,
'The Law might interfere?'
'I dread it', cried the Carpenter,
And shed a sterile tear.

The writer expressed his pity for these 'odious' people, dilated on the possible confusion between the word 'Urning' (Ulrichs's preferred term for a homosexual) and urinal, and suggested emigration as a cure. The British Medical Association's attitudes to 'unnatural and criminal practices' no doubt varied throughout the century, but as late as 1955, with its submission of evidence to the Wolfenden Committee, the Association restated its conviction that:

The public opinion against homosexual practice is a greater safeguard [than law], and this can be achieved by promoting in the minds, motives and wills of the people a desire for clean and unselfish living . . . Personal discipline and unselfishness have little place in their thoughts.[15]

It was not until 1972, in a *Family Doctor* pamphlet by F. E. Kenyon, that the British Medical Association felt it necessary to attempt a 'factual and non-moralizing' approach, which despite all efforts nevertheless remained glued to a deviance viewpoint.[16] The acceptance of the 'medical model' was gradual. It was not until the late 1950s, with the debate occasioned by the Wolfenden Report, that a sickness theory became general, in however vague a form. But, by 1965, 93 per cent of those polled in an opinion poll saw homosexuality as a form of illness requiring medical treatment. It was by then rapidly also becoming an aspect of big business. Roche Laboratories, whose drugs were to tranquillize a generation in the 1970s, published a leaflet in the 1960s advocating their psycho-pharmocologic drugs: 'In a discussion of homosexuality, psychiatrists would probably agree unanimously on at least one point: the belief that the homosexual is a sick person.'[17]

If you have a sickness model, you also need a briefcase full of cures. And following the individualization of the diagnosis, so you get the individualization of the cure. In this case the patient is subject to what Thomas Szasz has called the 'correctional zeal' of the doctor. English textbooks had been in the vanguard over masturbation, but seem to have been less enthusiastic over homosexuality.

Havelock Ellis records one or two cases of treatment,[18] but most of the really 'radical' attacks associated with the spread of the 'degeneracy' models occurred in continental Europe and the United States. Castration was the most radical 'cure' of all. In 1898 a Kansas asylum reported that forty-eight men had been castrated; after the turn of the century, castration was used on homosexuals, exhibitionists and child molesters in Switzerland; and during the 1930s it was applied to nearly two hundred sex offenders, including homosexuals, in Denmark. By 1956, almost six hundred men had been operated on in Denmark alone. Such is the price of deviance models.[19] The most widely used form of behaviour modification in the late nineteenth century was hypnotherapy, where the male patient was urged to think of women in the sexual act. Schrenck-Notzing reported twenty-seven cases of homosexuality treated in this way, six by himself, eleven by Krafft-Ebing. They were not remarkably successful, even in their own terms. Other behavioural methods were experimented with by Moll, Charcot and Magnan. The assumption was that homosexuality was a behaviour disturbance and therefore curable. But even for those who felt it to be 'incurable', new methods of psychoanalysis and other modes of adjustment were increasingly felt necessary. The most pernicious method of all, 'aversion therapy' – originally developed in the 1930s to treat alcoholism – was used occasionally from the 1960s for sexual offences. Based apparently on the notion that the task of medicine is to wrench people into line with the received sexual norms of society, it consists of making people nauseous and inflicting electric shocks on them while viewing pictures of same-sex people to whom they are attracted.[20] What has to be restated is that this has nothing to do with real medicine or proper science. It is medicine acting as the moral policeman of the mind and body.

Inevitably, the 'medical model' had its effects on the minds and behaviour of generations of homosexuals. If the law and its associated penalties made homosexuals into outsiders, and religion gave them a high sense of guilt, medicine and science gave them a deep sense of inferiority and inadequacy. Goldsworthy Lowes Dickinson, a well-known liberal humanist and rationalist of the early twentieth century, believed he had a 'woman's soul in a man's body'. But he also believed this to be a 'misfortune':'I am like a man born crippled.'

For Sir Roger Casement, who actually enjoyed his sex with boys, it was a 'terrible disease' which ought to be cured.[21] For countless others it was conceived of as a disability, a sickness, a personal disaster. Such was the force of the 'medical model' of homosexuality.

# 3
## A Way of Life

*Moral people, as they are termed, are simply beasts. I would sooner have fifty unnatural vices, than one unnatural virtue. It is unnatural virtue that makes the world, for those who suffer, such a premature Hell – Oscar Wilde in a letter of 1897*

Oppression does not produce an automatic response, but it does provide the conditions within which the oppressed can begin to develop their own consciousness and identity. In the nineteenth century, law and science, social mores and popular prejudice set the scene, but homosexual people responded. In so doing they created, in a variety of ways, self-concepts, meeting-places, a language and style, and complex and varied modes of life. The multicoloured patterns that emerge from the debris piled upon them by history belie the drab court-room images that have usually been offered.

Homosexual behaviour cannot be crammed into any one predetermined mould, because it pervades many different aspects of social experience. This was as true of Victorian society as of today's. Homosexual experiences could be absorbed into a wide variety of differing life-styles, with no necessary identity as a 'homosexual' developing. There is, first of all, the casual encounter, which rarely touches the self-concept.[1] It might be followed by guilt or even physical sickness, be seen as a drunken aberration or a 'passing phase'. Or it might be a result of a deliberate attempt to explore a new experience. The best nineteenth-century example of this comes from the anonymous author of the sexual chronicle, *My Secret Life*. After years of compulsive sex with all manner of women (but most enjoyably with servant girls or prostitutes), he experimented with homosexuality, and despite constant feelings of revulsion, persisted on several occasions without his own basic self-concepts being disturbed. There is even a suggestion in his recollections that he used the experiences to confirm his identity. He was excited when he could use the experience to stimulate himself further with women and particularly enjoyed copulating in another man's semen.[2]

The second type is the highly individualized, the deeply emotional, sometimes even sexual, relation between two individuals who are otherwise not regarded, or do not regard themselves, as 'deviant'.

The eighteenth and nineteenth centuries record a plethora of such relationships, female and male. Lady Eleanor Butler and Sarah Ponsonby, daughters of titled families from Ireland, refused to live apart from each other in the late eighteenth century, despite endless family anathemas, and became known to history as the 'Ladies of Llangollen'. In that town they led a placid and blameless existence, holding court to Scott, Wellington, Wordsworth and De Quincey. A later poet, Alfred Tennyson, celebrated what *The Times* censoriously called 'amatory tenderness . . . to a man, even though he be dead', in his famous lament for his friend Hallam, *In Memoriam* (1850).[3] But who could regard Tennyson, Poet Laureate and later peer, as anything but a pillar of the Victorian establishment?

Anglo-Catholicism seems to have been a particular breeding-ground for elevated passions, but it is highly unlikely that anything improper happened in most cases. And the British Empire, a market for the export of surplus sexual and emotional energy as well as of surplus capital, produced a similar crop of devoted and probably 'pure' relationships. Lord Kitchener had an inseparable companion in Captain O. A. G. Fitzgerald from 1907 to their deaths together in 1915, and Kitchener 'embellished his rose garden with four pairs of sculptured bronze boys'. Baden Powell, founder of the Boy Scouts, wrote to his friend Kenneth McLaren ('the Boy') daily during the siege of Mafeking, and later made him chief administrator of the Scouts.[4] It was widely accepted in Victorian society that strong relationships between men were normal, which is why W. T. Stead was so appalled at the consequences of the Wilde trial. Such relationships were deeply ambivalent, however, and became increasingly dangerous for the respectable as awareness of homosexuality grew. But while male friendships were suspect, no one questioned the legitimacy of strong emotional relationships between women. Highly personalized relationships such as these probably remained the most common form of lesbian relationship until very recently.

The third type of homosexual behaviour is situational: activity which may be regarded as legitimate in certain circumstances, for example in schools or the army and navy or prisons, but which is taboo in the wider society. The public schools offered the most notorious examples during the Victorian period, as the social-purity propaganda from the 1870s constantly illustrates. By the 1850s homosexuality was institutionalized in some of the major schools. J. A. Symonds piously described his horror at the situation in Harrow, where every boy of good looks has a female name, and was either a 'prostitute' or a 'boy's bitch'. Symonds was filled with a prudish disgust at the sexual maelstrom, 'animal lust' without passion or feeling, and at the hypocrisy of many of the teachers, who preached purity and practised covert sex. A little later, Lowes Dickinson described Charterhouse as a 'hot-house of vice'.[5] From the 1870s there was an attempted purge on 'school-boy immorality', but it was never wiped out. It might or might not have been the prelude to a later homosexual life-style, but it was acceptable within the narrow community of the school. The same is true of the notorious prostitution that characterized the Brigade of Guards, for which there is a long history between the eighteenth and the twentieth centuries. It could easily be justified as 'we are only doing it for the money', and no identification with being homosexual was demanded, but it was endemic: 'As soon as (or before) I had learned the goose-step, I had learnt to be goosed', as one particular practitioner put it.[6]

The prevalence of such situational homosexuality reveals more clearly than anything else the constant homosexual element which can be expressed whenever need arises or social restraints collapse.

There was only a fine dividing-line between these homosexual experiences and absorption of homosexuality into a total way of life. A young man of the Victorian upper middle class might progress from highly structured sexual encounters in his public school, to casual sex with a young working-class guardsman, to a full absorption into a complex homosexual underworld. This was not an inevitable step, and it was one fraught with increasing danger in the nineteenth century, but for those who did take it it meant involvement in an identity and sub-culture which, with its own system of values and ideologies, is the obvious forerunner of that of the present day.

Homosexuality has everywhere existed, but it is only in some cultures that it has become structured into a sub-culture. Homosexuality in the pre-modern period was frequent, but only in certain closed communities was it ever institutionalized – perhaps in some monasteries and nunneries, as many of the medieval penitentials suggest; in some of the knightly orders (including the Knights Templars), as the great medieval scandals hint; and in the courts of certain monarchs (such as James I of England, William III). Other homosexual contacts, though recurrent, are likely to have been casual, fleeting and undefined.

The development in England of a recognizable sub-culture seems to have been of comparatively recent date, In Italy there is evidence of a male transvestite sub-culture in the towns from the fourteenth century, and in France by a century later.[7] But in Britain there was no evidence for a similar sub-culture until the late seventeenth century. A sexual sub-culture is unlikely to arise when patterns of behaviour are acceptable within orthodox types of relationship. It develops as a response to the emergence of hostile norms: in the case of homosexuality, of a sharpening social oppression. And it has a two-fold function: for the 'deviant' it provides access to the outlawed sexual activity and relationships; for the wider society it has the effect of segregating the outlawed and stigmatized group from the population at large, with the purpose of keeping the wider population pure. A sub-culture does not arise in a vacuum. There needs to be both the felt need for a collective solution to a problem (group access to sexuality, in this case) and the possibility of its satisfaction. And it is the growth of towns with large groupings of people and relative anonymity which provides the possibility of both. Only with the breakdown of traditional value and status systems does it become possible to live a homosexual 'career', while the town offers the possibility of social institutions developing independently of the family and traditional responses. Such relative freedom has always been more available for men, which is probably why the development of a lesbian sub-culture has historically been minimal in comparison with the male. There were signs by the early 1700s of a distinctive male homosexual sub-culture in London.

Edward Ward, in *The Secret History of London Clubs* (1709), records the existence of 'The Mollies' Club', where a 'curious band of fellows' met in a tavern in the City and held parties and regular gatherings. A writer in 1729 described in more detail the homosexual life of the period. They had 'their walks and appointments, to meet and pick up one another, and their particular Houses of Resort to go to, because they dare not trust themselves in an open Tavern'. About twenty such places were known, most of them in the Covent Garden/Lincoln's Inn area. At about the same period, *Reports* of the Old Bailey, 1720–30, suggest the existence of pederastic brothels, while there is further documentary evidence for secret pederastic clubs.

There were several drives against homosexuality in the 1780s, with the discovery of homosexual groupings in London and Exeter. This embryonic sub-culture was closely associated with transvestism and stereotyped effeminate behaviour, in a mode which still characterizes the relatively undeveloped sub-cultures of areas outside the major cities of western Europe and North America:

Men would sit in one another's laps, kissing in a lewd manner and using their hands indecently. Then they would get up, dance and make curtsies, and mimic the voices of women, 'Oh, fie, sir' – 'Pray sir' – 'Dear sir' . . .[8]

This was reinforced by the words used for homosexuals in the period – 'Molly', 'Madge-cull', 'Marianne' – all conveying strong suggestions of effeminacy. Their transvestite attributes continued into the nineteenth-century sub-culture and beyond. The trials in 1870 of the transvestites Boulton and Park, the 'men in petticoats', was the best-dramatized example and evoked a crop of black jokes, especially as they were tried at the 'Middle sex' assizes. Of course, transvestite characteristics have continued to the present, not only as an essential individual response, but also in the ritualized forms of drag balls. It is significant that it is 'effeminacy' that is the most stigmatized form of behaviour, suggesting the deep underlying gender-role strains emerging. By the nineteenth century the homosexual stereotype was clear: 'lusts written on his face . . . pale, languid, scented, effeminate, oblique in expression'. The furtiveness and the effeminate stereotyping suggested by Symonds's description are characteristic of an emergent rather than a developed homosexual sub-culture.[9] During the nineteenth century, the spread and relative maturity of urban society made a more diverse pattern possible.

By the mid century the sub-culture is much more complex and variegated. The records of the court cases from this period show the spread of a homosexual underworld in the major cities (especially London and Dublin) and the garrison and naval towns. In the 1840s, London had brothels that supplied young boys as well as young girls for £10, while *The Yokel's Preceptor* in 1850 spoke of widespread homosexuality in the theatrical profession, and discussed the signs by which homosexuals revealed themselves to each other. A network of meeting-places developed, often located around public lavatories after the mid-century, the occasional public bath, private meeting places and clubs, and straightforward cruising areas. In London, the Regent's Street Quadrant, the Haymarket and areas towards Trafalgar Square and the Strand were favourite haunts for male (as for female) prostitutes, while in the 1880s, the circle of the Alhambra Theatre was a well-known picking-up area, as was part of the Empire Music Hall, the Pavilion, the bar of the St James's and a skating-rink in Knightsbridge.[10] In the developing homosexual underground, individuals could begin to learn the rules for picking up and watching for the law as well as the places to go. They could imbibe the rituals of social contact and behaviour, the codes for communicating, and the modes of living a double life. The sub-culture was thus a training-ground for learning the values of the world and a source of social support and information.

For those in the know, sexual contact was not difficult. The

American writer, 'Xavier Mayne', describes the use of cigarettes to establish initial contact, and vividly delineates a man cruising the streets in an account which, apart from period details, remains very familiar:

> . . . he meets a furtive, keen look from a man or a youth who passes . . . that signal and challenge everywhere current and understood among homosexuals . . . Before a shop window, or perhaps at a bench in a park, halts the Uranian. Soon another stroller . . . walks towards him – catches his eye expressively and sits near him . . . A conversation is begun. Little by little it slips on toward confidentialities. Presently they take a walk together; or go to some restaurant . . . The two men also are pretty sure to pause at the nearest latrine, by common consent . . .[11]

George Merrill, Edward Carpenter's lover for many years, found it equally easy:

> . . . it's certainly very odd how I meet people – but one day I was at the station there, and the Prince of Wales . . . was in the station just going off to Tranby Croft on a visit with some of his suite. Of course, they were all very smart with frock-coats and tall hats and flowers in their buttonholes; but one of them was a very good-looking fellow – real nice and kind-looking – and only about 26 or 7. And he got into the last carriage just where I was standing on the platform outside, and as soon as he got in he put his head out of the window and made a movement to me to speak to him; and directly I went up he said quite sharp – 'businesslike' 'Where will you be this evening at 9 o'clock?' And I said 'Here', and he said 'All right. Mind you come.' And the train went off. And in the evening he came all right – only in a tweed suit and cap. Oh! he was nice – such a real gentleman and such a sweet voice. And we walked along by the river, and sat on a seat under the trees, and he had brought some lovely grapes for us to eat.
> And after that we met several evenings the same way.[12]

The young aristocrat wanted Merrill to come and stay with him, but Merrill lost the piece of paper with the address, and in any case was too shy and class-conscious to let a relationship develop.

This suggests the casual nature of most sexual contacts. The sub-culture was overwhelmingly concerned with sexual encounters and overwhelmingly male. Its chief continuity, in fact, was not with the lesbian world but with male heterosexual values. And in this world the cash nexus determined most encounters. The most common form of the homosexual sub-culture today is peer-group contact, but the nineteenth-century male homosexual underworld was dominated by prostitution. The American sociologist Evelyn Hooker has described the homosexual sub-culture in terms of free markets that could arise only under a market economy, in which buyers' rights to enter are determined solely by whether or not they have the right attributes and ability to pay.[13]

This was true in more than a metaphorical sense in the nineteenth century. Abraham Flexner's study of European prostitution suggested just before the First World War that there were an estimated 1,000–2,000 prostitutes in Berlin, while 'Xavier Mayne' a little earlier suggested that male prostitution was no less than female.[14] But the evidence is scanty for Britain. One may speculate that the class of professional women detached from the rest of their class, which was increasingly the rule for female prostitution by the early twentieth century, did not apply to men. It is likely, on the contrary, that in most cases the exchange of goods and services was implicit rather than contractual. George Merrill records a liaison with an 'Italian count', who gave him presents, flowers, neckties, handkerchiefs and money, which he usually sent home to his mother.

The casual nature of most male prostitution is, above all, suggested by its association with the armed forces. This, according to 'Mayne', was evident throughout Europe. He wrote of the English situation: 'The skeptic has only to walk around London, around any English garrison centre, to stroll about Portsmouth, Aldershot, Southampton, Woolwich, large cities of North Britain or Ireland, to find the soldier prostitute in almost open self-marketing.'[15] The increase in the size of the armed forces in the mid century, the low pay, probably increased both the supply and the necessity of casual prostitution. And there was an increase in demand in the late century, as the impact of the social-purity legislation ground on its way.

But where the cash nexus rules in a society of gross inequalities of wealth, all sections of the working-class population are likely to be drawn in casually. Working-class youths featured prominently in all the major scandals, like the messenger boys in the Cleveland Street scandal. Oscar Wilde's life and trials underscored the web of casual contacts and monetary exchanges that dominated the nineteenth-century homosexual world. The presents he gave to his pick-ups (stable lads, labourers, newspaper boys), his wining and dining of them in expensive restaurants, scandalized the court which tried him and which saw the class barriers tumbling before its eyes. Edward Carson acidly asked at Wilde's first trial, 'What enjoyment was it to you to entertain groom and coachman?'[16] But the same question could be asked of the heterosexual man with regard to his servant girls and factory workers. Steven Marcus has commented on the scandalous situation where a working-class girl could get five times as much for masturbating a man as she could for a whole day of her work, and the temptation was similarly immense for working-class youths. The most facinating area of all to be explored is that of the self-image of these working-class boys. We know from other sources that it was precisely at this time that working-class life was consolidating itself into more rigid patterns of gender behaviour, and yet homosexual prostitution was rife. Certainly many (and, in particular, the middle-class homosexual) believed that the working class was not particularly bothered by homosexuality. As a correspondent of Havelock Ellis wrote:

> Among the working masses of England and Scotland 'comradeship' is well marked, though not (as in Italy) very conscious of itself. Friends often kiss each other, though this habit seems to vary a good deal in different sections and colonies. Men commonly sleep together, whether comrades or not, and so easily get familiar.[17]

The lives of many homosexuals record the development of close friendships across the class barriers. Oscar Browning, a master driven out of Eton because of his close friendship with the boys and with a taste for sailors and young workers, 'always had some boy or young man as a secretary, and for many boys and youths he did much to start them in life'.[18] The later life of J. A. Symonds was dominated by Swiss peasants and Venetian gondoliers: '. . . the way of thinking among the proletariat, honest citizens, etc., in Italy and Switzerland, where I alone have fraternised, is all in favour of free trade'.[19]

The money element inevitably intruded, even in the most nobly expressed panegyric. Roger Casement recorded in his diary not only the size of his pick-ups' organs, but also their price, and there is a strong element of sexual colonialism in the avidity with which the upper middle-class male approached his 'trade'. According to Sir Edmund Backhouse, Oscar Wilde preferred working-class youths because 'their passion was all body and no soul'. But there was also a yearning to escape the stifling middle-class norms. E. M. Forster wanted 'to love a strong young man of the lower classes and be loved by him and even hurt by him'. Edward Carpenter proclaimed his love for the poor and uneducated: 'The thick-thighed, hot, coarse-fleshed, young bricklayer with the strip around his waist.'

This was a recurrent theme in the literature of homosexuality from the 1880s to the 1930s and beyond.[20] It could even become the focus of a sentimental reconciliation between the classes. Symonds wrote to Edward Carpenter:

> The blending of Social Strata in masculine love seems to me one of its most pronounced, and socially hopeful features. Where it appears, it abolishes class distinctions, and opens by a single operation the cataract-blinded life to their futilities.[21]

This is an important and genuine theme which occurs again and again in the later reform movements, but is also indicative of the acute strains in the homosexual life of an upper middle-class man. For the dream of a liaison across class lines, which by the class nature of the culture was highly problematical, is suggestive of the guilt-ridden fear of relationships within their own class. Roger Casement, who revealed all in his diaries, never told his friends he was homosexual and Lowes Dickinson lamented the need for, and the impossibility of, an emotional relationship. J. R. Ackerley spent a lifetime looking for a close 'friend'. Others found that emigration was the better part of valour, and new vistas were opened up by the British Empire in the East. One captain found in Peshawar that 'to get a boy was easier than to pick flowers by the wayside'.[22] Britain offered no such simple joys.

Another major aspect of the sub-culture is a corollary of this, its 'part-time' nature. The lives of many homosexuals were dominated by their homosexuality and their search for partners, but this produced not an avowedly open homosexual life-style but a double life. A middle-class man's life was split apart by the need to be respectable in a job and home, where he would probably be married (most men brought before the courts for homosexual offences in the nineteenth century being married), and by his eager involvement in the homosexual sub-culture with its own codes and slang, itself a strong indicator of the sort of life-style that was emerging. 'Xavier Mayne' speaks of a vast homosexual argot, often international in character, in the early twentieth century.

The specific homosexual slang is known as 'parlare', which seems to have derived from 'parlyaree', which in the mid nineteenth century was the language of circus showmen and itinerant actors, and often merged with the language of tramps. The slang includes words such as 'bona' (attractive), 'varda' (look at), 'omee' (man), and 'polonee' (woman), which are directly derived from parlyaree, but it also includes words such as 'barnet' (hair), which is rhyming slang. The language is not so much concerned with sex (what people do in bed) as with how to behave in public. It is a language for evaluating appearances and mannerisms, and in which to gossip. Words describe parts of the body: 'lals' (legs), 'ecaf' (face), 'dish' (bottom), 'slap' (make-up), 'drag' (women's clothing). Much of the argot is highly esoteric, known only to a few homosexuals, but a large number of words are absorbed into the daily vocabulary of homosexuals. The most familiar are those words which characterize all members of the homosexual culture as feminine: 'Marianne', 'Nancy', 'auntie', 'queen'. But there are also terms and phrases to describe particular activities: for example, 'trolling' (for hunting for sexual contacts), 'tipping the velvet', 'rimming', 'on the game' (for prostitution).

The existence of such an argot is indicative of a fairly developed and stable sub-culture, and there is evidence of an extensive homosexual vocabulary throughout the eighteenth and nineteenth centuries. Words, of course, changed their meaning: 'gay' in the nineteenth century meant a prostitute, not a homosexual, while 'Nancy' meant a buttock; and there was an extensive international exchange. *'Tante'* was used for homosexuals in France in the nineteenth century, while the usage of 'queen' seems to have been transmitted from England to Australia by the 1880s, and then spread by American troops during the First World War.[23]

'Camp' is today the most familiar aspect of the homosexual language and style. 'Camp' is not just a vehicle of communication between peers, but a way of presenting the self to the straight world. It is deeply ambivalent, because it celebrates effeminacy while retaining a sharp awareness of conventional values. It can become a form of 'minstrelization', an ambiguous playing to the galleries which found its most skilled revelation in the work of Oscar Wilde.

The frivolous surface of Wilde's art conceals a fundamentally serious purpose, and most of his work is concerned with the contradiction between moral standards and mundane reality. His plays re-enact this contradiction in their glittering paradoxes. *The Importance of Being Earnest*, his most enduring achievement, is above all about the 'double life'. It is basically about two men who elaborately court females as a cover for bunburying, illicit pleasures, which, by extension, can easily be seen as homosexual in implication. There is a constant concern with the ambivalence of social institutions: 'The one charm of marriage is that it makes a life of deception absolutely necessary for both parties.'[24] And Wilde's work reveals an obsession with secret and unnameable vices, as in *The Picture of Dorian Gray*. Many of his works can be seen as metaphors for his ambivalent social position, as an artist mocking bourgeois pieties; and for his ambivalent sexual position, as a homosexual defying sexual orthodoxies.

But the consequences of this double life had their deep and long-lasting impact on the homosexual consciousness. Wilde saw his life as 'feasting with panthers', an exciting search after new and secret vices. As Rupert Croft-Cooke put it in *Feasting with Panthers*, 'he never ceased to believe that he was a pioneer from another class, adventuring in dangerous places'.

The world of fleeting contacts, casual sex, the excitement of meeting people from another class, was not unique to upper middle-class homosexuals; it can rather be seen as an aspect of the whole male ethos. But it was for the homosexual accompanied both by guilt and the added possibility of public exposure and disgrace, or blackmail and robbery. For many, the excitement and danger were an added incentive; for others, they were the accompaniment of deep shame. In the 'Uranian' poetry of the 1890s, 'shame' in fact became the synonym for homosexuality. As Lord Alfred Douglas ('Bosie') wrote, 'Of all sweet passions, Shame is loveliest.' The two were very often combined.

Symonds found in the crude graffiti of the backstreets of London 'the voice of vice and passion'.[25] But for others, who lacked the social gifts or the money to be able to indulge a semi-secretive homosexual life, the strains imposed by the need to deny were immense. One of Havelock Ellis's respondents recounted his excitement on hearing of the Wilde case, followed by his total inability to identify with the world thus revealed and dramatized. The rather frenetic life of the better-off homosexual world might establish the norms, but they were by no means universal. Nor did they, in a real sense, lead to public avowals. Oscar Wilde's famous defence of the 'Love that dare not speak its name' was a defence of 'that deep, spiritual affection that is as pure as it is perfect' rather than of the sexual life he actually led. André Gide complained in *Corydon*, *his* defence of homosexual love:

We have had Wilde, Krupp, Macdonald, Eulenburg . . . Oh,

victims! Victims as many as you please! But not a single martyr. They all deny it; they always will deny it . . . To try to establish one's innocence by disavowing one's life is to yield to public opinion. How strange![26]

But perhaps *not* so strange, given the ethos of the late nineteenth century.

The homosexual sub-cultural sensibility that was apparent by the end of the nineteenth century was deeply ambivalent. Firstly, there was the guilt, the sense of shame and of wallowing in evil which is one characteristic response. Secondly, there was the obsession with *style*, with a self-protecting individualism, even eccentricity, which deflected social criticism before it could hurt, which is another response. Then there is the avidly exploitative sexual colonialism, which marched, point counter-point, with the dream of class reconciliation. Finally, there was the complete absorption of homosexuality into one's life, so that one's identity became merged into it: the ultimate step in the acceptance of homosexuality as a 'way of life'. Few trod this path confidently by the turn of the century, but without it the reforming endeavours were necessarily marred by hesitation and compromise.

*Part Two*

# PIONEERS

# 4

## Speaking Out: John Addington Symonds

'*A few years ago . . . sexual inversion was scarcely a name. It was a loathsome and nameless vice, only to be touched with a pair of tongs*' – *Havelock Ellis*, Sexual Inversion (*1897*)

In 1867 the historian W. H. Lecky had spoken of 'that lowest abyss of unnatural love' as a topic to which it was extremely difficult to allude in an English book. Thirty years later, Havelock Ellis's moderate work on *Sexual Inversion* was labelled in a court of law as a 'lewd, wicked, tawdry, scandalous and obscene libel'. This serves to remind us of the oppressive atmosphere in which any reforming work had to survive. And yet this restrictiveness in the late nineteenth century does not indicate an ignoring of the subject; rather it underlines the growing concern with it. As Edward Carpenter put it, 'the subject has great actuality and is pressing upon us from all sides'.[1]

This actuality produced, on the one hand, a trickle of medical and legal texts, a gradual filtering through of the more sturdy European studies. On the other, it produced a number of more or less overt apologies. J. A. Symonds spoke of a vast subterranean literature on homosexuality little known to general readers. In the late nineteenth century some of this broke surface. Sir Richard Burton, the great traveller and adventurer, attempted to describe pederasty 'in decent nudity not in suggestive fig leaf or *feuille de vigne*', and described the 'Sodatic Zone' within which the vice was popular and endemic: the Mediterranean basin and Asia Minor, Mesopotamia and Chaldea, Afghanistan and Kashmir, China and Japan; all countries notably outside Christian and capitalist Europe.[2] Not surprisingly, Burton's wife destroyed others of his writings after his death.

The 1880s and early 1890s saw the appearance of a number of works of homosexual literature which achieved some minor notoriety, among them the anonymous *Telenny, or the Reverse of the Medal* (1891), Wilde's works and the somewhat etiolated poetry of the 'Uranian' poets.[2] Other writings appeared in a more hypocritically self-righteous form, cashing in on the notoriety created by the Wilde affair, including André Raffolovitch's Catholic apologetic *Uranisme et unisexualité* (1896).

The Wilde trial burst the main bubble of literary production, not only regarding homosexuality but other less 'dubious' subjects which threatened the moral consensus. But the writing went on. Lowes Dickinson, like J. A. Symonds earlier, wrote an honest autobiography of his homosexual life and fantasies which never saw the light during his lifetime. Others confessed their feelings to private diaries, or expressed themselves in mediated art form. E. M. Forster wrote in *Maurice* a whole homosexual novel, unpublished during his lifetime, and felt that sex had come between him and the writing of further novels.

So it was against a grey intellectual climate that works appeared which were designed to reform public opinion rather than subvert or confirm it. Among these, the writings of J. A. Symonds, Havelock Ellis and Edward Carpenter were most influential. These three figures set the tone for most of the discussion concerning homosexuality in liberal and left-wing circles, and through their work (particularly that of Ellis) was transmitted much of the most progressive of European thought on sexual matters (and especially the writings of Ulrichs, Magnus Hirschfeld and even Freud). Compared to the abundance of writings today, their work seems apologetic, even anaemic, but given the climate of opinion in which they worked it was an achievement – and the strain often shows. Their formulations, however distorted by existing preconceptions, set the tone for a generation of debate.

These three writers were very different personalities, with different aims, ambitions and achievements, but certain common themes do emerge. There is, first of all, their common association with a reaction against what they defined as the more restrictive norms of Victorian morality. Symonds sweepingly condemned Josephine Butler and W. T. Stead as:

A bourgeois Anglo-Saxon pack of Jesuits! Violating law and doing evil that good may come! Without even the solemnity, inscrutability, and perfect art of the real Jesuits![3]

For Ellis and Carpenter this became, more than a personal rejection, an important political stance: both were associated with the early years of the socialist revival from the 1880s, and with many of the most vigorous intellectual, moral and political as well as sexual movements at the turn of the century. This common thread was underlined by the devotion of all three men to the work of the American poet, Walt Whitman, the great hero and inspirer of such elements of the Victorian 'counter-culture' that got off the ground.

Whitman seemed to these bourgeois radicals to reject guilt and the notion of corruption: 'he begins anew with sound and primitive humanity'. Whitman's work offered the vision of health and wholeness, the restoration of a unity lost by the growth of industries, cities and fierce class conflicts, and the disintegration of old moral and religious certainties. All three writers can, in their different ways, be identified with a rejection of Victorian utilitarianism, determinism and materialism. In its place they yearned for an organic unity, a new social harmony, which thus places them in a long tradition of social criticism which has lingered throughout the present century.

The second unifying link between Symonds, Ellis and Carpenter, then, is their similar and more positive approach to the question of homosexuality. They wanted, above all, to humanize attitudes and make it more acceptable. Hence the typical manner in which they (like Hirschfeld in Germany) played down the role of buggery, still the most tabooed behaviour in male homosexual relations; insisted that 'effeminacy', the usual caricature for male homosexuality, was not necessarily linked with homosexuality; and rejected pederasty. On the contrary, they insisted on the potential health and normality of homosexual relations, their lack of morbidity, their complete separation from disease models. And to do this they contributed to the development of a concept of homosexuality as a congenital anomaly, a more or less harmless sexual variation. For them, a biological model, possibly even the notion of an 'intermediate' or 'third sex', offered the most productive way out of the trap of Victorian condemnation. The work of Ellis was particularly vital in this, and has to be seen as an aspect of the subdivision, labelling and classification of sexual phenomena which is a characteristic development of early twentieth-century social science. Finally, these common intellectual preoccupations dictated a common political approach: an emphasis on the dissemination of information, on education, and particularly on educating our masters as a prelude to reform of the law.

The emphasis on law reform was an obvious response to social oppression, but it was a long-term aim. For this reason, perhaps, we can say that the prime task of these pioneers of homosexual reform was to establish a view of homosexuality as a biological anomaly which would challenge both the medieval moralisms and the new, would-be-scientific definitions. But though these reformers were anxious to extend the understanding and definitions of sexuality to include sexual variations, none of them, in the last resort, was able to sustain a challenge to conventional views of gender and social roles. They attempted to fit homosexuality into existing concepts. In so doing they failed to develop a radical critique of sexual oppression. This will become clearer by examining in more detail their individual approaches to the subject.

John Addington Symonds (1840–93), poet and critic, complained towards the end of his life that he had never properly 'spoken out' about his homosexuality.[4] 'Speaking out' was, as several of his contemporaries were to find, a perilous business, and Symonds's writings, whether explicitly or implicitly about homosexuality, reflect a constant tension between the desire and the personal need to be honest and outspoken and his ultimate commitment to a bourgeois life. It is ironic but not unexpected, therefore, that after a lifelong effort to come to terms with his own homosexuality, his most important contribution to the propagandizing of a more rational view of homosexuality should appear, practically unsung, in his collaboration with a heterosexual, Havelock Ellis. The book, *Sexual Inversion*, was planned as a joint venture by Symonds and Ellis, but as we shall see finally appeared after Symonds's death in an edition devoid of his name and public presence.

Symonds was born into a comfortable upper middle-class family. His father was a senior physician, and a prominent citizen of Bristol. The young Symonds's sexual longings, as he described in his Memoirs, appeared very early. He was later to stress the vital importance of recognizing these early signs as a pointer to genuine congenital 'inversion'. As a child he identified passionately with sailors, but as a schoolboy at Harrow he was revolted by what he saw as the sexual excesses of his contemporaries and teachers. He was particularly appalled by the moral hypocrisy of the headmaster, Dr Vaughan, who preached purity and had sexual relations with his pupils. It is apparent from the Memoirs that Symonds was ultimately responsible for forcing Vaughan's resignation. He told his father, who threatened to reveal all publicly unless Vaughan renounced his claims to future office and preferment. In the event, Symonds lost friends at school, and spent many fruitless hours in later life justifying his own schoolboy prudery.

He became fully conscious of his own sexual longings after reading works of Plato at the age of eighteen. But conventionality and guilt inhibited him. He eventually married, on medical advice, in the 1860s, and for years his homosexual needs were partially sublimated in verse, where the gender of the loved ones was carefully altered to the feminine for publication. It was only after his marriage that he began fully to come to terms with his own needs. A year after his marriage he had by chance encountered a male prostitute in an alley off Leicester Square, and raced away in panic. Ten years later, he was to find a similar encounter, in Regent's Park, the very revelation of the superb comradeship which might exist between men, and especially men of a different social class.

Symonds experienced, in fact, a constant boiling up of his attraction for young men during the early years of his marriage, and in the anguish caused by one particular crisis he began to draft a study of Greek life and sexual mores, part of which was finally privately published in 1883 as *A Problem in Greek Ethics*. This can probably claim to be the first serious work on homosexuality published in Britain. The British Library in London has No. 10 of ten copies 'privately printed for the Author's use'. It was to achieve a wider circulation when it formed the basis for a section in Ellis's *Sexual Inversion*.

Greek life and Greek love were to represent for Symonds, as for many sexually tormented intellectuals of the period, an aspect of the ideal: '. . . here alone in history have we the example of a great and highly developed race not only tolerating homosexual passions but deeming them of spiritual value and attempting to utilise them for the benefit of society'.[5] He wrote in 1890 to the novelist and critic, Edmund Gosse, that this ideal had been the centre-piece of his belief, though to arrive at it he had to struggle through confusions and torments that were a major drain on his energies. But it had its polemical as well as its emotional significance. What he saw in Greek civilization was the role of homosexuality as part of the accepted way of life, part of an organic whole. This was a constant theme in his work. It reappears in the final chapter on Greek love in his *Studies of the Greek Poets*, which he was convinced lost him the Oxford poetry professorship in 1876. In actual fact the response was muted, as one would have expected; reviewers generally ignored the chapter, though one compositor protested at its iniquity, while a reviewer felt that Symonds's philosophy amounted to 'the total denial of any moral restraint on any human impulse'.[6] His idealization of Greek love had its limitations. He was not particularly interested in lesbian love, and it was only at Ellis's instigation that he included female homosexuality in his draft for *Sexual Inversion*. He argued, rather weakly, that, 'philosophically', lesbianism was put on the same footing as male homosexuality, though never as completely worked into the social system. He felt, moreover, that the male body 'exhibits a higher organisation of the human form than the female'. In fact, Symonds does not himself seem to have been particularly sympathetic to the Greek taste for pederasty, preferring strapping working-class young men or peasants. Only among these, he believed, could he find the genuinely spontaneous and 'natural' people who could satisfy his needs. It was for this reason that Switzerland represented for him the only hope of self-effectualization. He developed from the 1870s the series of relationships with Swiss peasants and Venetian gondoliers (particularly the handsome Angelo Fusato) who were at last to give him physical release if not emotional fulfilment.

His aim was to establish, by using the Greek analogy, that homosexuality *could* be accepted as part of the social mores. Giving him the personal confidence that this could be achieved was the influence of Walt Whitman. He first encountered Whitman's work on a visit to his friend, F. W. H. Myers, at Cambridge in 1865. There he heard for the first time the lines from the Calamus section of *Leaves of Grass*:

I proceed for all who are or have been young men,
To tell the secret of my nights and days,
To celebrate the need of comrades.

Symonds was transfixed and inspired: here were thoughts he had barely begun to confess to himself. As he later wrote: 'Whitman threw clear light upon truths which I had but dimly perceived, and gave me the courage of opinions previously held with some timidity.'[7]
In the first place, Whitman gave the rather sickly and tubercular Symonds a glory in the body, a realization of the mystical value of the physical. He quotes in his study of Whitman the phrase: 'If anything is sacred, the human body is sacred.' Whitman challenged 'those medieval lies regarding sexual sinfulness, those foolish panegyrics of chaste abstinence, those base insinuations of foul-minded priests . . .'. Secondly, Whitman gave a rationale for his own revulsion against what he saw as the rampant sexual colonialism of his friends Roden Noel and Lord Ronald Buxton. Symonds always laid great emphasis on the fact that there were two kinds of inversion: casual sex, which he deplored, even though he indulged in it, and pure, 'manly' sex. He was revolted by Wilde's *Picture of Dorian Gray* for the 'morbid and perfumed' manner with which it treated its subject.[8] Whitman's work was quite different from this. Alongside 'amativeness', ordinary heterosexual love, Whitman stressed some-

thing new: 'adhesiveness', love between men. This, as Symonds saw it, was a 'manly attachment', 'athletic love', 'the high towering love of comrades', 'a virtue', 'a passion equal in permanence, superior in spirituality, to the sexual affection'.

The actual role of sex between men in Whitman's philosophy was not, however, clear to Symonds. He was convinced it was there, but wanted confirmation from the great man himself. This Walt Whitman was too reticent to give. In a correspondence lasting twenty years from 1871, Symonds dropped constant hints about his own tastes and probed Whitman's own, but Whitman was as skilful in evading the question as Symonds was in posing it. Whitman had been flattered by Symonds's devotion and encouragement of 'Whitmania' in England in the 1870s and 1880s, but when disillusion set in after 1887, following a vicious attack on Whitman by Swinburne, Whitman felt that Symonds had been less than courageous in defending him. Nevertheless Symonds wrote on, and in 1890 at last posed the question openly: did adhesiveness include sexual relations between men? Whitman wrote back a scalding reply, denying that any such connotation should be put upon his work.[9] Symonds had his answer at last: a disingenuous but chastening one. It seems likely that Whitman was as reluctant finally to commit himself on paper as was Symonds, and he seems to have been exasperated with Symonds's own pussyfooting. J. A. Symonds, however, was now committed to a study of Whitman, and this he finally published in 1893. It is both a memorial to Whitman's influence and a celebration of his work. And in it, Symonds manages to present both Whitman's denial and his own reading of the American's meaning: 'Whitman never suggests that comradeship may occasion the development of physical desires. On the other hand, he does not in set terms condemn, deny, or warn his disciples against their perils.'[10] The ardent fervour of an impetuous young man was muted into the gently ironic and ambiguous inflections of middle age. Symonds manages to make his point while ostensibly denying it: he had perfected a technique of tasteful evasion.

Evasiveness was to characterize the moves towards publication of his own most explicit works on homosexuality. The last years of his life saw three significant literary efforts: the work for his essay on homosexuality, *A Problem in Modern Ethics*; the draft of his Memoirs; and the preparatory work for his joint venture with Ellis.

He began writing his Memoirs in 1889, but it was an idea which had long been germinating in his mind. They were intended, quite clearly, as a frank apologia for his life. Planned as an examination of the evolution of an 'abnormal' individual, it was founded on Symonds's fundamental belief that he was what his nature had destined him to be. He examines his childhood, his first sexual stirrings, his schooldays, the influence of his father, his experiences as a young man, his guilt, his marriage, his eventual coming to terms with his sexual nature. It is a fascinating insight into both the evolution of a nineteenth-century homosexual and the process of self-discovery and identity. He is anxious throughout to stress his own 'masculinity', his lack of effeminacy and absence of partiality for boys. His aim was to proclaim the lack of 'morbidity' in homosexuality as such, and through publication of the Memoirs to make others feel that they were not alone while perhaps helping the scientific understanding of sexual inversion as he saw it.

His other work, *A Problem in Modern Ethics*, was a counterpart to the Memoirs. There are two clear aims in this essay, completed in 1890: firstly, to elucidate the literature on homosexuality so as to reach a new view of homosexuality; secondly, to suggest the legal changes that should follow. He carefully studied the range of literature, particularly the European medico-forensic material and attempted to demonstrate the inconsistencies and inadequacies of most work up to Krafft-Ebing. As against these works, he sought to propose an alternative view, drawn specifically from his own insights into his own development and from ideas stimulated by the work of Ulrichs. Symonds, with his usual energy in following up leads, had established contact with Ulrichs and visited him in Italy, where he found the great pioneer to have lost some of his fervour. Ulrichs's elaborate schemes of homosexual types seemed to Symonds to be a little metaphysical, but he found his basic approach sympathetic. As he put it to Carpenter, 'The first thing is to force people to see that the passions in question have their justification in nature.'[11] He felt that physiologists still too easily thought that sexual instincts followed the build of the sexual organs, so that when they did not the phenomenon was assumed to be criminal or morbid, and that this was, in fact, 'due to science at this point being still clogged with religion and legal pre-suppositions'. In opposition to this, Symonds tentatively endorsed, following Ulrichs again, a spectrum theory of sexual behaviour, 'a rhythm of subtly graduated differences extending from the extremity of sexual inversion up to the most positive type of ordinary sexual instinct'.[12]

This led on logically enough to the social and legal conclusions of the work. 'I am eager about the subject for its social and justice aspects . . . I am therefore in duty bound to work for an elucidation of the legal problem.' This took up another theme present in Ulrichs's work: the law was unjust to a class of person guilty of nothing. This argument that Symonds presented was a mixture of utilitarianism (the law did not work) and natural law, but the work ends with a series of pragmatic arguments, that the law causes unnecessary suffering and should be repealed.

*A Problem in Modern Ethics* has an importance because it was the first work clearly to discuss the more advanced views then current, and to link them to the need to change the law. It was also pioneering in its use of terms – 'urning', 'inversion' – that were to remain current for many years afterwards. Some fifty copies were privately printed in 1891 (pirated editions appeared in 1896 and 1901) and distributed to various interested people, who were asked to return the copies with comments on the wide margins. There was a ready response and letters from many homosexuals came flooding in. As Edmund Gosse put it: '. . . the position of a young person so tormented is really that of a man buried alive and conscious, but deprived of sleep. He is doomed by his own timidity and ignorance to a repression which amounts to death.'[13] The secret circulation that the pamphlet enjoyed gave comfort to many such homosexuals, as the letters to Symonds testified. In this sense his 'speaking out' was not without its real significance.

This was the background to his planned collaboration with Havelock Ellis in the early 1890s. It was anticipated that *Sexual Inversion* would be a major study of homosexuality which would raise the issue in public discussion. But before the work could be realized, in 1893 Symonds died, and during the five years which followed, his writings on homosexuality were effectively suppressed. This has often been seen as an act of censorship by his family and literary executor, Horatio Brown, but it was in fact already prefigured in the hesitancies and caution Symonds himself had shown during his lifetime. He describes in his Memoirs how, as a young man, his love for a young Bristol chorister, Willie Dyer, had been thwarted by his father's edicts. He comments that the back of his life was broken by thus yielding to convention. Unfortunately, this yielding to convention was an ever-present danger. He complained painfully about the impossibility of ever getting acceptance for his homosexuality from his friends, of the 'impossible cul-de-sac' he was in. Then there was his family, to whom he felt obligated: 'I have to think of the world's verdict – since I have given pledges to the future in the shape of my four growing girls.'[14] Symonds's sexual radicalism never went to the extent of questioning either his outward respect-

ability or social roles. As he wrote to Carpenter: 'It does not interfere with marriage when that is sought as a domestic institution, as it
always is among men who want children for helpers in their work and
women to keep their households.'[15]

He even wondered whether *A Problem in Modern Ethics* ought
to be published: 'My best work, my least presentable.' The time was
not ripe, he felt, to launch the work on the world. So his family,
after his death, had ample justification for suppressing his writings.
His Memoirs were not published by Horatio Brown, his executor
and biographer, who had them locked up in the London Library
until 1976. Brown himself in his biography made Symonds's life
appear to be a search for religious rather than emotional satisfaction.
Symonds's name was removed from the joint work with Ellis. All of
this, it seems, was Symonds's own last cautious wish. Brown wrote
to Edward Carpenter in 1897:

> You probably do not know that the very last words he wrote
> when he was past speech, and within a few hours of death, were
> a strong injunction to me to regard his family in all matters of
> publication. An appeal from one of his family; the strongly
> expressed opinion of his oldest and most intimate friends when
> I go to London; the best legal and medical opinion I could
> obtain; all combine to make me take the step I did.[16]

The retreat from openness, from a full 'speaking-out', was prepared by Symonds's own lifetime caution. Edward Carpenter later
accused Symonds of timidity, of running away from his own conclusions, and thereby doing harm to the cause he valued.[17] Symonds's
final retreat still lay in the future, however, when he began his
collaboration with Ellis in the early 1890s.

## *Havelock Ellis and* Sexual Inversion

*'As a youth I had hoped to settle problems for those who came after me: now I am content if I do little more than state them'* – *Havelock Ellis (1898)*

Though not himself homosexual, Ellis had more than a theoretical interest in homosexuality from the start. He had, for instance, close friendships with such homosexuals as Edward Carpenter, and his own wife, Edith Lees, was lesbian. It is also possible that Ellis's own form of sexual variation, which he called 'urolognia' or 'undinism' – his sexual delight in seeing women urinate – made him more aware of the variety or 'naturalness' of sexual drives and the folly of trying to deny or obliterate them. Yet, in fact, Ellis showed a relative indifference to the subject of homosexuality until the early 1890s.

His first book, *The New Spirit* (1889), had contained a powerful essay on Walt Whitman, though he passed over the theme of 'comradeship' in relative silence. In this he had, however, suggested that here, for the first time since Christ, was a person who embodied the instincts of a complete man. The bourgeois reviewers were shocked by such blasphemy, and Symonds, needless to say, was delighted. He had had contact with Ellis in the 1880s, following a favourable review of one of his books, but he now wrote to Ellis, expressing his appreciation of the Whitman essay and delicately broaching the subject of homosexuality. Symonds had felt in Ellis's essay the 'aura' of a sympathetic soul. But in their correspondence, which was their only vehicle of communication as they never actually met, can be seen the development of an intellectual rather than a personal relationship. By 1892 they had finally agreed to collaborate on a major essay on homosexuality. The collaboration was to have a powerful impact on both writers. Symonds was anxious finally to launch forth with a major work to crown his life's involvement; Ellis was concerned, as he saw it, to help right a social wrong and to establish his own reputation as a student of sex. The work they jointly prepared was eventually to form vol. 2 of Ellis's *Studies in the Psychology of Sex*.[1]

Havelock Ellis (1859–1939) was a representative figure in the new radical/socialist intelligentsia that sprang up in the wake of the socialist revival of the early 1880s. He was born the son of lower middle-class parents in Croydon. His early years were uneventful. He read omnivorously, and imbibed many of the radical texts of the time – Renan's *Life of Jesus*, the poetry of Swinburne and Shelley – and questioned his evangelical religion. The inevitable crisis occurred during a prolonged stay in Australia as a young teacher in the late 1870s. Here, in isolation in the bush, he experienced a mystical insight which he called a 'revelation'. The immediate focus of this was a reading of a book by James Hinton, a doctor turned writer on moral and sexual matters. This seems to have crystallized the young man's vague discontents, given him a confidence in himself and a twofold determination: to make the study and understanding of sexuality his lifelong aim, and to train as a doctor to enable him to pursue this aim in the most practical way. With this double determination he returned to England in 1881. In the London of the 1880s he entered the new world of socialist discussion and agitation. He met most of the leading figures of the new left then emerging, including the Marxist pioneer H. M. Hyndman, Marx's daughter Eleanor, and her lover, Edward Aveling, the early Fabians, men like Edward Carpenter, and women such as Olive Schreiner, the South African feminist and novelist with whom Ellis developed a life-long friendship. At the same time he cultivated his literary abilities, writing on philosophy, travel, religion, politics, feminism, art. He edited for a while the 'Mermaid' series of unexpurgated Elizabethan plays, and shocked Symonds by printing as an appendix to his edition of Marlowe's plays the contemporary charges brought against him for blasphemy and immorality; Symonds feeling that 'the cause' was not helped by such wilful openness.[2] Ellis's socialism, so typical of the 1880s, combined a vague progressivism and a belief in the benevolent role of the state with a desire for personal uplift and freedom.

By 1890 he had already established a radical reputation. In *The New Spirit* he had made a passionate declaration of his belief in the 'new age', an era made up of the triumph of science, the emancipation of women and the growth of social democracy. And, with Fabian optimism, he believed that the traditional problems of the nineteenth century were on the road to solution: that the outstanding problem facing the new century was that of sexual relations.

In his second book, *The Criminal* (also published in 1889), based on Lombroso's theories of the biological basis of criminality, he had already put himself in line with some of Symonds's preoccupations. In this book he sought to show that the traditional belief that everyone had the germ of criminality was false, and that crime was a product of a certain type of individual, whose behaviour was determined by congenital factors. A simple and logical extension could be made to link this with congenital views of homosexuality. He was, moreover, beginning to clear the way for his major study of the psychology of sex by examining the differences between men and women. The results were published as *Man and Woman* (1894), and convinced him that major differences arose from biological predisposition. In other ways, too, his approach was compatible with that of Symonds. He shared with him, and indeed with Carpenter, the view that it was society which inhibited the real potentialities of human nature. Society, he believed, must be built on the 'sure and simple foundations of man's organism'. Whitman's work was the catalyst which brought all these strands together and facilitated collaboration between Ellis and Symonds.

By 1892 the lines of the proposed collaboration between the two men were clear. Symonds was to prepare the historical analysis (mainly on Ancient Greece) and provide most of the individual case-studies.[3] Ellis was to criticize the medical and 'scientific' theories. Ellis obviously felt that *A Problem in Modern Ethics* was a little too passionate for the book, and stated his intention of not going too far ahead of medical opinion. His aim, as he later put it, was always to be 'quietly matter of fact in statements, that at the time were outrageous'.[4] Symonds seems to have generally agreed that the book, to be acceptable, should not depart too far from the norm, and in fact he wanted a medical organization to publish it, to give it added weight, while Ellis preferred a more general publisher to provide a wider circulation. By the end of 1892 Symonds could write to Edward Carpenter, recording that he and Ellis agreed on all fundamental points, though he felt that Ellis was still a little too inclined to stick to 'neuropathical' theories. He intended to whittle this away to a minimum.[5]

After Symonds's death in 1893, Ellis continued work on the book along the lines agreed. It first appeared in print in Germany in 1896, translated by a friend of Ellis's, Dr Hans Kurella, under the title *Das Kontrare Geschlechtsgefühl*. Symonds's essay on Greece was published in full, as was an essay on soldier-love (not in the English editions), and *Modern Ethics* was liberally used throughout and in footnotes. The book was well reviewed in the German medical press. But in England publication was not so easy. An English edition, under the names of both Ellis and Symonds, appeared in 1897. Then, in the wake of the Wilde trial, Horatio Brown bought up the whole edition and instructed that all references to Symonds be expunged from future editions. In attempting to bring out a new edition thus revised, Ellis was faced with accumulating difficulties.

None of the orthodox medical publishers would take the book, and Ellis had in desperation accepted the offer of one Roland de Villiers, apparently a liberal-minded independent publisher, to produce the English edition. De Villiers was as it turned out less interested in the educational value of the work than in its commercial possibilities, but Ellis allowed himself to be taken in. It later became apparent that de Villiers was a notorious confidence trickster, wanted by the police of Europe and Britain. With these inauspicious auguries, the second edition of the book, this time without Symonds's name on the title page and with substantial deletions, appeared later in 1897. And almost immediately it was drawn into an unanticipated court case.

The book was warmly received by the Legitimation League, a small society dedicated to sex reform, and in particular to advocating changes in the law relating to illegitimacy. Its magazine *The Adult* was published by de Villiers, and through him the society came to display the book in its offices. Unfortunately for Ellis, Scotland Yard was keeping a close watch on the league, convinced it was the haunt of anarchists, then currently the terror of respectable London. The police obviously felt that a book on *Sexual Inversion*, especially in the post-Wilde atmosphere, would provide a convenient hammer with which to crush the society.[6]

The secretary of the Legitimation League, George Bedborough, was arrested and eventually brought to trial in October 1898 for selling 'a certain lewd, wicked, bawdy, scandalous libel', namely, Ellis's *Sexual Inversion*. Ellis himself was not charged, nor indeed was the book itself on trial as such. The membership of the Free Press Defence Committee, which was at once established to defend free speech, reads like a roll-call of the political and literary left: H. M. Hyndman, G. B. Shaw, Edward Carpenter, E. Belfort Bax, Grant Allen, George Moore. And the weather seemed set fair for a vigorous battle. But its efforts were not needed. The case ended in anti-climax. Bedborough was, under strong police pressure, persuaded to plead guilty and was bound over. This had the effect of preventing anyone giving evidence on the book's merits. Ellis himself was never called to the stand – luckily, since he was in any case too shy and reluctant to become a martyr – and the book was labelled scandalous and obscene, completely undefended. Nevertheless, like the Wilde trial three years earlier, the case dramatized the issue and had repercussions which rippled through the next few years. In the first place, and negatively, Ellis determined that future editions of his *Studies in the Psychology of Sex* would not be published in Britain. Thereafter they were printed in the United States, and to this day no full British edition of Ellis's most important work has appeared in his own country. In the second place, the police had achieved a double victory: they had crushed the Legitimation League as a supposed 'haunt of anarchists'; and they had effectively banned *Sexual Inversion* without even having to try it on its merits. The state had effectively capitalized on the pool of fear of homosexuality drummed up over the previous decade or so. The trial was another stage in the hostile labelling of homosexuality. It also marked *Sexual Inversion*, a sober book if there ever was one, as a 'dirty book' with a secure black market. The case confirmed Ellis in his belief in the difficulties of changing attitudes. The 'crusade' he had vigorously advocated in his early work became more a subtle tilt at outrageous attitudes, an attitude he justified in a pamphlet: 'The pursuit of the martyr's crown is not favourable to the critical and dispassionate investigation of complicated problems. I must leave to others the task of obtaining the reasonable freedom that I am unable to obtain.'[7]

Nevertheless, even this limited aim had its effect. The prosecution – as so often in this sort of case – had in one major way been counterproductive: it publicized the book. As a result hundreds of homosexual men and women wrote to Ellis, as they had earlier to Symonds, with their problems, their life-histories, information and views. Many of these he was able to reassure; others he referred to Carpenter and other homosexual friends such as George Cecil Ives. Many of his correspondents found their way, as examples, into his books. Given the conspiracy of silence, this was a major achievement. But the book had a major impact in another way: it set the tone for liberal attitudes to homosexuality for generations to come.

The aim of *Sexual Inversion* was to present a case *for* homosexuality, however mild its words may seem today, and its moral tone and method were the models for the later works that dealt with sexual variations. The two principles Ellis employed were a form of cultural relativism as applied to moral attitudes, and biological determinism as applied to essential sexual characteristics.

The first principle was useful in demonstrating the potentially transient nature of Victorian attitudes. By piecing together the anthropological, historical, religious and literary evidence available, he attempted to demonstrate its common incidence: among animals; among primitive peoples and in ancient civilizations; among famous literary and artistic figures; and in all social classes. His conclusion, written into his approach, was that homosexuality had always and everywhere existed; and that in many cultures, indeed, it had been tolerated and even socially valued.

Ellis's approach is still the most common among liberals in attempting to understand homosexuality. By collating all the available data, the aim is to show that it is not a product of particular national vices or periods of social decay, but a common and recurrent part of human sexuality. This was an important element in liberating ideas of homosexuality. But in Ellis's case (and in that of most of his successors) it stopped there. No attempt was made to explore why forms of homosexuality were accepted in some cultures and abhorred in others, and the only hints he gave as to why homosexuals were oppressed in contemporary society were vague references to the survival of religious taboos. Ellis's approach is basically descriptive: the material roots of sexual oppression are left unexplored. The result of this was to place a heavy emphasis on what he regarded as the basic truth about homosexuality, its biological roots.

This was the second major element in Ellis's approach. Ellis, like Krafft-Ebing and others, was in fact prepared to accept that some homosexual predilections were acquired, and in the final revised version of *Sexual Inversion* he made a distinction between 'homosexuality', which he defined as any sexual and physical relation between people of the same sex, and 'inversion', which was defined as a congenital condition. This implied that some people might indeed be 'corrupted' into homosexuality, and he was later to write in a typically liberal way that it was the task of a sound social hygiene to make it difficult to acquire 'homosexual perversity'. This opened up moral chasms and confusions that Ellis was never able to face. In the work of later would-be reformers in the 1950s and 1960s, it led to some peculiar distinctions between 'inversion', which was regarded as 'natural', and therefore unavoidable and tolerable; and 'perversion', which was vice adopted by weak natures and therefore to be condemned.[8]

Both 'inverts' and 'perverts' did the same things in bed, however, and the distinction relied on purely arbitrary judgements as to whether the homosexuality was inherent or acquired. And, of course, it implied that homosexual behaviour was only acceptable if it was involuntary and could not be suppressed. Havelock Ellis dodged the issue by concentrating his arguments on congenital 'inversion', which placed him in the main line of campaigners for homosexual rights, from Ulrichs through Edward Carpenter to Magnus Hirschfeld, but distinctly apart from the work on sexuality that Freud was beginning at about the same time.

Congenital theories had the propagandist advantage of allowing Ellis to reject current theories of 'degeneration', for a drive which was natural and spontaneous, he argued, could not simultaneously be a manifestation of a morbid disease. He took pains, therefore, to find a form of words describing homosexuality which did not suggest sickness, and the process can be traced in his correspondence with Symonds. Symonds originally felt that Ellis was too inclined to stick to 'neuropathical' explanations. Ellis countered this by suggesting that 'inversion' could best be seen as a technical 'abnormality', a congenital turning inwards of the sex drive and away from the opposite sex. He rejected J. A. Symonds's and Carpenter's description of homosexuals as an 'intermediate sex' or 'third sex', feeling that this merely crystallized into a metaphor the superficial appearances. Struggling to escape the notion of sickness, he suggested that perhaps 'inversion' could best be described as an 'anomaly' or a 'sport of nature'. Symonds was not so keen on 'sport' and suggested instead an analogy with colour-blindness, which was a harmless variation. Ellis, in return, felt that even this might appear a deficiency, and suggested a comparison with colour-hearing, the ability to associate sounds with particular colours.[9] In this terminology, inversion seemed less a disadvantage than a harmless quirk of nature.

His concern was to establish as far as he could the 'normality' of homosexuals. To do this he had to challenge certain stereotypes of homosexual behaviour, and even suggest the moral excellence of 'inverts'. In the first place, he questioned the association of buggery with homosexuality, suggesting it was rare. As Edward Carpenter put it, the law inhibited homosexual love by linking it with 'gross sensuality'; and, like Symonds and Carpenter, and Magnus Hirschfeld in Germany, Ellis deliberately played down this aspect for fear of jeopardizing his reform aims. In the same way he attempted to challenge the other stereotype of homosexual appearance, denying, for instance, that most homosexual men were 'effeminate'; and he regarded transvestism as an essentially heterosexual phenomenon. Here he followed closely Magnus Hirschfeld's massive work on transvestism. Ellis was striving, in other words, to emphasize that 'inverts' were essentially 'ordinary' people in all but their sexual behaviour. This had the positive effect, on the one hand, of allowing him to challenge conventional misconceptions; but, on the other, it had the danger, and one which sexual liberals have rarely avoided, of imposing new standards of behaviour for the supposed 'deviant' which may be as restrictive, if more subtly so, as the old. It offers, for example, the possibility of being accepted as homosexual so long as you are suitably 'masculine' in appearance and manner. Such an approach does not, in the end, challenge sexist assumptions, but helps to reinforce them.

Ellis was anxious, above all, to suggest the *respectability* of most homosexuals. He went to great lengths, for instance, to demonstrate that homosexuality was frequently associated with intellectual and artistic distinction. Some thirty-odd pages of *Sexual Inversion* are devoted to homosexuals of note, including Erasmus, Michelangelo, Christopher Marlowe, Sir Francis Bacon, Oscar Wilde, Walt Whitman, Sappho. Even here he showed a form of 'political tact': he carefully omitted names (like Shakespeare's) that might prove too controversial and thus obscure his case. The aim was to preserve a model of behaviour and abilities which would conform to a respectable if progressive middle-class mould.

Perhaps more revealing were the case-histories he gathered, some forty in all in final editions. These demonstrated very effectively the moral, personal and intellectual quality of homosexual people. The case-histories, often selected, as he said, from 'friends' (among them, carefully disguised, his wife, Carpenter and Symonds) were central to his argument. They were carefully picked (and in some cases doctored) to put the most favourable light possible. Just as earlier case-histories, in Krafft-Ebing's work for instance, had been biased towards sickness, so Ellis's were biased towards 'normality'. They illustrated the major part of his argument: the strength of homosexual feeling; its ineradicability despite moral repression; its wide distribution (the working-class 'inverts' cited seemed to accept their homosexuality more easily than those from the professional class); its lack of pathological forms; the absence of effeminacy; and the variety of sexual expression. The great majority of people cited found themselves fully able to accept their inversion. Those who could not nevertheless emerged as towers of moral strength.

If homosexuality was not a medical problem, then there was no necessity for a 'cure'. Ellis briefly discussed various methods of 'cure' – particularly hypnotism and psychoanalysis – and found them wanting. The various disorders often associated with homosexuality, he felt, were more often associated with society's attitudes than with the sexual orientation itself.[10] And this pointed to the necessity of changing the law. The whole force of *Sexual Inversion*, its tempered tone, its often muted evidence, was directed to suggesting this end.

The type of case Ellis argued was to have a long history among reformers. Three elements have been central: first, the argument that homosexuality is characteristic of a fixed minority and incurable;

secondly, that reforming efforts should be directed towards changing the law so that this minority may live in peace; and thirdly, the belief that such reform would only come about through a long period of public education. Few people until very recently argued for more.

But though liberal sexual ideology 'tolerates' homosexuality, it always begins with the assumption that homosexual behaviour has to be explained as a deviation from a norm of sexual behaviour. What has to be tolerated in this view is an 'abnormality', however gently this is stated. Ellis, despite his efforts to find a relatively neutral form of words, was no exception. He stressed, particularly in later writings, the impossibility of getting 'social opinion' to accept homosexuality and therefore found it difficult to advise a reluctant homosexual to 'set himself in violent opposition' to his society. There was, in his view, a need for a reluctant acquiescence in the moral views of society, and much the best result for the homosexual would be attained, 'When, while retaining his own ideas, or inner instincts, he resolves to forgo alike the attempt to become normal and the attempt to secure the grosser gratification of his abnormal desires.'[11]

He argued, in other words, that homosexuals had no choice but to endure the anguish and split morality that society had no choice but to dictate. Ellis's scepticism about the possibility of radical changes in attitudes stemmed from more than simple caution. He was locked at the end within a conservatism dictated by his biological theories.

Ellis's attitude to lesbianism is particularly relevant here. He claimed that his work gave special attention to female homosexuality, and by comparison with his predecessors this may well be the case. He was, as a matter of course, as prepared to defend publicly the rights of lesbians as he was of male homosexuals. His wife, Edith Ellis, was lesbian, a fact which became quite well known. A lecture tour of the United States in 1913 by Edith had reached the headlines of the Chicago press when she defended lesbian relations. In the 1920s Ellis, with typical diffidence, defended Radclyffe Hall's lesbian novel, *The Well of Loneliness*, and contributed a preface to it. He stated that his *Sexual Inversion* had, from its first edition, given special attention to lesbianism. Nevertheless, only one chapter of *Sexual Inversion* is entirely concerned with lesbianism and only six case-histories are properly described. References to it in later volumes of his *Studies* are similarly sparse. Two immediate explanations occur. First, there was possibly an element of personal embarrassment, given Edith's own lesbianism. Secondly, there was a great absence of easily obtainable information. There was no visible sub-culture

in Britain for lesbians until later in this century, unlike the situation
for male homosexuals. And lesbianism was not illegal, so there were
few spectacular court cases and no compelling reason for a political
campaign on the question. There is, however, a curiosity in Ellis's
approach. While he went to considerable lengths to stress that male
homosexuals were *not* effeminate, he stresses that lesbians *were*
inclined to be masculine. He believed the use of the dildo to be
common, and played down the importance of clitoral sexuality.[12]

Beyond this was his conviction that 'masculinity' and 'femininity'
were qualities based on deep biological differences. Male sexuality
was basically active. Female sexuality was essentially responsive to
the male's. If this was the case, lesbianism, which ultimately asserts
the autonomy of female sexuality, could only be explained by Ellis
as a deeply rooted element of masculinity in the woman. As a result,
Ellis was unable to challenge existing stereotypes of lesbian behaviour.

Ellis, in fact, flirted with certain ideas which restated an original
bisexual constitution in every individual. As an idea, it dated back to
Ancient Greece, and perhaps earlier, but it was just at this period, in
the late nineteenth and early twentieth centuries, that the notion
became the subject of scientific investigation. It was present in
Ulrichs's work, and other writers like Wilhelm Fleiss, Otto Weininger and Freud made it central to their theories. Ellis was at one with
these writers in recognizing that both sexes had elements of intersexuality, and he later adopted hormonal explanations for sexual
responses. But it was here that his disagreement with Freud was most
basic. He felt that Freud's theory of the Oedipus complex suggested
that bisexuality ought to be regarded as the primary state, so that
homosexuality arose through the suppression of the heterosexual
element. This opened up the possibility of similarly regarding
heterosexuality as the product of the suppression of homosexual
elements. Ellis recognized the dangers of this for his concept of
the congenital basis of sexual behaviour. If he were to accept Freud's
views, then he would have to accept, as he put it, that the 'most
fundamental' human instinct could equally well be adapted to
'sterility' as to propagation of the race. Such a view, Ellis believed,
would not fit into any 'rational biological scheme'.[13]

Ellis regarded this disagreement with Freud as of major significance, and it shaped their relationship. Freud, in later debates with
Hirschfeld's followers in Germany, was to concede that certain
elements of homosexuality might be congenital and was to believe
that perhaps hormonal theories might explain homosexuality; and
Ellis, as we have seen, conceded the possibility of environmental

influences. But at stake was the larger issue of the extent to which congenital influences could influence emotional and sexual patterns. Freud's theories left open the possibility that changes in personal and social circumstances might alter sexual behaviour and sexual roles. Ellis, wedded to biological theories, remained more rigid.

Ellis's work on homosexuality was not strikingly original in method or content. *Sexual Inversion* is essentially a work of synthesis, much influenced by Hirschfeld's researches, particularly on the importance of hormones, and on transvestism. Moreover, in comparison with later volumes of his *Studies*, it is thinner in detail and vigour, a fact underlined by his later revision of the first editions. Nevertheless, it was to prove a profoundly influential book. Its influence can be traced in most of the writings and campaigns that followed.

# 6

## Edward Carpenter and Friends

*'We call a man a criminal, not because he violates any eternal code of morality – for there exists no such thing – but because he vilates the ruling code of his time' – Edward Carpenter, 'Defence of Criminals' (1889)*

Just as Whitman was to provide the occasion for collaboration between J. A. Symonds and Havelock Ellis, so, earlier in the 1880s, he had been one of the common strands that brought Ellis into contact with Edward Carpenter. Ellis had purchased Carpenter's long Whitmanite poem, *Towards Democracy*, on a second-hand bookstall in 1885. At first he had been unenthusiastic, dismissing it as 'Whitman and water'. But when he eventually wrote to Carpenter, he was rather warmer in his appreciation. Ellis indicated a very useful comparison: 'I think that *Towards Democracy* compared to *Leaves of Grass* is (in no bad sense) feminine. Whitman is strenuously masculine.'[1] Over the years, the relationship between Ellis and Carpenter was to broaden beyond these early links. Carpenter developed in particular very close relationships with Olive Schreiner and Ellis's wife, Edith. The two men maintained a life-long correspondence, as well as a continuing interest and involvement in questions of sex psychology though their life-styles diverged greatly.

Edward Carpenter (1844–1929) was born into an upper middle-class Brighton family. He was destined for the Church, and in fact after Cambridge he took orders and was for a while curate to the early Christian Socialist, F. D. Maurice (and was also, at one time, approached to become tutor to the children of the Prince of Wales). In his autobiography, *My Days and Dreams*, he was to divide his 'early life' up to the 1890s into four periods: (1) 1844–64, when he was 'embedded in a would-be fashionable world which I hated'; (2) 1864–74, in Cambridge, with a more or less intellectual atmosphere; (3) following the rejection of this, half a dozen years searching for new paths (he began to give university extension lectures, and his long involvement in the life of the North of England); (4) finally, 1881–90, his espousal of socialism, his organizational and agitational work, and a life 'lived almost entirely among the working masses . . . engaged in manual labour'.

These periods represent a search for fulfilment, for new political, intellectual and emotional standards, and in this his evolving attitude to his own sexual orientation was to play a central role.

According to his own testimony, he had never found anything repellent in sex itself (unlike some of his contemporaries), but much of his early life was dominated by the acute nervous strains caused by guilt and emotional frustration. It is a recurrent theme of his autobiographical works. The influence of Whitman was therefore central: 'It was not till (at the age of twenty-five) I read Whitman – and then with a great leap of joy – that I met with the treatment of sex which accorded with my own sentiments.'[2]

He first read the 'little blue book' of Whitman's poems in 1869, and from this time he dated a profound change. And, as with Symonds, it was the poems that celebrated comradeship which attracted him. From 1874, the year in which he began his university extension lectures in the North of England, he began a long correspondence with Whitman. For Carpenter, Whitman was 'the most Greek in spirit' of contemporary writers, and during the same period he was to find a further inspiration in Italy, where he experienced 'the Greek idea of the free and gracious life of man at one with nature and the cosmos'. Throughout his life (as for many of the characters in E. M. Forster's early novels) Italy was to remain an 'inspiration', an antidote to the bourgeois materialism of his own milieu. While on a visit there in the 1880s, he confided to a friend, he found his sexual life reviving. The remnants of Greek civilization that he found in Italy seemed a complete antithesis to the stifling ideologies of commercialism and Christianity. This phase of his development culminated in 1877 with a visit to the United States, where he met Whitman and, like Ellis later, compared him with Christ as the embodiment of the 'whole man'. He was particularly impressed by Whitman's easy intimacy with common people. He saw in Whitman's belief in comradeship, in adhesive love, a counter-balance to materialism, a way of spiritualizing democracy and of drawing the classes together. This had a profound influence on Carpenter. He began work on the long poem *Towards Democracy*, which was to identify him in the 1880s as England's Whitman.

But 1877 was significant for Carpenter in another way. It was then that he first encountered the women's movement, as an extension lecturer in Leeds. He had long recognized the unsatisfactory nature of the bourgeois family, and its impact on both women and men. The life-style of middle-class ladies he felt to be 'tragic in its emptiness', and he recognized the absurdity of an ideology where his father could drive himself ill with work and worry so as to keep his daughters in respectable but destructive idleness. He drew a parallel with the working class: just as they had to sell their labour to survive, so women had to sell their sex. Carpenter felt an immediate and sharp sense of empathy with the women's movement. 'I realised in my own person some of the sufferings which are endured by an immense number of modern women, especially of the well-to-do classes, as well as by that large class of men . . . to whom the name of Uranians is often given.' He confided to Whitman his belief that 'the women will save us'.[3] As he moved in the late 1870s towards an espousal of socialism, his feminism, his sense of oppression arising from his homosexuality, and his identification with the working people were all essential elements.

Carpenter's socialism took a concrete form in 1883 when he read H. M. Hyndman's summary of the chief elements of Marx, *England for All*, which crystallized his vague aspirations. He met many of the leading personalities in the Marxist Social Democratic Federation – Hyndman, William Morris, John Burns, H. H. Champion, J. L. Joynes, Herbert Burrows – and helped to finance the federation's journal, *Justice*. But though influenced by Marxist concepts – he accepted, for instance, on a formal level, the theory of surplus value – his actual socialism was a more personal, ethically based system of belief. He found its main inspiration, not in the constructive pro-gramme of socialism (particularly, later on, in Fabian social engineer-ing), but in its basis as a searching critique of the old society and of the lives of the rich; and in its glowing vital enthusiasm towards the realization of a new society. His socialism had a moral rather than a 'scientific' foundation, with a natural bias towards anarchism. It might have been crystallized by *England for All*, but its roots were in Carpenter's rejection of a middle-class life, his revulsion against its over-consumption, the disjunction he felt between the classes, and the urge for a moral and social reintegration. It was fed, moreover, by various streams.

Through his involvement with the radical artisans of Sheffield from the late 1870s, he came into contact with the survivals of the Owenite and Utopian socialism of the 1840s. In the activities of his artisan friends, such as Albert Ferneyhough and Charlie Fox, he found the model of a 'life close to nature and actual materials'.[4] In 1880 he moved in with Ferneyhough and his wife, and this 'seemed to liberate the pent-up emotionality of years'. In the following year his mother died, which had a profound impact on him and further served to sever links with his background. At the same time he read the *Bhagavad Gita*, the central work of Hindu philosophy, which produced in him a mood of exaltation and inspiration, a heightening of his awareness of life and its meaning. The actual socialist encounters gave form to a change in his life which was already taking place.

During the 1880s he developed his ethical socialist analysis – in *Towards Democracy*, in articles and in a series of essays which were collected together into *Civilisation: Its Cause and Cure* (1889). In this latter work, he was to point to the heart of his belief: 'civilization' was not the culmination of human progress, as the Victorian age professed to believe, but a 'disease' which stunted human potentialities. 'Civilization' was a particular stage of human history, the stage based on private property. Loosely following the American anthropologist, Lewis Morgan (who greatly influenced Marx and Engels), he demonstrated the ways in which private property had created poverty, drawn man away from nature, from his 'true self', from his fellows, turned women into the property of men, and created the state to ensure that ownership remained the prerogative of the few. The result was clear, and disastrous: 'It had been the work of civilization – founded as we have seen on Property – in every way to disintegrate and corrupt man – internally to corrupt – to break up the unity of his nature.'[5]

Behind this was a belief in the purity and 'health' (the key word) of original man. It was society which had destroyed this noble savagery, introduced the sense of shame, undermined the 'sacredness of sex'. From this basis, Carpenter attacked modern bourgeois civilization for its artificial conventions, its stultifying manners and beliefs. He sought to undermine the ideology of science (and in so doing shocked the Fabian socialists in a famous lecture in 1889), which served 'civilization' and not man. And he challenged the moral and legal codes which expressed class power and not human aspirations. 'Law represents from age to age the code of the dominant or ruling class . . . Today the code of the dominant class may perhaps best be denoted by the word respectability'.[6]

Respectability! This was the voice of the bourgeoisie, of the commercial age, of property. It sought to impose its values on all, with disastrous effects. In the position of modern-day criminals, Carpenter saw a model for his own position as a homosexual, as an outlaw of society. But, 'The Outcast of one age is the Hero of another.' It was in the undermining of 'civilization', in the restoration of the real nature of man, the potential unity of his being, that Carpenter saw the hope for a better society. And, in this future society, sex and the body would be restored to their central position. 'Sex still goes first, and hands, eyes, mouth, brain follow: from the midst of belly and thighs, radiate the knowledge of self, religion, and immortality.'[7]

As with all utopian visions, the aspirations are highly dislocated from the practicalities. Carpenter sought to unify aim and practice by two unifying themes: intellectually, by his espousal of a form of moral evolutionism; and practically, by his own way of life. Carpenter rejected Darwinian themes of evolution because they relied on external influences, and on more or less accidental selective adaptation. He favoured instead a concept of internal growth, of spiritual development towards a higher form of consciousness. This evolutionism, loosely derived from Lamarckian theories, with elements from Eastern and Whitmanite mysticism, he called 'exfoliation'.[8] He believed that a higher order of consciousness was within everyone, waiting to be realized. Quoting Whitman, he spoke of 'Creation's incessant unrest, exfoliation', the shedding off of old forms and the gradual emergence of the new. There was in man, even under the toils of civilization, the growth of a higher awareness, of love and comradeship. In this Carpenter saw the hope for a better society which would transcend 'civilization'.

In his own personal life, Carpenter increasingly sought to cast off the weight of bourgeois conventions. In 1883 he bought Millthorpe, a house outside Sheffield, where he took up market gardening and, later in the decade, sandal-making. At Millthorpe he was, as he put it, able to escape from 'the domination of Civilisation in its most fatal and detested forms, respectability and cheap intellectualism'.[9] He aimed at the simplification of life, the casting off of the fripperies of civilization and the return to the essential roots of life. He advocated an outdoor life, a vegetarian diet, a 'return to nature'. But his life at Millthorpe was not just a personal life-style. He threw himself into building up the socialist movement in Sheffield, and became a popular and influential socialist propagandist elsewhere, especially in major provincial centres like Leeds and Bristol. The Sheffield Socialist Society, which he helped to establish in 1886, included local artisans and friends like George Adams, and George Hukin, a toolgrinder, but also had frequent visits from young members of the new intelligentsia, like C. R. Ashbee, Lowes Dickinson and Raymond Unwin (later a famous town planner and knight). More prominent figures in the socialist movement, like Hyndman and Annie Besant, and anarchists, such as Kropotkin and Charlotte Wilson, were frequent speakers at Sheffield socialist meetings.

The 1880s were years of hard political struggle and comradeship. They were also, as Carpenter tells in his autobiography, years of emotional conflict, of personal turmoil. Throughout these years, he sought to integrate his personal life into the political, to develop a single practice. In many of the socialist grouplets of the 1880s, as in the Sheffield Socialist Society, politics and friendship were inextricably bound together. For many of these pioneering socialists, living, loving and the revolution were inseparable: new forms of relationships, new ways of life, were seen as part of the practice of socialism. For many of the women and men who were seeking a new way of life, Carpenter was a key figure, a prophet. For many of the young bourgeoisie, breaking with their class, he lived their dilemma, as Sheila Rowbotham has put it. But the personal strains on Carpenter were often immense; they were years, too, as he later admitted, of 'personal tragedy'.

It is not surprising, therefore, that from the early 1890s there should be strong evidence that Carpenter's intellectual work and his sexual needs increasingly came to overshadow the publicly political. Beyond this, of course, was a transformation in the political climate. For those involved in the tiny socialist grouplets of the 1880s there seemed a heady feeling of the imminence of the millennium. By the mid 1890s, as we have seen, the intellectual and political climate was considerably gloomier. Carpenter's friend, Alf Mattison, produced a newspaper, *Forward*, which had a leader in 1897 asking, 'Will there be a Revolution?' Carpenter answered simply, 'No such luck!'[10] Carpenter's books continued to argue for specific reform – *Prisons, Politics and Punishments* (1905) and *Towards Industrial Freedom*, for example – and from the 1890s he was to produce a spate of works on the position of women and sex psychology. But his work placed increased emphasis on individual emancipation through spontaneity and mystical experience. And as the emphasis on the personal increased, so questions of sexuality came further to the fore: he felt the need to restore sex to centrality in people's lives. Personal changes in his own life encouraged this. In 1890 he had been deeply influenced by a visit to an Indian holy man, the Gñani, and in particular by the more open attitudes of Hindus towards sexual issues. And in 1891 he began his relationship with George Merrill which was to have a profound influence on the rest of his life. These new personal influences coloured his life and work, and the writings on sexuality appeared out of this new context.

In 1894 the Manchester Labour Press published three essays by Carpenter concerning 'Sex Love', 'Woman' and 'Marriage'. By 1895 he had prepared a large-scale work entitled *Love's Coming of Age*, which included a chapter on 'The Intermediate Sex'. This was immediately caught up in the aftermath of the Wilde affair. Carpenter's publisher, T. Fisher Unwin, withdrew from publication, and Carpenter reported a panic concerning homosexuality in London: '... the "boycott" has set in already. Isn't it a country.'[11] The Labour Press again stepped into the breach, so gaining the kudos of publishing one of the most radical works on sexuality to appear in the late nineteenth century. This was followed by a number of related works, chiefly on homosexual themes. In 1902 he published *Iolaus: An Anthology of Friendship*, a collection of writings with homoerotic themes. *The Intermediate Sex* (1908) gathered together various essays on homosexuality written over the previous ten years. In 1914 he produced a volume on *Intermediate Types Among Primitive Folk*. He also published several essays on Whitman, including *Days with Walt Whitman* (1906) and *Some Friends of Walt Whitman: A Study in Sex Psychology* (1924). And one of his last works was a study of the bisexual nature of the poet, Shelley. Though highly dated now, these works are still very revealing, and are vital stages in the evolution of a more liberal view of sexuality.

Carpenter's attitudes towards the women's question and homosexuality were closely linked. He felt that 'Uranian' men were instinctively close to women and more likely to identify with their cause, while he saw in the women's movement, with what we would now call 'sisterhood', the development of a 'homogenic passion', spiritually if not sexually.[12] The emphasis on the spiritual side of homosexuality is, in fact, very strong in his work, and had a double implication: it first challenged conventional notions of sexual debauchery, and therefore represented a form of political tact; and secondly it pinpointed Carpenter's own sense of a mystic unity within and beyond the body and the physical.

But it would be wrong to over-stress this, for what does distinguish Carpenter from most of his contemporaries (including Havelock Ellis) is his willingness to separate sex from procreation. This had important implications for women as well as homosexuals, male and female. He argued in *Love's Coming of Age* that public opinion had been largely influenced 'by the arbitrary notion that the function of love is limited to child bearing; and that any love not concerned in the propagation of the race must necessarily be of dubious character'.[13] He traced this back to the Hebraic and Christian traditions, and to the social need to encourage propagation, but he saw no contemporary need for it. As against this, Carpenter sought to stress the pleasurable nature of sex and its function as a binding fact in social relations; its prime object, as he put it, was *union*. And although he was anxious to stress that emotional love would be transmitted into spiritual, he emphasized that the physical must never be forgotten: without it the 'higher' things can never be realized. His aim was thus to free love from darkness and shame, and to place sex in the vital heart of the new awareness. This argument was central in his attitude towards homosexuality.

For Carpenter, 'Uranians' formed an 'intermediate sex' as bearers of the sexual characteristics of one sex and many of the emotional characteristics of the other: he was thus in the same tradition as many German writers, along with Symonds and, to a lesser extent, Ellis. But whereas Ellis spoke of 'hormones' and opted for a scientific framework, Carpenter's classifications have an indelibly vague and metaphysical air: 'Nature . . . in mixing the elements which go to compose each individual, does not always keep her two groups of ingredients – which represent the two sexes – properly apart.'[14]

He accepted a theory of sexuality which saw the two sexes as forming in 'a certain sense a continuous group'. He went much further than Ellis in accepting androgynous elements in individuals, and in his later works seems to be implying that androgyny was the state to be aimed for. He felt that there were many signs of an evolution of a new human type which would be *median* in character, neither excessively male nor excessively female. Bisexuality might thus become the norm of a new society. He broke away to a large degree from the positivistic and biological model that Ellis favoured, and in his philosophy saw not only a case for toleration of homosexuals, but a positive moral value. He felt that many 'intermediates' performed valuable social work, and he cited, rather cautiously, the influence of homosexual teachers on schoolchildren. But, more than this, he saw 'Uranians' as communicators and reconcilers, bridging the gap between men and women, becoming to a great extent 'the interpreters of men and women to each other'.[15]

In *Intermediate Types Among Primitive Folk* Carpenter went even further in seeing homosexuals as a 'forward force in human evolution'. He explained that, in primitive society, men are warriors and hunters while women attend to domestic work and agriculture. But the evolution of society demands more functions than this, and 'intermediate types', because they do not fit into the stereotyped roles, are able to become 'the initiators of new activities'. Carpenter, in fact, reverses the usual picture of evolution by arguing that it was the existence of a variety of sexual types which *led to* important differentiations in social life and activities. As a result, intermediate types were creators of many of the new activities: he uses evidence of the role of homosexuality in some cultures to show that homosexuals became inventors, teachers, musicians, medicine men, priests.[16] Western society, 'civilization', had to Carpenter's mind obscured this potential for human evolution. Above all, he argued, many homosexuals were bearers of the greatest potential for human development, linking up with his theory of exfoliation, for they had a special perception, a 'cosmic consciousness' which would flourish in a new society.

This sort of sexual millenarianism gave Carpenter a special aura among nineteenth-century sexual radicals. The utopian belief in a new era of sexual freedom was not unique – the work of James Hinton, Havelock Ellis's original mentor, had been a similar heady mixture of pantheism and sexual radicalism – but Carpenter was almost alone, after Symonds's death, in publicly asserting the possibly higher moral possibilities of homosexuality. Its flavour, of course, came from an emphasis on the spiritual qualities of a Whitmanite comradeship rather than an advocacy of sexual licence, but it was a potent brew.

However, Carpenter's work, like most contemporary views of sexuality, was constrained by its devotion to biological assumptions. Carpenter naturally assumed that the division of labour between the sexes was based on inherent biological qualities in men and women. He agreed with Ellis's analysis in *Man and Woman* that women were more primitive, emotional, intuitive, closer to nature. What gave Carpenter his radicalism for the period was his belief that society had *exaggerated* sex differences beyond sense and necessity. For this reason, he argued in *Love's Coming of Age* for the economic and social independence of women, which could only come with the end of the commercial system; for reform of marriage, involving a greater emphasis on spiritual rather than sexual loyalty; and for the central importance of birth control for women. His views on birth control are particularly revealing, especially given the inadequacy of most mechanical means at the time. He recommended 'Karezza', a method then currently advocated by Mrs. A. B. Stockham and practised in the American communal experiment run by J. L. Noyes of Oneida. This favoured prolonged bodily conjunction between the sexes, but a contact kept on the emotional level, with no orgasmic emission resulting.[17]

This theory provided a link with his attitude to homosexual love. Partly for political reasons (the actually illegality of what he was advocating), and partly for ideological motives (the Whitmanite 'adhesive' love), Carpenter wanted to stress the spiritual and emotional rather than the physical possibilities of love. So while he did not deny the physical, there is a strong moral element in his work which wants to make the purely physical a secondary issue. Carpenter's friend Charles Oates commented that the women he knew were 'either profoundly indignant or highly sarcastic' in response to Carpenter's views. The very ambivalence of his work caused a mixed response. *The Adult* criticized him for his devotion to monogamic views, while his friend, Kate Joynes, felt there was a 'clergyman's vein' in some of his arguments about sex. More conservative feminists were, however, appalled at the frankness of his arguments.[18] It is not surprising, therefore, that Carpenter's writings on sexuality do not always reflect his actual practice.

Carpenter wrote to Oates in 1887:

We are going to form by degrees a body of friends who will be tied together by the strongest general bond, and also by personal attachment – and we shall help each other immensely by the mutual support we shall be able to give each other. The knowledge that there are others in the same position as oneself will remove that sense of loneliness when plunged in the society of philistines which is almost unbearable.[19]

The position of someone like Carpenter, preaching a sexual politics, was peculiarly exposed. He preached a doctrine that was highly dangerous for the times. When the Oscar Wilde trial broke, he wrote to the *Star* protesting at the removal of Wilde's name from the billboards of the theatres where his plays were being performed – but he wrote under a pseudonym. Carpenter had a dual role: as a prophet, and as a person. He was compelled by his beliefs to practise 'propaganda by deed' – to live the life that he advocated. And, to a large degree, he did come out as a homosexual. By the 1890s most of his friends in the labour movement knew of his homosexuality, though he was always careful to obfuscate to a wider public. But, as an individual, he had emotional needs of his own, and his public position imposed enormous strains. His socialist propagandizing of the 1880s was constantly bedevilled by his emotional conflicts. Later, as a guru, he was to find his fame a strain in itself. Henry Salt was to recall his frequent offhandedness and his need to go off on his own. But what Edward Carpenter sought above all was a close relationship which would be the focus of a 'body of friends'. It was not until the 1890s that, in his relationships with George Merrill, he was to find such a focus.

The relationship with Merrill was not his first attempt to form a close emotional attachment, and during the 1880s Carpenter became deeply involved with some of his closest political comrades. In 1886, at the time of the formation of the Sheffield Socialist Society, he was closely attached to George Hukin. They apparently had a sexual relationship, but Hukin was unfortunately on the point of marrying and deeply in love with his future wife, Fannie. 'Yes, Ted, it did help me a great deal, that talk we had in bed that Monday morning. Oh, how often I had wanted to tell you about it: ever since that first night I slept with you at Millthorpe.' The anguish continued for some time, and Hukin was reluctant to make an emotional break, even after his marriage. 'I do wish you could sleep with us sometimes, Ted, but I don't know whether Fannie would quite like it yet.'[20]

The friendship was, in fact, to continue and strengthen over the years, until Hukin died at the age of fifty-seven, but in its early stages it caused Carpenter considerable pain. There was a series of other relationships with local artisans and socialists. In 1890 he drew close to Bob Muirhead, the Glasgow socialist. He wrote to his friend, James Brown:

> You will be surprised to hear that I slept last night with Bob – at Derby. I hope you won't be jealous. But I don't think you are. It was so good to have him . . . He was loving and good and we did not forget you.[21]

But it was with George Merrill that Carpenter was to achieve a lasting and firmly based relationship. They met in early 1891, when George was about twenty. He came into a railway carriage where Carpenter was travelling; Edward was struck immediately. 'We exchanged a few words and a look of recognition.' George followed Carpenter after they left the train, and gave him his address. The acquaintance, thus so casually begun, became 'almost immediately close and intimate, and has remained so ever since'.[22]

George came from a large working-class Sheffield family. His father was an unemployed former engine driver who had taken to drink, and his mother assumed firm control of the family. Up to the time when Carpenter met him, he had had a variety of dreary jobs – in a public baths, file-grinding, in a public house.

> The world so far to George consisted on the one hand of bar-room life – drunks and smutty jokes and the sentimentalities of boozy customers; and on the other hand of dreary and dingy works, with ill-paid monotonous toil, and no earthly prospect

of deliverance . . . Through it all, the great need of his nature
– the 'need of real love' – remained unsatisfied; nor was much
prospect of satisfaction to be discerned.

In Edward Carpenter, Merrill found a complementary soul. And
Carpenter found in Merrill that spontaneity, closeness to the earth
and devotion that, while struggling against his bourgeois upbringing,
he had always craved. He would excuse some of Merrill's excesses in
later life by referring to his 'childlike spontaneity'. Merrill was quick-
witted and direct, with a devastating repartee that often crushed
Carpenter. But he was also self-distrustful, with a slight stammer:
he felt acutely his lack of knowledge of politics and his inability to
help 'the social cause'.[23] Sexually, however, he was full of self-con-
fidence, and Carpenter noted his 'strong sexuality of temperament and
habit'. His language was often a little 'Elizabethan' in its vulgarity,
and his behaviour often offended some of Carpenter's staider friends.
But the two men were soon devoted. 'Our lives had become necessary
to each other so that what anyone said was of little importance.'[24]
The relationship did not entirely transcend the class or intellectual
differences, and there was a strong romanticism on each side: in the
early days, George would address Carpenter as 'My Dearest Dad',
in the manner of Pete Doyle and Walt Whitman, but there was more
to the relationship than paternalism. There was a deep and persistent
affection. 'It is impossible for me to love anyone as I love you and I
always shall to my dying day.'[25] The relationship was to provide
warmth and necessary stability for both partners.

Despite the intimacy established from the very first, it took a number of years before they felt able to live together. And when Merrill
did eventually move into Millthorpe, after Carpenter's erstwhile
companions, George Adams and his family, had moved out in some
acrimony, the sight of two homosexuals living more or less openly
together caused some controversy even among friends. Carpenter
later noted:

I received no end of letters, kindly meant, but full of warnings
and advice – deprecating the idea of a ménage without a woman,
as a thing unheard of, and a step entered on, it was supposed, in a
rash moment, and without due consideration: hinting at the risk
to my health, to my comfort, at bad cooking, untidy rooms, and
abundance of cobwebs, not to mention the queer look of the
thing, the remarks of neighbours, the certainty that the arrangement could not last long, and so forth.[26]

But Merrill took to housework with a passion, and while Carpenter left most of it to George, he participated more than previously. He gave up market gardening and tended a small kitchen garden. He found himself, he wrote later, in a new and unimagined state of comfort.

Carpenter's new, more open life-style alienated some of his friends. Henry and Kate Salt were never quite so close after Merrill moved in – Salt later referred to him as Carpenter's evil genius. Some of the neighbours were taken aback by the strange household, and spread stories, especially about Merrill. But others, like Edith Ellis, preferred the new atmosphere. And with this new emotional security, Carpenter felt able to make Millthorpe what he had always wanted it to be, 'a rendezvous for all classes and conditions of society'.

The house became almost a centre of pilgrimage for many in the labour and progressive movements. Vegetarians, dress reformers, temperance orators, spiritualists, secularists, anti-vivisectionists, socialists, anarchists: all attempted to recruit, and some succeeded in recruiting, Carpenter to their cause. Sheffield artisans, pioneering socialists, Cambridge and London intellectuals like Lowes Dickinson and Ashbee, close political associates like Edith Lees, Olive Schreiner, Isabella Ford and Alf Mattison, the Whitmanite Charlie Sixsmith: all found a warm welcome and sympathetic political and social response at Millthorpe. And, growing from this, Millthorpe became a focus for the hopes of many isolated homosexuals. Hukin wrote to Carpenter in 1906 describing a young man, Lionel Ash, who had come all the way from London to see Carpenter: 'He was evidently very troubled about himself. He had been reading *Unknown People* and other books on that subject, more or less, and didn't seem to know quite where he was – sexually.' Others were more stridently self-confident. In 1904 Hukin observed that:

> . . . two very pretty young ladies turned up with a donkey and cart and a dog. They had come all the way from Essex with bare feet and sandals and just a thin sort of Holland dressing gown – with no head gear. They said they were pilgrims and your disciples, they loved you and so sorry to have missed you.[27]

Carpenter's works had a particular warmth and insight that struck a chord for the young (especially among the middle class) of the period. The adolescent Robert Graves wrote to Carpenter from Charterhouse in 1914, confessing that *Iolaus* and *The Intermediate Sex* had taken the scales from his eyes and crystallized his vague feelings.[28]

But Carpenter's delicate avoidance of direct confrontation with the guardians of morality was not always successful. In 1909 he was the victim of a sustained local onslaught from a right-wing Irishman, M. D. O'Brien, a member of the reactionary Liberty and Property Defence League and a strong upholder of social purity. After harrying Carpenter at meetings and in the local press, he published and distributed to Sheffield householders a vitriolic attack on all that Carpenter stood for, entitled, graphically enough, *Socialism and Infamy: The Homogenic or Comrade Love Exposed. An open letter in Plain Words for a Socialist Prophet.* O'Brien sought both to blacken the socialist movement by linking it with the hellish horrors of an international Whitmanite plot to undermine morality, and with breaches of the criminal law; and to destroy Carpenter's local personal credibility. Carpenter was outwardly calm, calling the episode 'a sort of Gilbertian farce in the gutter', but he was inwardly badly shaken.[29] He wrote to the papers, stating that his views could be better read in his books. And he gained support from various local worthies, including the vicar, himself rather unfairly attacked by O'Brien. Nevertheless, he felt constrained to ask respectable friends to come and stay with him. And, in 1910, he was dropped from the parish council. The slanders had their poisonous impact.

Carpenter had to live his role as a prophet of homosexuality in the shadowy area between honesty and public scandal. He was, as the O'Brien episode revealed, anxious to remain on the right side of respectability. At about the same time the *British Medical Journal* viciously reviewed *The Intermediate Sex*, and Carpenter's reply neatly details his careful approach.

I am certain there is not a single passage in the book where I advocate sexual intercourse of any kind between those of the same sex. I advocate sincere attachment and warm friendship, and allow that this may have fitting expression in 'caress and embrace' – but I suppose that to some minds this is sufficient, and it is immediately interpreted as an advocacy of lust.[30]

On a formal level, Carpenter's protestations were justified. But for those who wanted to see, the message of his work was clear enough. The general vagueness and ambiguity which looks so obvious now was in large part a product of social necessity.

But there was a more fundamental vagueness in his work which partly accounts for its ambivalent impact on succeeding generations. In Carpenter's total work, the writings on homosexuality can be seen as part of a wholesale social critique of the values of 'civilization'. But the actual emphasis on the personal in his writings on sexuality could easily be detached from the broader context. His work was quietly absorbed, for instance, into the Bloomsbury emphasis on personal relationships, via Lowes Dickinson and E. M. Forster, whose novel *Maurice* owes a great deal to Carpenter's inspiration. It also formed part of the background to D. H. Lawrence's sexual dialectic; in his early life, Lawrence seems to have come into close contact with friends and associates of Carpenter, only to spit out this influence in the later works. But it was in the labour and socialist movements that his influence was most incalculable and ambiguous. It was clearly and passionately taken up by feminists like Isabella Ford of Leeds, by socialist Whitmanites like Charlie Sixsmith of Bolton, and by groups of socialists at home and abroad, particularly in Germany and Italy. The publication of *Love's Coming of Age* led a group in Italy to found a 'Union of Young Men' for the discussion of sexual problems.[31] And when the British Society for the Study of Sex Psychology was established in 1914, Carpenter was the obvious choice as its president.

In the wider labour movement, Carpenter's influence in 'making socialists' must have been vast. But to what degree his sexual radicalism was absorbed is another matter. By the turn of the century, the socialist movement – with its emphasis on the trade unions and parliamentary representation – was already quite different from the millenarian groupings that Carpenter had known in the 1880s. The support he gave to industrial militancy after 1910 further alienated him from some of his old Independent Labour Party friends, like the Bruce Glasiers. The First World War saw further snappings of the links, as his lukewarm opposition to the war (his nephew was a naval hero during it) alienated some on the left. On his eightieth birthday in 1924 he received a testimonial signed, among others, by members of the first Labour government. Merrill recorded that their home was like 'a flower and fruit store' besieged by 'taxis, cars and telegram boys and reporters waiting in long queues'.[32] But this was a celebration of the pioneering past rather than a signal for the living present. Carpenter's works were by then already a little dated, their optimism and mystical flavour a little passé in the face of the unemployment and depression and retreat of feminism that marked the 1920s and 1930s.

The last year of his life was sad and lonely. George Merrill died in 1927, and Carpenter was heartbroken: 'They have laid him in the cold earth,' he moaned, and within the year he was dead himself, already a figure of the past. An effort was made to keep his memory alive. In Sheffield, Edward Carpenter's friends and admirers organized a Carpenter Fellowship, and an annual memorial service which went on till 1948. But the fellowship could not raise enough money to buy up Carpenter's property for a museum. In 1944 E. M. Forster, Gilbert Beith, his literary executor, and other friends tried to revive interest in his work to celebrate the centenary of his birth. Forster spoke on the BBC on 25 September 1944. Special articles were carried by *The Times Literary Supplement*, the *Spectator*, the *Listener* and the *New Statesman*. *Towards Democracy* was reissued. But the centenary was not, on the whole, a success. He had been largely forgotten. His socialism and sexual radicalism were not only old fashioned – they were irrelevant to the managerial capitalism and Welfare State security that developed in the long boom after 1945. It was only in the new era of renewed social instability and sexual radicalism that emerged from the late 1960s that Edward Carpenter's work and example were rediscovered. Now, perhaps, is an appropriate time to reassess and celebrate his memory and life's work.

*Part Three*

INVISIBLE WOMEN

# 7
## Lesbianism and the Position of Women

*'The Lesbian is one of the least known members of our culture. Less is known about her – and less accurately – than about the Newfoundland dog'* – Sydney Abbott and Barbara Love, Sappho Was a Right-on Woman (*1973*)

By the end of the nineteenth century, male homosexuality was beginning to find a voice, but it was to be another generation before female homosexuality reached a corresponding level of articulateness. While intimations of lesbianism persist in European history, our knowledge of a lesbian life-style and identity remains shadowy, almost non-existent. Even the literature referring to female homosexuality, which seems to have boomed in the nineteenth century, was written largely by men, for male delectation. Out of over thirty authors who wrote on lesbian themes in the last century, Jeanette Foster can find only four who were women. And of all these authors, most either condemned lesbianism explicitly, or made it responsible for murder, suicide or ruin. Only one or two were relatively tolerant, and even they generally married or killed off their lesbian characters.[1]

These negative literary images are echoed in what we know of a lesbian milieu. A lesbian sub-culture of sorts did exist, but was a pale version of the male, and even more overwhelmingly upper class. Berlin and Paris had several meeting places by the turn of the century. In Paris, the Rat Mort in the Place Pigalle attracted poets by day and lesbians by night; while the more extensive sub-culture of the 1920s has been vividly if not encouragingly described by Radclyffe Hall in her portrait of Alec's Bar – 'that meeting-place of the most miserable of all those who comprised the miserable army' – and the Paris Salon of Valerie Seymour (alias the real-life Natalie Clifford Barney). Even in a more cautious England there are hints of lesbian meeting-places. 'Xavier Mayne' mentions the London 'vapour bath' on Ladies' Day as a frequent place to meet, and by the 1920s well-off lesbians could meet in the new night clubs, such as the Cave of Harmony, the Orange Tree and the Hambone.[2] Here you could encounter more 'out' lesbians, often flamboyant and defiant in appearance and manner. One young observer of the then notorious Radclyffe Hall and Una Troubridge in the 1930s remembered them with fascination as 'very unusual looking, Una with her monocle, and both of them smoking little green cigars'.[3] Others, like the novelist Naomi Jacobs, who lived in the Lake Garda village of Sirmione, were aggressively 'masculine' in behaviour. The portrait of Radclyffe Hall – short-haired, bow-tied, betrousered, left hand defiantly in pocket, smoking a cigarette – that adorned the vicious *Sunday Express* attack on *The Well of Loneliness* was the image of lesbianism that persisted. Only by asserting one's identity so vehemently, as Radclyffe Hall recognized, could you begin to be noticed and taken seriously. But the numbers who could dress this way and could afford to defy conventional opinion were minuscule, and the lives of the vast majority of women with lesbian inclinations are unknown – perhaps unknowable.

Even 'science', which in the early twentieth century strove to classify and label every social phenomenon, stopped short at female homosexuality. In 1901 Krafft-Ebing noted that there were only fifty known case-histories of this strange phenomenon, and even today two modern writers on homosexuality can note that, 'The scientific literature on the lesbian is exceedingly sparse.'[4] Where efforts were made to 'explain' lesbianism, it was assimilated all too easily into a more (for males) comprehensible activity, prostitution. 'Xavier Mayne', following Moll, felt that a quarter of prostitutes had lesbian leanings, while a German researcher noted that forty-one out of sixty-six prostitutes he studied were homosexual. Even Magnus Hirschfeld, whose study of homosexuality aimed to treat both male and female alike, saw a tendency in lesbians to turn to prostitution.[5] It was as if lesbians had to be explained and justified always in terms of a largely male phenomenon. Writers like Hirschfeld and Havelock Ellis, whose 'scientific' and polemical interest was genuine, seemed to have found it difficult to discover much information, or many lesbians whose case-histories they could record. The aim was, it often seemed, not so much to trace the characteristics of lesbians as to establish that they existed at all. The truth is that if male homosexuals are the 'twilight men' of twentieth-century history, lesbians are by and large the 'invisible women'.

One reason for the absence of knowledge is the legal situation – the fact that lesbianism was not generally subject to legal sanctions – and there were thus no pillorying scandals to seize the public imagination. Kinsey listed some eleven reasons to explain this vacuum, from the social situation of women in Hittite and other ancient cultures to fears about marriage.[6] But the basic reason for the indifference towards lesbianism is more fundamental, and it relates precisely to different social assumptions about the roles of men and women, and to prevailing notions of female sexuality. Havelock Ellis, whose wife was lesbian, felt the need to stress that female homosexuals were often particularly masculine, and in Radclyffe Hall's apologia it is the 'masculine' woman who is the true invert. In *The Well of Loneliness*, Stephen, 'masculine' in name and behaviour has to endure the agonies of her 'nature', while the feminine Mary can keep her options open.

This concern with maleness in asserting an identity is only explicable in terms of the overwhelming weight of assumptions concerning female sexuality, which acted as a barrier both to 'science' understanding lesbianism and women taking control of their own sexuality. If the taboos against male homosexuality can only be understood by reference to assumptions regarding the male social role, so attitudes to lesbianism are only understandable by reference to the position of women. For, as J. H. Gagnon and W. Simon have put it, 'the patterns of overt sexual behaviour on the part of homosexual females tend to resemble closely those of heterosexual females and to differ radically from the sexual patterns of both heterosexual and homosexual males'.[7] There are therefore several intertwined elements which determine attitudes to lesbianism: the role that society assigns women; the ideology which attempts to control this; the prevailing definitions of female sexuality; and the actual expression by women of their sexual nature. The key to the social situation of lesbians lies within this matrix.

Assumptions about the 'natural' basis of the separate social roles of men and women were deeply based, and were actually reinforced by post-Darwinian scientific speculation in the late nineteenth century. Scientific knowledge was fed into pre-existing models of social behaviour and used to confirm them. Female homosexuality was inexplicable to many because it challenged so many assumptions held by men and transmitted to women. Many of the early sociologists and social scientists, from Comte to Herbert Spencer, assumed as a matter of course that social life, and the differences between the sexes, could be explained by reference to biological capacities. Spencer, for instance, concluded that sex differences were a result of the earlier arrest in the woman of individual evolution, necessitated by the reservation of vital powers to meet the cost of reproduction. Female energy was not available for intellectual growth.[8] By the end of the nineteenth century the tendency to seek explanations in the *genetic* make-up of men and women became more pronounced in many quarters. The work of Patrick Geddes and J. Arthur Thompson, particularly their book, *The Evolution of Sex* (1889), set out to synthesize what was known about sex differences and to interpret the social and economic significance of this knowledge.

Geddes was convinced that sex differences should be viewed as arising from a basic difference in cell metabolism. The physical laws concerning the conservation and dissipation of energy applied to all living things. At the level of the cell, maleness was characterized by the tendency (katabolic), to dissipate energy, and femaleness by the capacity (anabolic) to store or build up energy. By making sperm and ovum exhibit the qualities of katabolism or anabolism, Geddes was able to deduce a dichotomy between the sexes which, like Spencer's, could easily be assimilated to the conventional ideal of male rationality and female intuition. The conclusion of this was apparent: male and female roles had been decided in the lowest forms of life, and neither political nor technological change could alter the temperament which had developed from these differing functions. 'What was decided among the prehistoric Protozoa cannot be annulled by an act of Parliament.' The germ plasm, it seemed, had all the qualities of a male-dominated middle-class society. Moreover, it had implications for concepts of sexual behaviour. For male homosexuality, however odd it might be, was clearly an aspect of katabolic activity, of men's energy and activity going outwards. But female homosexuality suggested a more violent wrench from female anabolic capacities, women's receptivity and passivity.

The views of Geddes and Thompson did not go unchallenged, even in the world of social science, but their approach was a formative pre-Freudian one. Their book was published in Havelock Ellis's influential 'Contemporary Science' series, and many of its assumptions are traceable in his own work. Like theirs, his work can be seen as part of a tradition which expected change to come only from an extension of the area allowed for female sex-determined characteristics. Anything else would challenge what Ellis saw as a 'cosmic conservatism', a natural harmony between men and women which had become 'as nearly perfect as possible and every inaptitude is compensated by some compensatory aptitude'.[9]

For a just society, therefore, each sex must follow 'the laws of its own nature'. For Ellis the fundamental truth of natural life was that the two sexes were separately defined in evolution only as a method of favouring reproduction, and this could only partially be overridden. Nature therefore sanctified the social roles that men and women inhabited: 'Woman breeds and tends; man provides; it remains so even when the spheres tend to overlap.'[10]

These beliefs were actually reinforced from the 1890s by a renewed ideological emphasis on the importance and joys of motherhood. The crisis of imperialism at the turn of the century, with the prolonged agonies and uncertainties of the Boer War, had encouraged a renewed emphasis on breeding a healthy imperial race. From the 1900s the eugenics movement attempted to interest an unquiet professional middle class in the merits of scientific breeding, and few of the more radical writers, even among socialists and feminists, failed to succumb. Military metaphors abounded, and Havelock Ellis, a pacifist by inclination, quoted with approval a particularly vivid metaphor from the Swedish feminist, Ellen Key (who influenced his work a great deal): '. . . as a general rule the woman who refuses motherhood in order to serve humanity, is like a soldier who prepares himself on the eve of battle for the forthcoming struggle by opening his veins.'[11]

The theme of racial betterment becomes increasingly dominant in Ellis's work. He advocated that every *healthy* woman should at least once in her life exercise her supreme function in the interests of the race. Moreover, in opposition to the socialist tradition which, theoretically at least, favoured the socialization of housework and child-rearing, he believed that the rearing of children would be best served by each mother being responsible for each child's individual upbringing. This was in keeping, as he saw it, with both the aptitudes of the mother and the best interests of healthy childhood. These theoretical excursions inevitably had their impact on definitions of women's sexuality.

It was not so much that women were seen as sexless. In some ways this myth was a creation of the post-Victorian sexual modernists themselves, who in their anxiety to condemn some of the excesses of the past exaggerated the significance of some of the chief protagonists, such as William Acton. As Havelock Ellis pointed out, the notion of female sexual passivity was curiously unique to the nineteenth century, and to certain countries, particularly Italy, Germany and the Anglo-Saxon nations. And even within the ideology there were conflicting tendencies: the 'Madonna and the Magdalen', that of the all-devouring, voracious woman, *la belle dame sans merci*, and that of the angel of the home, the passive homekeeper, pure and angelic. (As Edward Burne-Jones put it, 'The more materialistic science becomes, the more angels shall I paint.') Someone like William Acton could describe the idea that women enjoyed sex as a 'vile aspersion', but this was less a description of reality than an injunction to middle-class women on how they ought to behave; it probably reflected more on the fears of middle-class professional men than it did on the reality of women. Elizabeth Blackwell, the pioneering woman doctor, who was clearly within a sturdy puritan tradition, had no doubt about the reality of female orgasm – which she called 'sexual spasms' – and recognized the importance of sex in cementing marriage, though she did at the same time inveigh against female masturbation and clearly felt that coitus was the special need of men rather than women.[12]

The next generation of writers, including Havelock Ellis, even recognized the legitimacy of women having their sexual needs satisfied, and attacked male clumsiness and brutality in the sex act. But, typically, Ellis could not resist suggesting that female orgasm had a utilitarian function in that it facilitated procreation. And assumptions persisted about the male role that tended to deny female sexual autonomy. The male displayed in the sex act many of the *social* characteristics that middle-class men were prized for. According to Havelock Ellis, the male must generally take the initiative in sexual matters: 'The female responds to the stimulation of the male at the right moment just as th  tree responds to the stimulation of the warmest days in spring.' Hᴄ believed that the sex life of the woman was largely conditioned by the sex life of the man, so that while a youth spontaneously becomes a man, the woman 'must be kissed into a woman'.[13] Against this background it was very difficult to see any clear image of lesbianism emerging.

But all these speculations were on the level of theory. It is less easy to trace the influence of these ideas on the actual lives and sexual practice of women. In his massive *Studies in the Psychology of Sex*, Ellis described a number of case-histories of women of all tastes and aptitudes, many of them his friends (Olive Schreiner and Edith Ellis among them). Several were lesbian; all reveal the reality of female sexuality, and the various pressures which limited or controlled it. But these cases were self-selecting, and how representative they were is difficult to estimate. Wider surveys of female sexual behaviour were not common before the 1920s and 1930s, culminating in the full-scale surveys of Kinsey and his associates of the 1940s which fully established the varieties of female sexuality. In the early 1930s, Dr Robert Latou Dickinson published the results of 5,200 case-histories. Some 1,200 of these gave their sexual history. Eighteen of his patients, it seemed, had remained virgins for one or more years after marriage, and a high proportion experienced unsatisfactory sexual activities thereafter.[14] Carl Degler has recently discovered an earlier survey, begun in the 1890s and conducted by Dr C. D. Mosher, of the attitudes of some forty-five middle-class American women. Of these some twenty-four felt that sex should be a pleasure for both sexes, thirteen thought it was a necessity for both, but thirty felt that reproduction was the prime aim.[15] But no similar survey exists to give insight into the attitudes of working-class women.

It is clear that the medical profession, the main transmitter of scientific assumptions, did little to enlighten women, and in fact largely conveyed its own preconceptions about the roles of women. Most doctors at the turn of the century had little acquaintance with women's sexual feeling or sex organs. Advances in endocrinology led to a recognition of the importance of ovaries to reproduction, and increased knowledge of female anatomy was largely a result of technological innovation in anaesthesia and antiseptics which made possible operations on female reproductive organs. But a lack of detailed information persisted, and there was debate in the medical press on the extent to which women should be examined at all. One doctor doubted whether unmarried, non-working women should be examined, lest 'local manipulation directed attention to the sexual organs'.[16] What is most clearly absent is any recognition of the significance of the clitoris to women's sexuality. The extremes of clitoridectomy were usually avoided, but even sex researchers like Ellis at first played down the importance of the clitoris. This was a long and persistent tendency. Peter Fryer has noted that while the nineteenth-century book *The Slang of Venery* lists over 1,000 popular and literary English synonyms for the female pudenda as a whole, it gives only nine for the clitoris – and only three of these are genuinely popular synonyms.[17] There was a constant use of the metaphor of the male sexuality of the sex organs. The clitoris is consistently described in medical texts as analogous to the penis, but not vice versa. Doctors and scientists felt they were looking at a lesser penis – in Freud's view, a 'vestigial penis' – so that it was never seen in its own right. The metaphor of 'penis envy' thus became a major one in sub-Freudian speculation. Modern sexologists, on the other hand, particularly Mary Jane Sherfey and Masters and Johnson, have shown the existence of a complex clitoral system, at least as potent as and probably more potent than the penis.[18] But it was not until the 1960s that the 'myth of the vaginal orgasm' was finally exploded. This myth had all sorts of consequences in interpreting female sexuality, not least the assumption that to satisfy herself a woman needed some substitute for the penis. Havelock Ellis believed that most lesbians used a dildo, even though there were (and are) no grounds or justification for such an assumption.

The theory of an 'absence' obsession often dominated discussion of lesbianism, particularly from the 1920s with the Freudian debate that followed Freud's first long study of a lesbian. Freud postulated in the young girl a castration complex sparked off by her awareness that she had no penis. To resolve this, she had to transfer her early libidinal attachment from her mother (when sexual interest was attached to the clitoris) to the father (and sexual interest to the vagina). She did so because of her wish to obtain a penis, something her mother could not give her but her father could. Should this process have failed, the girl would have been stuck at an earlier, 'immature' phase of development. The way was thus left open by Freud for his epigones to explore the 'immaturity' of lesbians. Most agreed that the key to lesbianism was mother-fixation resulting from inadequate emotional warmth; beneath all the bravado of lesbians there was therefore a little girl lost. Helen Deutsch, in writing about this, quoted Colette:

. . . two women embracing are a melancholy and touching picture of two weaknesses; perhaps they are taking refuge in each other's arms in order to sleep there, weep, flee from a man who is often wicked, and to taste what is more decried than any pleasure, the bitter happiness of feeling similar, insignificant, forgotten.[19]

Until the 1930s, at least, most discussion of lesbianism in Britain was in the physiological terms endorsed by Ellis rather than the psychological framework of Freud. But the mood – of isolation, desolation and sorrow – was the common one.

Nevertheless it is likely that most women with lesbian inclinations fitted inconspicuously into the general world of women. There is abundant evidence in eighteenth- and nineteenth-century diaries and letters (and this has been especially explored in the United States) that women as a matter of routine formed long-lived emotional ties with other women.[20] Such relationships ranged from the close supportive love of sisters, through adolescent enthusiasms to mature avowals of eternal affection. Relationships like those of the 'Ladies of Llangollen', whatever their sexual connotations, were acceptable because they were not a million light-years away from the feminine norm. Relationships were formed along, not across, the cleavage between men and women, which is why marriage nights were often nights of pain, anguish and mutual confusion. 'With marriage both women and men had to adjust to life with a person who was, in essence, a member of an alien group.'[21] And as a result, as Ellis put it, more women had been raped in marriage than outside it. The emotional segregation in middle-class homes was stronger than in working-class ones, because here the division of labour was most strongly stratified. But stratification of women probably proceeded apace as the century developed – with women excluded from many areas of social labour, with a new ideology of domestic work which underscored this tendency, and with the development, from the 1870s, of a gender-divided educational system.

Inevitably, a sense of feminine identity was engendered around what were defined as almost exclusively female concerns: women were bound together by certain exigencies – frequent pregnancy, child-birth, nursing and family care, menopause – which worked towards physical and emotional intimacy between them. Many of the early writers on lesbianism spoke of the greater emphasis on cuddling, on physical warmth and comforting, of kissing and holding hands between female homosexuals, at the expense of exclusively sexual activity. This was precisely the line of continuity between all women, whatever their sexual orientation. Indeed, deep and passionate declarations of love recur without any obvious signs of sexual expression. Charlotte Brontë wrote to her friend Ellen Nussey in 1836:

Ellen, I wish I could live with you always. I begin to cling to you more fondly than I ever did. If we had a cottage and a competency of our own I do think we might love until Death without being dependent on any third person for happiness.

And, later, she wrote again: 'Why are we so divided? Ellen, it must be because we are in danger of loving each other too well.'[22]

It is almost meaningless to attempt to analyse this along the modern polarity of lesbian/heterosexual, because for very few women up till the present century was such a polarity even conceivable. The physical and social conditions of most women encouraged a feminine solidarity around common concerns. Many of the close relations might have become 'physical' in a modern sense; others did not. To say more than this would be to push modern definitions on to an alien scene. It was only with the widening public awareness of lesbianism, especially after the First World War, and the series of public pilloryings of lesbians in the 1920s and afterwards, that a commitment to a lesbian identity became both more necessary and, for the majority, possible.

# 8
## Lesbianism and the Women's Movement

*'Lesbianism is the one issue that deals with women responding positively to other women as total human beings worthy of total commitment. It is the one area where no male can tread' – Rita Mae Brown (1971)*

'If we had a cottage and a competency of our own . . .' Few women ever had this possibility. Until the expansion of clerical and secretarial jobs at the turn of the century, consequent upon the growth and new scale of capitalism and industry, single middle-class women had little scope for employment outside the overcrowded ranks of governesses, while single working-class women were either trapped in domestic service (replacing their own home roles) or in work in the secondary and tertiary sectors of industry, where labour was often sweated and wages low. It was not easy for a woman to survive without a man. From the 1850s the unemployment of single middle-class women was one of the charges behind the energy of the early women's movement.[1] The movement implicitly raised the issue of male patriarchal dominance. It stressed the importance of the idea of women's social and economic independence, and in political action it displayed the merits of 'sisterhood', of solidarity produced by common struggle. Inevitably the question of lesbianism was touched on in various controversies, but always indirectly, and rarely with any positive force.

Even progressive contemporaries like Edward Carpenter feared that the movement would come to be dominated by unrepresentative 'masculine' women. But the idea was given its most concrete form in the 1930s in George Dangerfield's glittering and mischievous book, *The Strange Death of Liberal England*.[2] In particular, in not over-subtle hints, he suggests Christabel Pankhurst's lesbianism, and cites her pamphlet *The Great Scourge* (1913) as a tract against men. Undoubtedly there was a homoerotic element in the women's movement. In Germany Magnus Hirschfeld claimed that 10 per cent of feminists were lesbians, and there was certainly some discussion of lesbianism; and from around 1900 lesbian fiction was regularly reviewed in Hirschfeld's *Yearbook* (though, as usual, such works displayed an extraordinary incidence of suicide and/or physical and mental illness).[3] But in Britain feminists largely avoided the question. Most feminist leaders aimed, on the contrary, to play down the more controversial issues. Mrs Fawcett deemed it a great merit of Mary Wollstonecraft's that 'she did not sanction any depreciation of the immense importance of the domestic duties of women',[4] and there was anxiety among many that their cause (particularly the vote) would be damaged by association with sexual radicalism. The London suffrage organization had split in the early 1870s over Josephine Butler's campaigns against the Contagious Diseases Acts – not because they did not support them (Mrs Fawcett, who was among the conservatives at that time, later became the biographer of Josephine Butler), but because of the controversy it would arouse. For the same reason, and even more so, most feminists carefully distanced themselves from outrageous radicals like Ellis and Edward Carpenter.

The women's movement, however, never ignored sexuality. In many ways it was to the fore. The whole campaign over the 'State Regulation of Vice' was, after all, about the use of women as objects of male sexual lust, and the social-purity flavour, which was largely about sex, was very strong. This is the real significance of Christabel's pamphlet. The arguments of this tract were clear enough. Male sexual vice was the real reason why men prevented women getting the vote. Ruling-class men wanted to protect prostitution and the sexual abuse of women. But the result was the 'scourge' – venereal disease, inflicted on innocent women, and the great cause of physical, mental and moral degeneracy, and ultimately of 'race suicide'. Prostitution wasted the energy and health of men, and sacrificed women on the altar of the double standard.[5] Sexual disease and social disaster were the result of the subjection of women owing to the 'doctrine that woman is sex and beyond that nothing'. The only way out of this male-created trap was for women to get the vote and enforce chastity – hence the double slogan which stubbornly beats through the pamphlet: 'Votes for women and chastity for men.' The main enemy is not men as such, but the male-orientated 'double standard' of morality.

The circumstances which immediately produced the work bear an uncanny resemblance to events in the 1880s preceding the 1885 Act, including the Mrs Jeffries case of 1884. The Pankhurst pamphlet was stimulated by a scandal known as the 'Piccadilly flat case', involving a prostitution ring. There were strong hints that prominent persons were concerned, and as in the Mrs Jeffries case, suggestions that leniency was exercised in 'semi-secret' hearings because of the names that might come to light.[6] What particularly outraged feminists was that the procuress at the heart of the case, one Queenie Gerald, only got three months in the prison second division, while almost simultaneously Emmeline Pankhurst was given three years' imprisonment for her suffragette activities. Christabel wanted not so much to castrate men (though many might have thought so from her tone), but, like the social-purity campaigners of the 1880s, to raise them to the conventional standards of respectable women; and, indeed, to raise the female age of consent to twenty-one. Even the issue of race suicide echoes the imperialist fears of the 1880s. *The Great Scourge*, not surprisingly, was distributed by army chaplains to the troops during the First World War.[7] The pamphlet exalts rather than undermines traditional puritan morality.

This is true of most of the literature that discussed female sexuality. In the early 1890s the 'fiction of sex and the new woman' caused something of a sensation.[8] Grant Allen, with his notorious novel, *The Woman Who Did*, is the most familiar name today, but there were many others – Sarah Grand, 'Iota', George Egerton, Emma Frances Brooke, Mona Caird. The heroines depicted by these popular novelists were new women in the sense that all rejected some, though not all (or, indeed, all the same), features of the female role. They all employed a new degree of frankness about sexual behaviour, and recognized that women had to be freed from the constricting male middle-class view of femininity, though none questioned the existence of fundamental differences. But even in this would-be radical tendency, the impact was tame. There were two main types of novel. The first, and less radical (later typified as the 'purity school'), was represented by Grant Allen. The women of these novels did not shirk venereal disease, prostitution or adultery, and rejected absurd female delicacy. But while a work like Allen's *The Woman Who Did* challenged conventional views of marriage, it did not attack traditional concepts of human relationships. The heroine, Herminia, refuses to marry on principle, but remains monogamously devoted to her chosen, Alan. When he dies, leaving her with a technically illegitimate child, she is martyred to social convention, but not to her real aspirations. 'It is a woman's ancestral part to look up to man; and she is happiest in doing it, and must long remain so.'[9] The sensation here lay in the treatment, not the theme. The second tendency was more aware of the all-encompassing tyranny of traditional sex roles and saw their heroines striving, and usually failing, to achieve a wider emancipation. But only Mona Caird, in *The Daughters of Danaus*, went so far as to challenge the 'maternal instinct'. The heroine, Hadria, reflected that throughout history:

. . . children had been the unfailing means of bringing women into line with tradition. Who could stand against them ? They had been able to force the most rebellious to their knees. An appeal to the maternal instinct had quenched the hardiest spirit of revolt. No wonder the instinct had been so unimpeded and exalted![10]

The issue of motherhood was central in the early twentieth century, and one which most feminists exalted rather than challenged (as we have seen with Ellen Key). Mona Caird represented a thin line of resistance.

Inevitably, though, the challenge that the women's movement implicitly offered to traditional sexual relations, and the bonds of sisterhood engendered by close political cooperation, produced a number of close emotional relationships, many of them lasting for years. There is some evidence that these were tacitly accepted but never discussed at any great length in the movement. And it is probable that the barriers against overt physical expression were high. The only feminist forum where there was some attempt to raise the issue was the journal, *The Freewoman*, in 1912–13. Its columns in January and February 1912 saw a discussion on the nature of homosexuality which drew on the theories of Edward Carpenter and Weininger as well as Mendelism and traditional morality. Later, Carpenter wrote an article in *The New Freewoman* which discussed the status of women and the incidence of homosexuality in Ancient Greece, and there was the occasional letter on lesbianism. But the issue was never broadened out and related to the central issue of the nature of female sexuality.[11]

Stella Browne, an ardent feminist, pioneer birth-controller and later advocate of abortion-law reform, did defend lesbianism, if somewhat less staunchly than she defended contraception. And it was precisely the question of a woman's control over her own body that involved her. In a paper read in October 1915 at a meeting of the British Society for the Study of Sex Psychology,[12] she rejected the myth that women have no strong, spontaneous and 'discriminating' sex impulse, and that their sexual life is subordinated to the male. She defended masturbation and also questioned whether 'great love is the sole justification of sexual experience'. She thus explicitly raised the separation of sex from procreation. With regard to lesbianism, she followed Ellis in arguing that normal sexuality includes the beginnings of most 'abnormal instincts', and felt that society should begin to recognize the 'vital, very often valuable' role of homosexuality in civilization (thus echoing Edward Carpenter). But, following Ellis again, she makes a sharp distinction between what she sees as 'artificial' inversion, acquired through temporary influences, and 'true' inversion, firmly believed to be congenital. 'Artificial or substitute' homosexuality was, she felt, widely diffused among women, 'as a result of the repression of normal gratification and the segregation of the sexes which still largely obtains'. She felt that the suppression of desires and the delay of marriage would encourage homosexuality, so that here lesbianism was used as an argument *against* itself. Congenital homosexuality was, by this argument, acceptable because unavoidable, but the same was not true for 'artificial' homosexuality: 'I repudiate all wish to slight or depreciate the love-life of the real homosexual; but it cannot be advisable to force the growth of that habit in heterosexual people'.[13] In adopting this mechanistic division between congenital 'inversion' and artificial 'perversion', Stella Browne was closing the doors to exploration of that 'great plasticity of women's sex impulse' which she had earlier lauded, and so was artificially containing female sexual experience.

This was, it should be remembered, the most advanced feminist opinion. A similar ambivalence can be seen in the work of the American anarchist and feminist, Emma Goldman. Like Stella Browne, she drank deeply of the heady wine of Havelock Ellis's philosophy, and like almost all feminists, implicitly accepted his biologistic assumptions. She wrote to Ellis (27 December 1924) telling of an essay she had written on her friend Louise Michel.[14] She had written it, she said, because she 'was shocked' when she saw a photograph of her in Magnus Hirschfeld's home among a collection of homosexuals. 'I was shocked not because of any squeamishness . . . but because I knew Louise Michel to be far removed from the tendencies ascribed to her. I am so anxious that Louise Michel should be saved the unfounded charge of Homo Sexuality.' If it was not something to be condemned, why was it so unfortunate? No one seemed able to confront this issue.

# 9
## Emerging Identities

*'When . . . I read* The Well of Loneliness *it fell upon me like a revelation. I identified with every line. I wept floods of tears over it, and it confirmed my belief in my homosexuality' – a lesbian, quoted in Charlotte Wolff,* Love Between Women *(1971)*

Male homosexuality and lesbianism have different social implications. For men, homosexuality is seen as a rejection of maleness, with all its socially approved connotations. For women, it can be an assertion of femaleness, of separateness from men, and of identity. But, for this to occur, there need to be models, personal and literary, which are both positive and assertive. Several women writers in the twentieth century did write about lesbianism, both in polemical articles and in literature, though it is the literary figures, such as Virginia Woolf, who are now best remembered. Most famous of all is Radclyffe Hall.

The publication in 1928 of her novel *The Well of Loneliness*, along with the controversy that surrounded it and her, was a crucial stage in the evolution of a public image of lesbianism; in many ways it had for women an equivalent social impact to the one the Wilde trial had for men. It is important, therefore, to begin to understand the constituents of the image articulated. Three quite different writers, Edith Ellis, Violet Paget/Vernon Lee and Radclyffe Hall herself, illustrate the stages in this development. None of them, it should be noted, was particularly concerned with the major questions of feminism.

Edith Lees Ellis (1861–1916), as her husband Havelock Ellis put it in explaining her relative indifference to feminism, refused to work 'at some single spot', and her writings, like her life, are erratic.[1] She met Havelock through the Fellowship of the New Life which she joined after the split with the Fabians. There she undertook secretarial work and later helped to organize the cooperative boarding-house in Doughty Street, near Mecklenburgh Square, Bloomsbury, where eight to ten people (including at one time the future Labour prime minister, James Ramsay MacDonald) made their home. After her marriage she gladly retreated from these activities – later explaining it by parodying (and reversing) the popular socialist saying into 'Fellowship is Hell, and the lack of Fellowship is Heaven'. She was, in fact, a far more gregarious person than the diffident Havelock, and she led a busy social life. She developed a very close friendship with Edward Carpenter, being one of his middle-class friends who enjoyed the unconventional atmosphere and bawdiness of Carpenter and Merrill's male ménage. She enjoyed visiting them and corresponded frequently. But she had a touch of unconventionality about herself, and was subject to sharp bouts of severe depression and bursts of temper. Margaret, James Hinton's daughter, sometimes played the piano for women in Bethlem. When asked what they were like, she said, 'Like that Miss Lees.'[2]

Married life, from December 1891, was not without its turbulence. From the start Edith and Havelock lived fairly unconventional lives (Havelock had to be almost dragged to his wedding reception), keeping separate incomes and homes (though not names: strangely, Edith Lees published her books under the name of 'Mrs Havelock Ellis'). From early on each had separate emotional involvements, Havelock's generally asexual, it seems, but Edith's passionately involved with women. Edith's novel, *Kit's Woman* (originally published under the uninspiring title of *Seaweed*), was a parable of her marriage. In the book the wife is married to a husband who, through an accident, has become impotent. She is driven by physical passion to find a lover (a man in the novel), but returns to her husband because of his unique spiritual qualities. In his autobiography, Havelock Ellis saw this as a parable of the deep love between him and Edith which stopped short at physical passion. It is possible, on the other hand, that it reflects negative feelings on Edith's part about her lesbianism, and a regret that she could not be fulfilled within marriage. Whatever her deepest personal misgivings, she stated her public position, close to her husband's, in an early pamphlet, *A Noviciate For Marriage*, near the start of their relationship: 'Hounding abnormal sexual offenders to death, and wearing white ribbons as a sign of our own worthiness, will not help poor, suffering, ignorant humanity to a new vision of healthy sexuality.'[3]

There is an obvious ambiguity in the last words. She took up the same theme more positively in her later book, *Three Modern Seers*. The three gurus were James Hinton, Friedrich Nietzsche and Edward Carpenter, and the plea throughout the book is for the breaking of artificial social conventions and the realization of individuals' true nature. The work climaxes with a study of Carpenter, who had found, Edith felt, a deep personal serenity. 'Carpenter has found out what he believes in and he is living it.'[4] This is what Edith strove for.

In a paper prepared for the Eugenics Education Society in 1911, Edith attempted to assimilate homosexuality to the latest bourgeois preoccupations and to the planned future of 'the race'. She spoke of Oscar Wilde, and reflected that, 'Even in abnormality, in its congenital manifestations, nature may have a meaning as definite in her universal purpose as the discord is in music to the musician.' And she pleaded:

> There is surely a place in the great scheme of things, even for the abnormal man and the abnormal woman, but it is not an easy place. Possibly it is a very high place: the place of clean living and renunciation.[5]

This was hardly a rallying-cry to sexual freedom. Her prime significance was her assertion of a lesbian existence: 'We must give abnormal people a chance to be their best'. This, limited as it may now seem, was the best her generation allowed.

A similar initial separation from the mainstream of feminism characterized the work of Violet Paget, better known under her pseudonym of Vernon Lee (1856–1935). She was undoubtedly lesbian, though her biographer, Peter Gunn, who had access to her private papers, does his best to obscure the fact. The rare glimpses of her emotional life that he allows us are therefore all the more raw. Gunn comments at one point: '. . . any emotional contact she had with others was through women, and the repeated failure of these relationships left her with only a more intense feeling of loneliness and spiritual isolation.'[6]

But, as with Edith Ellis, a strong sense of her fundamental feelings breaks through in her writings. A good example of this is her chapter on 'The Economic Parasitism of Women' published in her *Gospels of Anarchy* (1908), which takes as its starting point a book by Mrs Stetson, *Women and Economics*. Vernon Lee found in this book a sentence which, she says, converted her to the cause of female emancipation: 'Women are over-sexed.' She did not take this to mean that women had too much sex: rather that women were treated purely as objects of male sexual affection, and their lives were dominated by their sex-dominated activities. She argued that, 'The different position of the female who we call *woman* is due to a difference not in physiological but in sociological functions' – by which she meant specifically the long period of child dependence, a historical creation which made the female dependent on the male. Unfortunately, Vernon Lee does not go on from this to advocate the socialization of child care to relieve women of their burden. But she does end her chapter on a note which has a modern ring: a recognition of the inadequacies of rigid divisions of the sexes, and a veiled advocacy of androgyny:

> It is not just the most aesthetic but also the most athletic and the most intellectual, people of the past which have left us those statues of gods and goddesses in the presence of whose marvellous vigour and loveliness we are often in doubt whether to give the name of Apollo, or that of Athena.[7]

Although it is never made explicit, extensions could be made from this towards a positive lesbian position.

The third of these writers to explore lesbian themes is the most famous, Marguerite Radclyffe Hall (1886–1945). She had touched on lesbianism in her writings for some twenty years before the publication of *The Well of Loneliness* in 1928 brought her a culminating notoriety. As early as 1908, in *A Sheaf of Verses*, lesbian love had been celebrated. The themes are constant: the reality of lesbian love, but also its painfulness and its supposed barrenness, as in this verse from *Poems of the Past and Present* (1910):

> For what is all her ardour,
> Whose fruitfulness doth mock us,
> To our enduring passion,
> That yet remaineth barren.

It was a puzzling anomaly to be endured:

> O thou mortal weary minded,
> Thou who wert alone created
> As a pastime for the gods –
> When thou treadest thy sad measure
> Making songs to ease thy spirit,
> With the laughter on Olympus
> Mingles falling tears![8]

Radclyffe Hall had lived more or less openly as a lesbian since the 1900s, certainly so far as family and friends were concerned. From 1915 she lived openly with Una Troubridge, wife of the well-known Admiral, Sir Ernest Troubridge. And a certain amount of scandal became attached to her name when some researches into psychic phenomena prepared by herself and Una Troubridge during the latter stages of the Great War proved controversial. They had outraged more well-established members of the Society for Psychical Research, particularly Sir George Fox-Pitt (son-in-law of the notorious Marquess of Queensberry who had hounded Oscar Wilde). Sir George took it upon himself, in the context of these internal quarrels, to accuse Radclyffe Hall of being immoral and of breaking Troubridge's marriage. Hall's name was already in the public eye following the huge success of various sentimental verses of hers, set to music, which echoed a winsome war-time mood. Now, following in the fatal footsteps of Wilde, she sued for libel. The case was heard in 1920 and aroused considerable interest. Even *The Times* devoted eight column inches to it in its Law Report. The court found for Hall, but on appeal a retrial was ordered for technical reasons. Radclyffe Hall did not pursue the case, evidently believing that the issue had been essentially settled. But some of the mud stuck.

What makes this of particular note is that lesbianism was, to a certain extent, beginning to emerge from the shadows during this period, if not into a particularly shining light. During the war several novels had appeared with lesbian themes, including D. H. Lawrence's *The Rainbow* (1915), which portrayed lesbianism as life-denying (the chapter dealing with a lesbian relationship is entitled 'Shame'). Another novel, A. T. Fitzroy's *Despised and Rejected* (1918), was more positive, portraying both male and female homosexuals as well as the campaigns of conscientious objectors. As a result the publisher was prosecuted and fined £160.[9] But a more dramatic dénouement followed the court case in 1918 when Maud Allan, a Canadian classical dancer, sued the self-publicizing and opportunist right-wing Member of Parliament, Noel Pemberton Billing, for criminal libel. Pemberton Billing, playing on current xenophobic feelings, claimed to have uncovered a 'Black Book' prepared by the German Secret Service, which had the names of some 47,000 Englishmen and women who were 'sexual perverts'. This provided the excuse for a public morality crusade, into which Maud Allan was unfortunately dragged. She was advertised to perform the Dance of Seven Veils in Wilde's *Salome* in private performances in early 1918. In the first edition of Pemberton Billing's new paper, *The Vigilante*, in February 1918, a paragraph was inserted in the editorial, headed 'The Cult of the Clitoris', clearly implying that Maud Allan, and likely attenders at the performances, were on the list of 47,000. In the trial that followed there were extraordinary scenes of ultra-chauvinistic support for Pemberton Billing. Lord Alfred Douglas ('Bosie'), who had originally translated *Salome* from French into English, in attempting to tear up his own homosexual past described Oscar Wilde as 'the greatest force for evil that has appeared in Europe during the last three hundred and fifty years'. Against such a background, Maud Allan's case was lost by default.[10]

It was against the backcloth of this new concern with lesbianism that Parliament in 1921 attempted for the first time to bring lesbianism within the scope of the criminal law. At the report stage of the new Criminal Law Amendment Act, which was proceeding uneventfully through the House of Commons, a Scottish Tory M.P., Frederick Macquisten, moved a new clause, under the heading of 'Acts of Gross Indecency by Females', which would have extended the Labouchère Amendment to women. In supporting his new clause, Macquisten made much of the decline in female morality, doubtless reflecting on the appalling impact of feminism. This had been documented in a book, published the previous year, which may have had some influence. Arabella Kennealy's *Feminism and Sex Extinction* saw the chief feature of the women's movement as 'masculinism'. She had attempted to document women's part in 'Human Decadence', and, in particular, the 'Impending Subjection of Man'. The main threat feminism posed, it seemed, was to parenthood:

> In aiming at Hermaphroditism, Feminism is contriving not only at frustration of all that Evolution has achieved in Life and Faculty, but it is making for the extinction of Life itself. The Hermaphrodite is incapable of parenthood.[11]

This was the theme taken up in the House of Commons debate. Sir Ernest Wild complained that 'it stops child-birth because it is a well-known fact that any woman who indulges in this vice [lesbianism] will have nothing whatever to do with the other sex. It debauches young girls, and it produces neurasthenia and insanity.' Even those who opposed the clause did not quite slough this off. Colonel J. T. C. Moore Brabazon commented: 'We are dealing with abnormalities of the brain, and we have got to look on all these cases from that point of view.' The House of Commons nevertheless passed the clause.

In the House of Lords, however, there was less enthusiasm. Lords Malmesbury and Desart pointed out the probability of blackmail, and the latter made the comment:

> You are going to tell the whole world that there is such an offence, to bring it to the notice of women who have never heard

of it, never thought of it, never dreamed of it. I think that is a very great mischief.

Lord Birkenhead, the Lord Chancellor, made the same point:

> I would be bold enough to say that of every thousand women, taken as a whole, 999 have never even heard a whisper of these practices. Among all these, in the homes of this country . . . the taint of this noxious and horrible suspicion is to be imparted.

The Lords rejected the clause, the Commons neglected to take it up again, and the proposal fell.[12] The significant point is not so much that it was proposed as the ways in which it was rejected. These were essentially on two grounds, the more 'advanced' being the sickness theory; but the most persuasive view was the pragmatic one: better not discuss it in case it might spread like a contagion. Neither approach augured well for future rational debate.

Radclyffe Hall had long brooded on her urge to publish a novel which would set forth the truth, as she saw it, of lesbian love in all its joys and pains, and would help to produce a new attitude to homosexuality. She clearly saw herself in the line of sexual enlighteners speaking up for afflicted minorities. She informed her publisher:

> I wrote the book from a deep sense of duty. I am proud indeed to have taken up my pen in defence of those who are utterly defenceless, who being from birth set apart in accordance with some hidden scheme of Nature, need all the help that society can give them.[13]

As the reference to 'Nature' suggests, her theoretical position came from Havelock Ellis. She wrote to him shortly after *The Well of Loneliness* was committed to trial that she was stumbling along after him and Edith, a 'humble but very gladly willing disciple'.[14] She had delayed working on the book until she had established a name which would justify a hearing for her work, and by 1927 the time seemed ripe. She had made a reputation as a novelist with her first novel, and her second, *Adam's Breed*, just completed, had proved a major success. It carried off the two major English literary prizes of the time, the only previous novel to have achieved this being E. M. Forster's *A Passage to India* (1925). After Forster's success he had written no more fiction, and his earlier and positive homosexual novel *Maurice* was kept in the closet. Radclyffe Hall's success, on the other hand, spurred her on.[15]

She was anxious that the book should be properly received. She wanted it to be both psychologically accurate and respectably endorsed. Havelock Ellis was asked to write a preface. With reluctance – for he announced his fear that his name would do more harm than good – he agreed. His fears were unfortunately well-founded. In his brief 'Commentary' to the published novel, Ellis remarked on its 'notable psychological and sociological significance' which presented a faithful picture of an aspect of contemporary sexual life. It was this 'Commentary' that the editor of the *Sunday Express*, James Douglas, took up in his notorious attack on the book in August 1928, soon after its publication.

With a typical Beaverbrookian mixture of moral outrage, prurience and pretence at expressing the voice of the people, Douglas (a forerunner of the equally egregious John Gordon) declared the novel 'an intolerable outrage': 'The English people are slow to rise in their wrath and strike down the armies of evil, but when they are aroused they show no mercy . . .'[16]

The attack was carefully timed and prepared. The novel had come out shortly before to varying reviews. Douglas's article appeared in the dog days of August and had all the characteristics of a silly-season stunt. The article appeared on 19 August. Hall's publishers, Jonathan Cape, received proofs of the article on the 17th, and on Saturday the 18th, the *Daily Express* puffed the forthcoming attack. The carefully contrived publicity had its effects. On 18 August, Cape, without consulting Radclyffe Hall, wrote to the Home Secretary, Sir William Joynson-Hicks ('Jix'), a highly reactionary member of the Conservative administration, enclosing a copy of the book, a sheaf of reviews and an offer to withdraw the book if the Home Secretary felt it appropriate. By 21 August 'Jix' had replied, that he did feel withdrawal would be appropriate. Cape, again without consulting the author, withdrew the book, but secretly sent the moulds to Paris, where the novel was reprinted by the Pegasus Press. Imported copies from this press were then seized under the Obscene Publications Act of 1857. The distributors were summoned to show good cause why the books should not be destroyed as an obscene work.

This background is essential for understanding the way in which the case was conducted. Hall herself – like Ellis thirty years before – was not brought to trial, as she neither occupied the premises from which the books were seized, nor did she own the books. She had no say in the conduct of the case, as the presiding magistrate, Sir Chartres Biron, made clear; nor any direct say over the way in which the case was handled. Her single verbal protest during the trial was quickly silenced. Norman Birkett, for the publishers, even attempted at first to deny the central point about the book – its defence of female emotional and *sexual* relationships. Only a burst of anger from Radclyffe Hall during the lunch adjournment forced Birkett to change his tune. Moreover, the book was trapped by an antiquated law which prevented any witnesses being called to plea for the novel's 'literary merit'. But, once the book was in the public eye, fundamental to the trial's outcome was the weight of prejudice against lesbianism. As Birkett later pointed out, Sir Chartres Biron found against the novel because Radclyffe Hall 'had not stigmatised this relationship as being in any way blameworthy'.[17] Predictably, the novel was judged obscene, and the seized copies were burned in the furnaces of Scotland Yard.

Reaction, as ever, was mixed. Many literary luminaries were outraged. Some forty writers who had been prepared to testify signed a protest letter to *The Times*. These included E. M. Forster, Desmond MacCarthy, Storm Jameson, V. Sackville-West, Leonard and Virginia Woolf, G. B. Shaw – a fair proportion of whom were themselves of unconventional sexual tastes. Bertrand Russell helped to raise the issue at the 1929 International Congress of the World League for Sexual Reform. But others, often homosexual themselves, were more ambiguous. Hugh Walpole felt that 'abnormality' was best left unspoken about, but nevertheless he pointed out the unprecedented publicity given to homosexuality by 'Jix' and Biron.[18] This perhaps is the outstanding feature of the case: the publicity it aroused did more than anything to negate the hopes for reticence expressed by Lords Desart and Birkenhead in 1921.

What is so surprising about the result is that the furore should have been about a book that in the end turned out to be so mild. As Vera Brittain put it, Hall was ultimately a 'lady' and the treatment of her theme was 'essentially lady-like'. It was no more sensational in treatment than other novels with lesbian themes which appeared contemporaneously. These included Compton Mackenzie's mildly satirical novel *Extraordinary Women* (incorporating a wicked caricature, which infuriated her, of Radclyffe Hall) and Virginia Woolf's *Orlando*. It was Hall's didactic purpose, combined with the opportunism of Cape and Beaverbrook newspapers, which trapped her. The novel itself is resolutely 'moral' in every sense but the most conventional. Its clear intent was not to show the joys of homosexuality, but the pains that those who were homosexual had no alternative except to endure. This was picked up at the time by the less purblind reader. Vera Brittain, in her review, saw lesbianism as a painful anomaly, and spoke of 'all who are fortunate enough to have escaped one of nature's cruellest dispensations'.[19] The plea of the novel is for *toleration* and public acceptance of those who were 'afflicted'. The novel is a celebration of pain, love and sacrifice.

The heroine is Stephen Gordon, a tomboy product of a well-off county family. *The Well of Loneliness* (and, of course, the title is indicative) follows Stephen's odyssey, from isolated child, fonder of her horses than of her contemporaries, to sexual awakening with the awful Angela Crossby, who uses and betrays her, to a literary career and an encounter and love affair with Mary, a young, pretty and 'feminine' woman. This relationship is the core of the novel, and is passionately evoked. Sex is clearly present, as is a sharp role-differentiation. The novel follows their relationship, their encounter with English prejudice, their sojourn in Paris, their encounter with the chilling homosexual underworld and fellow lesbians.

But Stephen's fate, the inherited tragic fate of the born invert, catches up with her. Martin, a rejected youthful love of Stephen, enters the women's lives, and the climax of the novel is a tug-of-war for the soul of Mary (in a literary tradition going back at least to Henry James's *The Bostonians*). Stephen, with painful self-sacrifice, decides that Mary must leave her and begin a 'normal' life with Martin. Through a stratagem, Stephen finally convinces the reluctant Mary that she is having an affair with their friend Valerie Seymour, and in anguish Mary leaves – for the waiting arms of Martin. Stephen is left to her own anguish and pain: '. . . her pain, their pain . . . all the misery at Alec's. And the press and the clamour of those countless others – they fought, they trampled, they were getting her under . . .'[20] The novel ends in a welter of religiosity underscoring its theme:

> 'God,' she gasped, 'we believe; we have told you we believe . . .
> 'We have not denied You, then rise up and defend us. Acknowledge us, oh God, before the whole world. Give us also the right to our existence!'

Within its own liberal terms the novel is successful. Pervading the whole is a sense of the tragedy of these lives, the need for painful adjustment, the claim to tolerance. Interestingly, Radclyffe Hall's own life belies her dismal portraiture in the novel. She lived in close harmony with Una Troubridge for close on thirty years. Her last letter spoke movingly of 'my love which is much stronger than mere death'.[21] This is the authentic tone of her life, not the pain of unnecessary separation which dominates *The Well of Loneliness.* But the novel does epitomize the most advanced current theories, from the congenital nature of homosexuality to the difficulty of social acceptance. Certain of its elements were criticized even at the time by feminists. Vera Brittain picked up the role-stereotypes that pervade it, pointing out that Hall 'appears to take for granted that this over-emphasis of sex characteristics is part of the correct education of the normal human being; she therefore makes her "normal" woman clinging and "feminine" to exasperation'.[22] Radclyffe Hall's novel is trapped within stereotypes of human behaviour, and this, to modern eyes, is its most fundamental weakness. It is at the heart of the 'tragedy' which is the theme of *The Well of Loneliness.*

Radclyffe Hall was undoubtedly upset that the book had achieved notoriety as a salacious work rather than as an earnest moral text (countless numbers of dirty-book seekers must have been gravely disappointed by its contents). And around her a posthumous halo has developed. But Radclyffe Hall and Una were less broken than they might have been. As with Havelock Ellis and others earlier, the controversy inadvertently publicized – thus subverting the very intention of the legislators. And the book was read – it enjoyed a clandestine circulation in copies emanating from the United States, where, after a successful court case, it was circulated without hindrance. By 1968, when a paperback edition was issued in Britain, 551,910 foreign copies of the novel had been sold in fourteen languages.[23] Radclyffe Hall made a moral stand, and it had had its effect. Towards the end of her life she wrote:

> I have always stood for fidelity in the case of inverted unions. I have tried to help my own kind by setting an example.
>
> Thousands have turned to me for help, and have found it, judging by their letters. I have a debt of honour to pay.[24]

The debt she spoke of was to Una and their relationship, but many lesbians felt a similar debt to Radclyffe Hall. For another thirty years or so her novel represented the clearest moral stand on lesbianism, and a position beyond which few women were prepared or able to venture.

*Part Four*

# APPROACHES TO REFORM

# 10
## Creating a Consciousness

*'Oh, a deal of pains he's taken and a pretty price he's paid*
*To hide his poll or dye it of a mentionable shade;*
*But they've pulled the beggar's hat off for the world to see and*
*   stare,*
*And they're haling him to justice for the colour of his hair.'*
*– A. E. Housman, 'O who is that young sinner'*

The Oscar Wilde débâcle and the successive controversies and scandals of the 1890s made the public avowal and defence of homosexuality a perilous project. The major published works, those of Havelock Ellis and Edward Carpenter, had appeared in a difficult climate, trailing whiffs of notoriety and marked by public controversy and private reticences. Ellis, as we have seen, felt it necessary to reject the 'martyr's crown', and Carpenter delicately pirouetted on the verges of respectability. Nevertheless, despite the difficulties, a flame for reform was kept flickering throughout the period, kept burning by the endeavours of such as Ellis and Carpenter. Their ideas travelled along a narrow transmission belt to small circles of men and women who were prepared, in a variety of inconspicuous but often significant ways, to begin to piece together a new consciousness of the need for reform.

'I have no doubt we shall win,' Oscar Wilde wrote to the criminologist George Cecil Ives in 1897, 'but the road is long, and red with monstrous martyrdoms. Nothing but the repeal of the Criminal Law Amendment Act would do any good. That is essential.'[1] But this hope for law reform seemed only a long-term aspiration in the 1890s and early 1900s. As an early pamphlet on *The Social Problem of Sexual Inversion*, published by the British Society for the Study of Sex Psychology in 1915, made clear, the time was not opportune for a direct campaign to change the law because 'before the Law can be amended, it is clear that the subject with which it deals must be better understood'. This pointed to an orientation which dominated the campaigns for homosexual rights up to the 1950s and beyond: the need for public education as a prelude to reform. This was expressed in the famous slogan of Magnus Hirschfeld, leader of the German reform movement, *Per Scientiam ad Justitiam* ('Through knowledge to justice'). This set the tone for the public activities of sexual reformers, but beneath the surface there were interesting cross-currents which suggest that some, at least, were developing not only modes of adjustment but also patterns of resistance.

Havelock Ellis adopted a characteristically indirect approach in 1907 when he published a short article in the socialist literary and political journal, the *New Age* (14 November 1907). The article discussed a homosexual scandal, then gripping the German public amid frantic political intrigue: the Eulenberg–Harden case, which involved people close to the Kaiser. Ellis quoted Hirschfeld's evidence in court that 'to be abnormal is not to be unnatural', and he took this as a text to attack the absurdity of the English law. The article is not particularly significant in itself; its importance lies in its appearance in such a socialist journal. Under the editorship of A. R. Orage, the *New Age* was to build up during the Edwardian period a glittering reputation as a radical literary and political journal. Its contributors included a long list of famous journalistic luminaries, from Carpenter to H. G. Wells and G. B. Shaw. Some of the contributors were distinctly cranky, and Orage's enthusiasms notoriously wide. The paper embraced, at various times, arts and crafts, post-impressionism, imagism and vorticism, Nietzsche, Victor Grayson (the socialist M.P. elected in 1908, who shocked the then new, but already conventional Labour Party), Guild Socialism, and after the war, Major Douglas's social credit schemes. But, although always a shaky publication, perpetually on the verge of bankruptcy, the *New Age* had a wide readership in the vaguely radical-socialist workers, the sort of people who might be active locally in the Independent Labour Party or the women's movement. D. H. Lawrence was associated with a small group in Nottingham that met regularly to discuss the articles in the *New Age*. His ideas, influenced in the early days it seems by Carpenter and his circle, later became bitterly anti-homosexual, even while he extolled the virtues of male bonding, but in 1907 people like him would have read and discussed articles such as Ellis's, and been introduced to what then passed for advanced sexual theory.[2]

That was one way of keeping the issue alive. Another was tried by Carpenter a little later when he launched a campaign, partly tongue-in-cheek but with a deep underlying seriousness, against the powers-that-be in the British Museum Reading Room. In 1909 his book *The Intermediate Sex* had been published to mixed reviews. The *Journal of Education* had noted it for its 'wholesome plain speaking', the *Schoolmaster* (3 July 1909) gave a favourable notice, while the

*British Medical Journal* sneezed at it. Carpenter, however, quite rightly saw the book as an important intervention in public debate. He sent copies to various libraries, including the Masters' Library at Eton College (by whom it was politely acknowledged); the major provincial libraries (the Manchester Free Library had it on its shelves); and the National Libraries. Here the problem occurred.

On a visit to the British Museum in July 1911 Carpenter noticed that the book had not been entered in the catalogue; a year later he wrote to the Superintendent of the Reading Room, asking if this had now been done. The reply was brief and pointed:

> As the above book is only available upon special application, it has not been entered in the General Catalogue.
>                 Yours faithfully . . .

Carpenter replied immediately, enclosing copies of favourable reviews, mentioning appreciative comments from teachers and others, and asking *why* the book was so treated. The reply, on 29 June, was as brief as the first.

> Books that are only available upon special application are thus placed by order of the Keeper of Printed Books, and the reasons are many and various . . .

On 4 July Carpenter asked for details of these 'various reasons'. By 8 July the Keeper himself felt obliged to respond that it was his custom 'to reserve books dealing with certain sexual phases. Among such books is the work of which you write . . .' In his reply to this, Carpenter raised a more general point:

> The withdrawal of my book from the open shelves of the library and from the Catalogue does certainly seem annoying to me as an author, but (what is more important) it does not seem consonant with what is due to the General Public of which the author is one member . . . when such a book is banned from the B.M. Catalogue, one can only speculate on the great number of other serious works (some no doubt more important than this one) which may be so banned . . .[3]

The issue, of course, opened up important questions, questions that still remained unresolved in the 1960s when a new wave of books on sex began to appear which had broadly similar problems.

In 1912, the Keeper of Printed Books stood firm: 'The question which you ask has, I think, been sufficiently answered in my former letters to which I have no further information to add.'[4]

Carpenter was not satisfied, and in the next year or so kept the issue bubbling, gathering information about American and European library policies, consulting friends and lawyers, and helping in the preparation of an article on the subject which appeared in the *English Review* in December 1913. A few years later, the newly formed British Society for the Study of Sex Psychology, with Carpenter's prompting, continued the battle, when they requested access to the catalogue of the Private Case books to help in the preparation of their own bibliography. In a letter to Sir George Kenyon for the British Museum Trustees, the Society's committee stated:

> The object of the bibliography is purely scientific, but it has to be said that in view of the psychological investigations of Freud and Jung, Stekel and others, and the wide adoption of psychological methods in modern medicine many observations and enquiries in sexual science – which a few years ago and under old fashioned views – were relegated to obscurity and neglect, are now seen to be of considerable importance.[5]

The Trustees agreed to meet with the committee, but no special access was ever granted. These were small deeds, and not always very successful. But they established the lines of conflict, and clarified the areas of work. They also had local achievements. In the late summer of 1913, Carpenter's *The Intermediate Sex* was entered in the British Museum catalogue.

Carpenter was a direct influence on another and quite different endeavour which he was certainly aware of that centred on George Cecil Ives. From the mid 1890s Ives was chief luminary of a secret homosexual society, the Order of Chaeronea, which seems, from the fragmentary evidence, to have acted both as a support group for its members and as the focus for homosexual resistance and reform campaigns. Both its obsessive secrecy and its form and structure were products of the heightened sense of oppression felt by its members from the 1890s.[6] Ives's career is particularly revealing of the pressures and influences that gave coherence to the order. He was born in 1867 in Germany, the illegitimate offspring of two aristocratic families. His father was Gordon Maynard Ives; his mother the Baroness de Molarti, apparently the daughter of a Spanish grandee. As he told Janet, wife of C. R. Ashbee, in 1899:

'Our family is a mass of scandal – many of them I couldn't publish – what with divorces, elopements, suicides, hopeless love affairs and other tragedies. In fact my own advent into the world was a deep tragedy . . . you see?' He added meaningfully . . .

He was 'adopted and brought up' as he put it, by his grandmother, the Hon. Emma Ives, daughter of the 3rd Viscount Maynard, and he grew up in an ambience which was privileged, especially when living in France in his early years, and materially comfortable, if spiritually barren. His guardians could not understand, as he later put it, 'a nervous boy's grievous problems and unanswered perplexities'. He appears to have felt the pangs of his homosexuality from an early time and to have developed a precocious political sense about it. Mrs Ashbee asked him in 1899 when he first joined 'The Cause': 'Oh as far back as I can remember, when I was a small boy and I *could* not understand why such a wonderful thing should not be sanctioned.'[7] His own taste leant towards youths, and his poems reflect his interests, tempered as they are with a necessary caution. In his voluminous private diary, some three million words in length, parts of it in various codes, he is a little more explicit,

> . . . in my room alone night after night while the household slept, I dreamed if only I had another boy living by my side, I should have been in such a splendid setting, but my fate left me in solitude, alone with my own soul. And thus I grew apart – saw what I had to do. To set all loves free.[8]

'The Cause' – homosexual liberation – dominated Ives's life; and his own vague aspirations were given form and force by contacts with Edward Carpenter and Oscar Wilde in the early 1890s. He recorded in the volume of tributes to Carpenter, edited by Gilbert Beith, his first contacts with the socialist. A schoolmaster neighbour of Ives's parents in Nice, G. E. Comerford Casey, introduced him to Carpenter's *Towards Democracy* in 1892, and Ives found in it, as Carpenter had found in Whitman, a key that unlocked his perplexities: 'The first grip of sense and sanity I got from the outside world was received from the writings of Edward Carpenter.' Carpenter represented both that homosexual idealism that he craved for, and a sense of solid moral identity. 'Here was a man whose eyes were looking into the heavens, but yet whose feet were standing upon firm ground.'[9]

Ives's own temperament was quite different from Carpenter's. He had a wide range of interests; was an accomplished linguist; he became a Fellow of the Zoological Society, while his recreations included music, chess, swimming, cricket and 'anything to get hot and work hard at'. But he was also prone to deep introspection and gloom, and predictably found Carpenter's Sheffield life a little difficult. He visited Millthorpe in 1897, before Merrill moved in, and thought its gregariousness trying, himself being 'so much more cloistral and hermitic by habit and temperament'.[9] But Carpenter and Ives corresponded regularly, and Carpenter frequently called on Ives in London. Carpenter's influence was permanent.

The relationship Ives had with Wilde and his circle was possibly even more personal, and it seems that there was an emotional and sexual involvement with Lord Alfred Douglas. Certainly, again from around 1892, he identified strongly with Wilde's fight against 'the Philistines'. In his diary, which is an important untapped source on Wilde's last decade, Ives linked *Towards Democracy* and Wilde's work as part of the same endeavour. His comment is revealing:

> Well, the cause must be sacred and followed by all sorts of men, each to work in their particular sphere – the issue and the hope is great enough to bind even the most heterogeneous society and if only organised which we have never been before, we shall go on to victory.[10]

Already, however, before the Wilde trial cast a pall, Ives had experienced the difficulties of these chiliastic flights. He had been warmed by Grant Allen's article on 'The New Hedonism' in 1894, which had attacked Christianity and exalted the 'sex instinct' as 'the origin and basis of all that is best and highest within us'. Ives, like others, took this to be an acceptance of homosexuality, so that when Grant Allen declared in a later contribution that 'On this issue . . . I am a Social Purity Man', Ives was impelled to wet his own pen in reply: 'To pronounce any opinion upon Roman, and especially Greek love, upon the data our opponents furnish, would be so sweeping and absurd that only utter ignorance of history could afford any excuse for so doing . . .'[11] At this the *Review of Reviews*, in outrage, lumbered out its own heavy artillery. Ives was sharply rapped over the fingers by name, and, pained, retreated into his shell.[11] But it was the Wilde trial that most sharply underlined the difficulties. Ives was shattered by the conviction, and equally by the prison conditions which Wilde (whom he visited in jail) had to endure. A poem in his *Book of Chains* (1897) refers to the Wilde trial:

Oh, brutish herd, is this your service then?
To what strange god? What potent fiend on high
Gloats to smell blood, and see the helpless life
Gasp out its soul for human wantonness?
True type of earthly justice this indeed,
To make the weak suffer the wrongs of power.[12]

It confirmed him in the first place in his retreat into a defensive secretiveness which characterized the rest of his life's activities. Even Wilde was to be infuriated by this, and he wrote from Paris in 1900: 'Don't have with *me* the silly mania for secrecy that makes you miss the value of things.' But the events of the 1890s also gave Ives a heightened sense of his mission, a burning sense of his oppression, and a desire to fight, as he put it in his diaries, 'the fires of persecution'.

In his diaries he calls on the 'children of the Faith' to stand fast; and in his published works, less openly, he makes the same point.

It may be greater light will come
And cast a shadow of the rays
That flash from our terrestrial sun,
Though bright they look in these dark days.
We may a deeper wisdom learn
Than that for which our reason groped,
And hidden beauty yet discern
In things for which we never hoped.[13]

Ives deliberately made his public persona an enigma. Several of his books were published anonymously, including his early work *Book of Chains*. But the unifying threads of his life are clear enough in his relatively small published output as well as in his diaries. He described himself in his *Who's Who* entry as 'author and criminologist', and several of his books are concerned generally with penal reform, but have obvious extensions. His *A History of Penal Methods: Criminals, Witches and Lunatics*, which dealt with the legal treatment of deviants through the ages, had explicit relevance for homosexuals. Similarly his last book, *Obstacles to Human Progress* (1939), examined the ways in which religion, prejudice, ignorance and blindness distort the 'Wonders of Instinct' and 'The Dignity of Nature'. In his pamphlet, *The Continued Extension of the Criminal Law* (1922), he touched on the intervention of public authority in the personal life. The conclusions for penal reform that flowed from this body of work were the obvious complements of his homosexual poetry. He recalled in his diary that he had been called to 'the War of Liberation' as a lad; for the rest of his life the persecution of homosexuals weighed heavily on him, and he was determined to fight for justice to the end. The Order of Chaeronea was seen as part of this struggle.

The order was a secret society, bound together by ties of friendship, loyalty, a sexual-political awareness and a symbolic ritual. Masonic in form, in practice it was a homosexual support and pressure group. It is quite likely that it existed from the mid 1890s, but there are more accountable references to it from the late 1890s. On one level, it was similar to Carpenter's hoped-for 'body of friends', a homosexual coterie and network which, in countless echoes, remains a familiar part of the homosexual sub-culture up to the present. But it was obviously intended to be much more than this. Ives and Laurence Housman, another prominent member, made sure that only those prepared to work for reform of attitudes should be admitted; they did not want it to be a hunting-place for sexual contacts, though bonds of close friendship inevitably arose. Its members viewed it with deadly seriousness. The name of the society was significant. It was derived from the Battle of Chaeronea in 338 B.C., when troops of Philip of Macedon crushingly defeated the Athenians. In the battle the 'Sacred Band' of Thebans, a highly trained strike force of three hundred young men bound together by ties of loyalty and love, held their position and were annihilated by the Macedonian cavalry. A gigantic marble lion, restored in 1902, marks their mass grave. The legend of the Theban band persisted for obvious reasons among certain layers of homosexuals, educated as many were in classics and Greek love. Lowes Dickinson cites it in his study of Greek civilization,[14] and E. M. Forster mentions it in his novel *Maurice*. The image of homosexuals dying for 'The Cause' could be a potent inspiration.

The date 338 B.C. was given a mystic significance by the order as year one of the Faith, and communications between members were dated from that base. This had the additional advantage of hiding the significance of the correspondence.[15] Communications between members of the order were deliberately obscured in other ways. Ives and Housman wrote to each other as 'One to Another', and used a form of numbers to identify their fellow members. Members were bound to each other not only by their sense of solidarity in secrecy but also by the ritual of initiation ceremonies and by common symbols. The order had 'Services of Initiation', revised regularly. One for '2237' (1899) began with 'Rememberina':

1. Thou shalt not trifle with Souls.
2. Thou shalt not break A Promise given with Intent, Freedom and Knowledge.
3. Thou shalt not Command nor Obey.
4. Cultivate Every Gift.
5. Be ruler of Thyself.
6. Feel True in thine own Heart.

This was followed by solemn vows:

> That you will never Vex or Persecute Lovers. That all real love shall be to you as sanctuary. That all heart-love, legal and illegal, wise and unwise, happy and disastrous, shall yet be consecrate, for that love's Holy Presence dwelt there. Dost thou so promise?[16]

Once within the order, members could recognize each other by seals and insignia, several of which survive among Ives's private papers. The symbol of the order was 'the Seal of the Double Wreath'. The outer wreath represented 'calammus', referring to Whitman's flower representing comradeship; the inner wreath was myrtle for love. In the middle was a chain, with open links at each end, representing the unity of the order; then the date 338, and the letters z, L, D. z stood for zeal, enthusiasm for 'The Cause', which came before all things, for without it there was no worldliness. L was for learning, since knowledge is power (thus echoing the Hirschfeld motto). D was for discipline, needed to fight for 'The Cause'. These symbols were taken with obvious earnestness. Ashbee recorded how Ives always wore a heavy silver ring 'with the name of the battle of the Greek lovers and the little device like a double fork'.

The Commentary on the 'Rule and Purposes' made clear the aim of the order: it represented 'A Religion, A Theory of Life, and Ideal of Duty. We demand justice for all manner of people who are wronged and oppressed by individuals or multitudes or the laws.' Its membership and mode of operation is less apparent. Members were exhorted to be secretive about their comrades:

> Thou knowest the two who received thee in the Order. Thou dost not need to know any others. Thou art forbidden to mention who belongs to anybody outside it.

It is not easy therefore to piece together those who were actually involved. Among the most likely members are those who were associated with Ives in the British Society for the Study of Sex Psychology (which will be dealt with at greater length in the next chapter). Timothy d'Arch Smith speaks of this society as being little more than a 'cabal of homosexuals'. In its early days, at least, this is misleading, but certainly many homosexuals were involved in both societies. Housman, chairman of the society, is the most obvious figure, but there were several others.

Laurence Housman (1865–1959) was, like Ives, a minor poet, but also a writer on varied topics, a playwright and an illustrator. In 1900 he had published anonymously *An Englishwoman's Love Letters* which had been regarded as very daring at the time, and two earlier poems by him had raised some eyebrows, carrying, as *The Times* obituary in 1959 put it, 'introspective glimpses of his own soul of a disturbing oddity'. Coming from a Tory background, by the new century he had been deeply influenced by the twin strands of socialism and feminism. He knew Carpenter from the mid 1890s, and was present in 1908 when the Irishman M. D. O'Brien began his demented attacks on Carpenter. He was also closely acquainted with Wilde, and deeply influenced by his downfall. Years later, in his ninetieth year, Housman was to recall that 'His unhappy fate has done the world a signal service in defeating the blind obscurantists: he has made people think.'[17] He was an ardent feminist, and an early member of the men's group that supported the militant Women's Social and Political Union (WSPU). In June 1909 he was at the centre of disturbances in the Central Lobby of the House of Commons, but left the WSPU finally in 1912 over its policy of violence. During the First World War that followed he was a pacifist. Like Ives, his involvement in homosexual reform was obsessive and life-long, and found a natural focus in the Order of Chaeronea and the British Society for the Study of Sex Psychology.

Other certain members of the order were Montague Summers (1880–1948), who was secretary of the BSSP sub-committee on homosexuality until 1921; and John Gambrill Francis Nicholson (1866–1931), hon. treasurer of the society.[18] Both were poets, writing on 'Uranian' themes, and again are a direct link with the more extravagant activities of the early 1890s. Laurence's brother, A. E. Housman (1859–1936), scholar and poet (author of *A Shropshire Lad*), was also possibly a member of the order, as was C. R. Ashbee after 1899. C. Kains Jackson, editor and publisher of 'Uranian' material from the early 1890s, certainly belonged, as did Samuel Elsworth Cottam, a collector of 'Uranian' material.[19] Several of these people were associated with *The Quorum: A Magazine of Friendship*, produced by Kains Jackson in 1920, and which involved Housman and Nicholson. One edition only of this appeared, and was circulated to members of the society. Also linked with this journal was the Rev. E. E. Bradford, another writer of verse with pedophile undertones, as was Leonard Green (1885–1966), a writer of 'Uranian' prose, friend of T. E. Lawrence and later chairman of the Save the Children Fund. It seems that membership of the order was in fact worldwide. There were probably members in America, France and Italy, and certainly members in Germany. According to Ives's Diary, meetings were held in various international localities, including Vienna and Paris.

From the limited evidence it would appear that most of the leading elements in the order were born in the 1860s or early 1870s, and thus would have been in their twenties or early thirties during the traumatic period of the Wilde trials. Most had some connection with Wilde and his circle, and we can speculate that his downfall might have been the precipitating element for the order's establishment. Most of its known members were upper middle-class, literary or professional men who, by the nature of their relatively privileged social situation, could develop a sustained homosexual life-style while simultaneously needing to protect themselves from social disgrace.

There is some evidence that Una Troubridge and Radclyffe Hall applied to join the Order of Chaeronea after the publication of *The Well of Loneliness*, but it is not certain whether they were accepted. Most of the known male members seem to have shared an interest in youths, usually of working-class origin. In the curious way that was common in the early decades of the century, it seems often to have extended from a sexual to a political identity. In 1914 Ashbee began a relationship with a young man, and Laurence Housman wrote in the following terms:

I haven't a doubt of the extraordinary humanising and educative values which do come out of these rapprochements – especially when it is between class and class that the union takes place . . .

Comradeship with women made me an ardent suffragist; comradeship with man makes me more and more of a socialist . . .

I know two very dear gentlemen – one a policeman and the other a cobbler; and it is only comradeship that has revealed it to me.[20]

Of course, as we have seen earlier, there was often a fine line between this and a sexual colonialism. The class barriers never completely dissolved. Comradeship was one theme. Another, again echoing Carpenter, and also a strong German tradition, stressed the moral superiority of 'Uranian' love. Unpublished works in the George Ives papers strongly suggest this theme.

The general political commitments of the order are less clear. Certainly Ives believed in the early years of the century in a comprehensive ethical socialism which, like Carpenter's, looked to a transformation not only in economic relations but also in social and spiritual atmosphere. He wrote to Janet Ashbee in 1904:

> There is a curious kind of 'Socialism' in this country, which is allied with Christianity and even with Grundyism. That, to my mind, is more hateful than the present order. The socialism to which I belong, and to which solid millions adhere on the Continent, refuses all compromise with the religious parties, all compromise with existing sexual morality, all compromise with the class system in any shape.[21]

Sexual freedom was seen as an essential aspect of all freedoms. Typically, this moralistic socialism was not located in any social force; it was utopian in spirit and vision. But it was a representative mood among many early sex-reformers. This may or may not have been shared by other members of the order, but it can be traced as a central tendency in the early sex-reform organizations.[22]

It is far from clear how influential the order actually was. Its most important function was undoubtedly to serve as a support group for its members. It helped to provide a sense of solidarity in a hostile world. Its ambitions were certainly wider than this, and wider than those of the reform organizations that worked publicly. It appears that one of its characteristic activities was to encourage homosexual non-members to propagate 'The Cause', especially Members of Parliament, other people in authority, and especially writers and artists. Contact was especially close with the 'Uranian' writers of the early part of the century. The order probably outlived, as a social circle, any of the organizations to which it gave support (several of its members lived until the 1950s). But it is equally certain that, without these enthusiasts, particularly Ives and Housman, an organization like the British Society for the Study of Sex Psychology would have lost some of its impetus. The Order of Chaeronea was perhaps not quite the mythical 'Homintern' that was alleged, in a famous joke, to march arm in arm with the Comintern, but, on a smaller scale, it might conceivably have had a trifle more reality. And under-lying its existence was an important assumption otherwise rare until the 1970s: that the liberation of homosexuals could only be the task of homosexuals themselves.

# 11
## Reform Societies

**In Memoriam.** *In loving memory of my dear friend 'Dave', who took his life in May 1938 aged 19 years. We kissed in the park and they caught us. | I got nine months – He died. | He used to say 'We'll make it together'. | It's been a long time Dave! | And a lonely journey. | I wish I could say 'We'll meet again' | But I have no faith – only memories. – Harry. May I pay tribute to all those who suffered and died with us during the dark years.*
– Gay News, 95

The British Society for the Study of Sex Psychology (BSSP) was finally established in July 1914. Edward Carpenter was made a life member and first president. In an obituary address to the society after Carpenter's death, Cecil Reddie, founder and headmaster of the progressive school at Abbotsholme, which Carpenter had also played an early part in inspiring, observed that, without Carpenter, the society would never have come into being: 'sex study was in England almost totally tabued [*sic*]'. And Reddie pointed out the special qualities Carpenter had to contribute:

> . . . it required courage to start a society for sex study. More even than courage, it required extreme care and tact. Here Carpenter's inimitable gift for discussing problems moderately and persuasively yet firmly and frankly, was invaluable.[1]

This 'extreme care and tact' was already felt to be a little old fashioned by younger elements. Laurence Housman, who became chairman of the society, felt that Carpenter was often too indirect and evasive for his pleading to hit home, and that he was too hedged in with appeals to extenuating circumstances.[2] But only Carpenter and Havelock Ellis, who was another early backer, stood as giants of an earlier British generation who could provide the necessary prestige to get a reform society off the ground.

Another important influence was external, that of Magnus Hirschfeld. Hirschfeld was a major pioneer in the foundation of modern sexology, and the inspirer from the late 1890s of the German homosexual movement. Born in 1868, the son of a physician in the Baltic town of Kolberg, he had studied comparative philology and philosophy before turning to medicine in 1893. Thereafter he practised as a doctor, first in Magdeburg, then in Charlottenberg, until 1909; later he practised as a neurologist in Berlin. But it is as a writer on homosexuality and leader of the Scientific Humanitarian Committee in Germany that his influence was most direct. He founded the committee, in effect the first homosexual reform organization, in Charlottenberg in 1897. Other committees were founded in Hamburg, Munich, Leipzig, Hanover and Amsterdam. In 1899 he established the *Jahrbuch für Sexuelle Zwischenstufen*, a yearbook which appeared regularly until the 1920s, often of vast size (and with a disappointingly small circulation) and incorporating a vast amount of historical, sociological, psychological, anthropological and personal information about homosexuality.

Hirschfeld's work proceeded on two levels: theoretical and practical-political. It was in the former that he felt most at home, living out his famous motto (already quoted on p. 115). His massive studies on 'sexual inversion', which culminated in 1914 in his *Homosexuality of Men and Women*, are the definitive statements of the biological-congenital model of homosexuality, and were among the most influential works of his generation, influencing not only co-thinkers such as Havelock Ellis, but also people who eventually made radical breaks with his tradition, such as Freud. In Hirschfeld's work we can observe at its peak that categorization of behavioural phenomena and the classificatory passion which is a mark of late nineteenth-century studies in sexuality. His earlier study of *Transvestites* (1910), a term he coined, carefully distinguishes cross-dressing from homosexuality for the first time in a detailed study. Ellis's work was proceeding along the same lines, but his volume on *Eonism and Other Supplementary Studies* did not appear until the 1920s. Even before the major work of Steinach, Hirschfeld put a central emphasis on the importance of the sex glands (testicles and ovaries) in determining sexual characteristics, and the 'internal secretions' (hormones) were given a central role. He made strenuous efforts to explain homosexuality in terms of the irregularities of hormonal secretions, in the belief that sexual characteristics could be seen as resulting from hormonal balances.[3]

In fact, the mechanistic connection between the internal chemistry of the body and social behaviour is the most dubious aspect of his work, though it had the politically useful capacity of justifying the conclusion that homosexuality (because it was 'natural') was a harmless anomaly or intermediate stage. But there was another characteristic of his work which, like Ellis's, served to put contemporary attitudes in their place. He observed that morals were relative and changing things, not fixed or given or eternal. A visit to Africa in the early 1890s apparently convinced him that 'the sexual prejudices of the civilized world were only social conventions'.[4]

Hirschfeld was less happy as a political organizer in a reform campaign, often making ponderously 'scientific' interventions in public debate, but it was a role he performed up to the 1920s. By the early 1900s the Scientific Humanitarian Committee had succeeded in raising the issue of homosexuality in Germany on a comparatively wide scale. A 'Petition' Campaign had been launched in 1897 with the aim of collecting as many signatures as possible of important political, social, artistic, medical and scientific people on a call for the decriminalization of male homosexual acts. Over the years, more than 6,000 prominent people signed it, from Krafft-Ebing and Albert Einstein to leading socialists such as Karl Kautsky and writers such as Herman Hesse and Heinrich and Thomas Mann. Many leading figures of the then Marxist Social Democratic Party gave the repeal campaign full support. August Bebel, the veteran socialist, spoke for it from the floor of the Reichstag in 1898. The committee questioned candidates at elections to establish their position; gathered elementary statistics through the efforts of Hirschfeld; and disseminated information through the *Yearbook* and pamphlets. By June 1908 more than 5,000 homosexuals had been in touch with the committee, and it had over 1,000 members by 1910.

Nothing on this scale seemed possible in Britain, but Hirschfeld's work was well known among homosexuals and reformers. Ellis and Carpenter were in contact, as were various other interested parties. Hirschfeld had received two letters from England after the publication of *Sappho and Socrates:* one from Max Müller, the Oxford Sanskrit scholar, and another from Robert Ross, Wilde's close friend and literary executor.[5] George Cecil Ives was in frequent touch with him. There were also links between British reformers and other tendencies in the German movement. Certainly Ives was in correspondence with Adolf Brand, who broke away for a time from the Scientific Humanitarian Committee. Brand edited *The Special* from 1896, and also published *Friendship and Freedom* and *Eros*. He was associated with Benedict Friedländer in an organization called the

'Community of the Special', which had a cultural rather than a political emphasis, extolling the virtues of masculine culture and Hellenic love. Its tone was closer to Carpenter's cosmic adventures than to Hirschfeld's positivism, and there was possibly a direct link with Ives's and Housman's Order of Chaeronea.

Whatever the exact nature of the links, there was obviously a basis in personal contacts for a public British reform organization, and the informal ties began to crystallize after 1912 when a British branch of the Scientific Humanitarian Committee was first mooted. The crucial event seems to have been the Fourteenth International Medical Congress, held in London in 1913. Hirschfeld was one of the leading speakers, and he brought over some of his famous exhibits of 'intermediate types' – diagrams and photographs of male and female homosexuals. These caused a minor sensation. Ellis secured admission for Carpenter, and Carpenter encouraged others to attend. Housman recorded that it was a letter from Carpenter which brought him to the congress, there to hear Hirschfeld lecture and see his exhibits.

Important links were strengthened at the congress, and Carpenter was invited in return to speak on homosexuality at the First International Congress for Sexual Research planned for Berlin in November 1914. Only the outbreak of war prevented this taking place.[6]

But the 1913 congress had been a revelation also for many of the ordinary medical people who attended, especially on the subject of homosexuality. One of the complaints of the British doctors, according to Housman, was that there was no 'informed public' in Britain to encourage research along the lines that Hirschfeld detailed. It was apparently in the minds of the founders of the British Society for the Study of Sex Psychology, encouraged by the contacts and these reactions, to help to develop the nucleus of such a public.

By 1914 the time seemed opportune to launch the society publicly. It was established, in the words of its 'Policy and Principles', 'for the consideration of problems and questions connected with sexual psychology, from their medical, juridical and sociological aspects'. The aim was to adopt a 'scientific' (that is, humane and rational) approach to the problems of sex. But inextricably linked with the research and investigation was the question of public sex education. The society's ambition was, through lectures and the issue of pamphlets, 'to organize understanding in the lay mind on a larger scale, to make people more receptive to scientific proof, and more conscious of their social responsibility'. By laying the basis of a new informed awareness, the society hoped to pave the way to needed reforms.[7]

The immediate point of reference was obviously the women's movement, which inevitably, if indirectly, posed the sharpest problems of sex relations. The militant presence of feminism had struck home like a clarion at the 1913 congress. As Sir Edward Grey, the British Foreign Secretary, was delivering his welcoming speech, cries of 'Votes for women!' had rung through the Albert Hall. Hirschfeld was amazed at the vast array of police which appeared and bundled the women off with great violence. The links of Ellis and Carpenter with the women's cause were well established, while Laurence Housman had come to political commitment through support of the suffrage campaigns, and saw his work in the society as an important continuation. Housman gave a lecture on 'The Relation of Fellow-feeling to Sex' to the society in 1916, and was delighted that it went down well with a mixed audience of men and women who listened carefully without discomfort or embarrassment. He commented to Janet Ashbee, 'That is what the BSSP is doing; and I am pleased for it is my main contribution to the suffrage cause during wartime.' Although never worked out in detail, there was the clear assumption that the women's cause and sex reform were part of the same battle. As Housman put it in his chairman's statement:

> We believe that nothing concerning sex can be rightly dealt with apart from the full equation – men and women thinking and working together for a common understanding – and that no sex problem has ever yet been rightly dealt with by one sex deciding and acting alone, and that in consequence of decisions so formed and so acted on society is suffering today.[8]

The society involved women from the start, and among the most important participants in 1914 was Stella Browne, who appears to have acted as a stimulant. In 1917 she confided to her friend, the American birth-control pioneer Margaret Sanger, that the society was now 'getting a move on – thanks partly to my efforts, I must admit!'[9]

These links were important, because they implied that homosexual oppression was not seen as an isolated problem but was part of a wider issue. Nevertheless, the question of homosexuality itself was taken with great seriousness, and public education on homosexuality was a major theme from the beginnings of the society. Its 'List of Aims' declared that: 'We have faced that problem with a petulant and a disgusted ignorance, priding ourselves on a refusal to consider it at all'. The problem was, of course, how to tackle it in a way which was not biased, but which would not bring the risk of prosecution to members. Carpenter had himself experienced the risk of public calumny, and during the early years of the First World War there were hints of the police taking a more than usual interest in his books on homosexuality. Particularly in the context of war-time hysteria that almost immediately overtook the new society, homosexuality was not an easy question to examine dispassionately. The conscious use of his homosexuality by the British government to blacken the name and reputation of the Irish patriot, Sir Roger Casement, was a notorious example of the issues' exploitation by the authorities.[10] Nor was there a ready public opinion willing or able to defend homosexuals. In such a climate, the society moved with more caution than aplomb in its process of public education.

The disruptions caused by the war inevitably meant that the society got off to a slow start (indeed, in Germany, the Scientific Humanitarian Committee largely went into abeyance). A library sub-committee of the society was established, and, as we saw in the previous chapter, under the direction of C. R. Ashbee took issue with the British Museum to try to gain access to the Private Case Catalogue. Efforts were also made to build up a private library for the use of members. This was bedevilled by the lack of permanent premises, but Ives seems to have assumed responsibility. Among his surviving papers in England is a library catalogue which indicates that a wide range of books was eventually available: books by Ellis, Carpenter and Hirschfeld obviously, but also books by Northcote, Frere, Dendy, Coghlan, Robinson, and covering such topics as sex education, sex in different societies, the attitude of the Church, works on biology, venereal disease, moral purity. There is more Hirschfeld than Freud, and a bias towards biological theories, but this is to be expected.[11] Ives also continued his own personal activity of collecting newspaper cuttings on homosexual issues. By his death there were some forty volumes, which were offered in his will to the British Museum, but never reached there. Ives himself made voluminous use of them in his own works; indeed, some of his articles and papers are little more than press snippets strung together by a narrative line.

At the heart of the work of the British Society for Sex Psychology, however, was the process of self-education, and of attempting to educate a sympathetic public. The intention was, through exchange of views, discussion, assembly of information and encouragement of research, to build up a body of information. Talks were often given monthly in the 1920s, and open to a wider public. Many of the lectures and talks to members were later published as pamphlets, either under the society's imprint (seventeen were so published between 1915 and 1933) or privately. The pamphlets covered a wide range of topics, from the first, *Policy and Principles; General Aims*, which set out the outlines of the society's policy, to the seventeenth, *A Plain Talk on Sex Difficulties*, the substance of a lecture by F. B. Rockstro on 'Some Difficulties in the Technique of Conjugal Relationships' given before the society in March 1933.

Several of the pamphlets were relevant to feminist politics, such as Stella Browne's *Sexual Variety and Variability among Women* (No. 3) and Havelock Ellis's *The Erotic Rights of Women* (No. 5). Others raised more general issues on sexuality. The Rev. H. Northcote wrote on *The Social Value of the Study of Sex Psychology* (No. 7), and the leading anthropologist, Edward Westermarck, on *The Origin of Sexual Modesty* (No. 8). Eden Paul published a pamphlet on *The Sexual Life of the Child* (No. 10), and Paul and Norman Haire jointly produced one on *Rejuvenation: Steinach's Researches on Sex Glands* (No. 11), which discussed the function of the sex hormones in determining personal characteristics. All these touched on what are now seen as central questions in the exploration of sexuality: the nature of sexuality in the young and in women, the factors that determine sexuality, the significance of monogamy and the nuclear family. No consistent BSSP view emerges from an examination of these questions, apart from the overriding willingness to explore the meaning of sexuality.

The discussion of homosexuality was inevitably at the heart of the society's work. Nor is this surprising. There were, after all, other societies dealing with related aspects of the 'sex problem'. The long-established Malthusian (later New Generation) League and the Eugenics Education Society concerned themselves in differing ways with birth control, and after 1921 were joined by Marie Stopes's Society for Constructive Birth Control and Racial Progress. Stella Browne was very active in such work. Ives maintained contact with the Divorce Law Reform Union and the Howard League for Penal Reform. The special contribution of the British Society for the Study of Sex Psychology could be in the wide field of sex psychology, and in the particular field of homosexuality. This is even less surprising when we consider that most of the leading lights who dominated the society from the 1920s, from Carpenter on his pedestal to Housman and Ives, and later Norman Haire, were homosexual.

The society's second pamphlet had indicated this involvement. It was an English digest of a famous German pamphlet, originally published in Germany in 1903 and into its nineteenth edition within four years. The English version, *The Social Problem of Sexual Inversion*, was published with suitable caution: 'Issued by the BSSP to members of the Educational, Medical and Legal Professions'. But as the Introduction noted: 'That any courage should be needed in a demand for facts to be recognized and scientifically investigated, is in itself a sufficient condemnation of the obscurantist attitude which prevails so largely among us in regard to this question.'[12] And despite its belief that changes in the law were not yet on the agenda, it called for the harmonizing, as far as possible, of social and juridical practice with scientific investigations and conclusions.

The 'scientific conclusions' themselves were a straightforward summary of third-sex notions: they cited relevant testimony from Krafft-Ebing to Hirschfeld, quoted Bebel and the views of headmasters and authorities, and ended with the text of the petition to the legislative bodies of the German Empire. It was a cautious but clear statement of argument, based entirely on German figures, but it provided a useful summary of current theoretical views. No details of distribution or circulation are available, but it was reprinted.

Certain other BSSP pamphlets were directly concerned with homosexuality. Laurence Housman's *The Relation of Fellow-Feeling to Sex* (No. 4) touched on the theme of comradeship, and discussions in other pamphlets published later in the 1920s were more openly concerned with deviant sex. Harold Picton published *The Morbid, the Abnormal and the Personal* (No. 12), and Edward Carpenter published a frank article on Whitman's homosexuality, *Some Friends of Walt Whitman: A Study in Sex Psychology* (No. 13). In this he criticized John Addington Symonds for his timidity and issued his own credo: the existence of inversion 'proves to us that perhaps after all the continuation of the race is not the main effect of love and sex intercourse'. Two other pamphlets looked at homosexuality from a more ostensibly scientific viewpoint: F. A. E. Crew's *Sexuality and Intersexuality* (No. 14), which explored the bisexual characteristics of all people, an important theme in early twentieth-century debates, and H. D. Jennings White's *Psychological Causes of Homoeroticism and Inversion* (No. 15), which touched on Freudian themes not otherwise notably current in these papers.

The special sub-committee devoted to the study of homosexuality (which inevitably overlapped with the Order of Chaeronea), had various papers read to it. Montague Summers as secretary of the sub-committee (during his last year in office in 1921 the sub-committee met at his house in Hampstead), delivered a paper on the

Marquis de Sade, later published by the society,[13] and also gave talks on 'Sidelights on English Kings and Roman Pontiffs' and 'Noteworthy Tendencies in Modern English Literature'. Ives read to it a paper on the 'Graeco-Roman View of Youth', which was later published by Philip Sainsbury at the Cayme Press (1926) with a limited circulation. This is an interesting pamphlet, for Ives ties his argument about homosexuality to the way in which society labels other deviant minorities: the 'insane', he says, are only those whom society cannot tolerate; normality is not something given by nature but a matter of taste and opinion of the majority.[14] But this idea is never developed, the overall theme being not unexpectedly love of youths. At an annual meeting of the society (14 October 1921) Ives took up a related theme in a paper on 'The Plight of the Adolescent'. He speaks of the tyranny of age over youth, giving cross-cultural comparisons, and complains of the monstrous laws on solicitation, wriggled through Parliament in 1898. Ives expostulated that no young person of either sex was safe from what any two detectives, hunting in pairs, might allege against them.

His central concern had a curious way of coming through even in the most apparently disparate field. A talk he gave to a 'Study Group' (not specified, but presumably of the society) on 'The Sexes, Structure and "Extra-Organic" Habits of Certain Animals', found in the curious habit of flat-fish in swimming on their side 'no little philosophy' for humans: 'They accept life, and make natural history, by living out their instincts and mysterious promptings; they are making the best of things as they find them.'[15] This was the message the society attempted to bring home.

It is difficult to estimate what influence the society (which became, in the 1920s, the British Sexological Society) could have had. In July 1920 there were some 234 members, and this was probably the median size. Up to forty or fifty people often attended its meetings, and the pamphlets had a fairly wide circulation. But it is highly unlikely that it made any deep penetration into public consciousness, though the more sexually aware atmosphere of the 1920s meant that it had a wider constituency to influence. Its membership and support was wide among progressive intellectuals. George Bernard Shaw was a member (a life member from 1930), as were E. M. Forster, Maurice Eden and Cedar Paul (two early advocates of birth control in the Independent Labour Party, and later in the Communist Party), Vyvyan Holland (Oscar Wilde's son), the playwright, Harley Granville-Barker, and Harriet Weaver Shaw, editor of *The Egoist* and patron of James Joyce. Other supporters included Radclyffe Hall

and Una Troubridge, Bertrand and Dora Russell, Norman Douglas
and Edward Westermarck. Abroad, the society maintained important links: with Hirschfeld and his colleagues, of course, but also
with Margaret Sanger in the United States, and many others. The
society affiliated to the Society for Human Rights in Chicago in 1925,
while a French Sexological Society was formed in 1932. Alexandra
Kollontai, the Russian feminist, sat on its Honorary Committee in
the early 1920s.

It is doubtful, however, whether the society greatly extended its
own natural audience, and it certainly could never claim to have
revolutionized attitudes. Neither did it have any influence on government policy. At the most it may have strengthened the self-awareness
and sexual knowledge of a relatively small layer of people. But in its
talks and publications, it did attempt to extend the pre-1914 concern with feminism and sex reform. And during the 1920s it was to
become part of a wider current, with the development of the international sex-reform movement. Until the early 1930s it was the major
British organization concerned with the issue: that, in itself, is an
achievement of sorts.


The immediate post-war years had indeed seemed to herald a new
era of sex reform. In post-revolutionary Russia the Bolsheviks had,
as a matter of course, legalized divorce and abortion, encouraged
birth control and decriminalized homosexuality. Dr Grigorii Batkis
in his book *The Sexual Revolution in Russia* had explained the
underlying principle of Soviet legislation:

> It declares the absolute non-interference of the state and society
> into sexual matters, so long as nobody is injured and no one's
> interests are infringed upon . . . Concerning homosexuality,
> sodomy, and other forms of sexual gratification set down in
> European legislation as offences against public morality, Soviet
> legislation treats these exactly the same as so-called 'natural'
> intercourse. All forms of intercourse are private matters.

In actuality, the immediate penetration of this 'sexual revolution'
was limited, given the immense backward nature of Soviet Russia,
and it was to be followed by a massive retreat in outlook after the
degeneration of the revolution under Stalin in the 1930s; but, for
progressive opinion in the 1920s, Soviet Russia seemed like a
beacon. Norman Haire, far from being a socialist revolutionary

himself, saw the sexual code of the USSR as a 'fascinating experiment which we sexologists in other countries are watching with great interest'.[16]   In Germany, too, during the 1920s there seemed to be the possibility of great advance. In the wake of the political revolution which had overthrown the Kaiser, the Scientific Humanitarian Committee was revived and hopes ran high that Paragraph 175 of the penal code would be repealed. And in 1919 Hirschfeld fulfilled a long ambition and opened the Institute for Sexual Science – 'A Child of the Revolution', as he called it. This was to be a living centre for sex research and the dissemination of scientific knowledge. He presented his huge archive to the Prussian state, which in turn funded the institute as being of major public importance. It was housed in one of the finest old buildings in Berlin, and became an unequalled repository of biological, anthropological, historical and statistical data, a sexological museum, an important library (with over 20,000 books on sex psychology) and a Mecca for sexologists from all over the world. But it was of vital importance, too, to lesser mortals. It housed a marriage-guidance bureau which was consulted by thousands, and on the second floor it housed the Scientific Humanitarian Committee. Every German citizen who entered the building was given the opportunity of signing the Petition.

At the same time it was clear that the sexual-reform movement needed an international focus if it was to achieve its maximum influence on public opinion and existing institutions. In 1921 Hirschfeld convened in Berlin the first International Congress for Sex Reform, reviving the abortive pre-war plans. At a further congress, held in Copenhagen in 1928, the World League for Sexual Reform, already mooted earlier, was formally established. Appropriately, Hirschfeld, August Forel and Havelock Ellis were its first honorary presidents.

According to Wilhelm Reich, the league in the 1920s 'comprised the most progressive sexologists and sex reformers in the world'.[17] It developed no single theoretical line or approach, nor did it have a single political line. It had representatives from the USSR (including Alexandra Kollontai, the great Bolshevik feminist) as well as from the Western capitalist countries, but its method was essentially reformist, interested primarily in putting forward a definitive programme – 'a sexual sociology', as Hirschfeld called it – which could be presented to the legislators of the world. The 1928 Congress appealed 'to the legislatures, the Press and the Peoples of all countries, to help to create a new legal and social attitude (based on the knowledge which has been acquired from scientific research in sexual biology, psychology and sociology) towards the sexual life of men and women'. This approach suggested implicit contradictions in its attitudes to sexual politics from the first, but these did not come to a head until the mid 1930s. Up to 1932 at least the league did its utmost in its cautious way to build up a basis of sexual knowledge and awareness.

Its declared aim, in the tradition which Havelock Ellis and the British sex reformers had always espoused, was to harmonize social and judicial practice with the 'laws of nature'. Its specific planks included support for the political, economic and sexual equality of women and men; reform of marriage and divorce laws; improved sex education; the control of conception; reform of the abortion laws; the prevention of venereal disease and prostitution; and the protection of unmarried mothers and the illegitimate child.

But the emphasis on the 'laws of nature' also allowed for the inclusion of homosexual reform. There had, indeed, been a demand in the German homosexual movement since the early 1920s for closer international cooperation – 'Uranians of the World, Unite', as the more radical German homosexual reformers had urged – and apart from the frequent informal links already noted, the World League for Sexual Reform was the main agency for this. Its platform called for 'a rational attitude towards sexually abnormal persons, and especially towards homosexuals, both male and female' (Point 6), while Point 9 made a more general statement, echoing the Russian practice: '. . . only those sexual acts to be considered criminal which infringe the sex rights of another person'.

British reformers, members of the British Society for the Study of Sex Psychology and other organizations, were drawn into the work of the league from the start. A British section of the league was established in 1928, with an extensive overlap of membership with the old BSSP. One of its members, Norman Haire, was chairman, while Dora Russell became its secretary. Norman Haire was a flamboyant and dynamic character who dominated the British sex-reform movement from the late 1920s. He had been born in Australia in 1892, and settled in England finally in 1919. A gynaecologist and obstetrician who had studied at Hirschfeld's Institute, he became deeply involved in the birth-control movement, and in 1921 was a founder and medical officer in charge of the Walworth Welfare Centre, the first such centre to give contraceptive advice. It was as an advocate of and expert on birth-control techniques that he became internationally respected, but he was also a prolific writer under both his own name and a pseudonym (Wykeham Terris), an editor, and a fashionable consultant in Harley Street. Dora Russell, who worked closely with him in the late 1920s, describes him as a lover of opulence.

> His consulting rooms in Harley Street were richly furnished with Chinese carpets, scarlet, black and gold lacquer cabinets, Chinese porcelain. He shocked people by his brutal frankness about birth control and sex. 'Sex, for the proletarian', he used to say, 'is fourpence and find your own railing'.[18]

As the latter comment suggests, his instinctive sympathies were not with the political aspirations of the working class. In an ambience where most of the international sex reformers were socialists of one sort or another (Hirschfeld, for instance, was a supporter of the German Social Democratic Party), Haire, like Freud, was, in his own words, 'an old fashioned Liberal . . . an opponent of egalitarianism'.[19] Indeed, so faithful was Haire to his credo that he refused to enrol as a practitioner with the National Health Service after its establishment in 1948. But he was a dedicated advocate of sex reform in the inter-war and immediate post-war years.

Dora Russell was quite a different sort of person. In the 1920s she had been married to Bertrand Russell, but was independently active in the labour movement and an enthusiastic advocate of birth control. She was considerably further to the left than Haire, and had opposed the non-political stance of the World League for Sexual Reform. At one meeting of the British section, Robert Boothby, later a Tory M.P. and peer, stood up and accused her of dragging the class war into the organization.[20] But there was no real danger of this while Haire remained in command; the section remained resolutely non-political. This remained so even on a parliamentary level. The only M.P.s to support it were John Strachey (a left-wing socialist, later one of the founders of the Left Book Club, and later still a right-wing anti-Communist Labourite) and Oliver Baldwin, the eldest son of the Tory leader Stanley Baldwin, but himself a labour supporter and homosexual. Its chief supporters came from the traditional areas, mainly those already involved in the British Society for the Study of Sex Psychology.

The prime function of the British section was to organize the 1929 World Congress, which was held in London on 8–15 September 1929. In international terms the meeting was a success. Over 350 delegates attended from all over the world, including Russia, and of European countries only Portugal was without a representative. This compared with the seventy delegates who had attended the 1928 Congress in Copenhagen. A large number and variety of papers were presented, and papers covered topics from abortion and birth control (the single most important topics) to issues of censorship. Hirschfeld gave a magisterial presidential address, surveying the origins and development of the science of sexology, and firmly placing Ellis high in the list of its founders. Messages were delivered from the USSR, the model nation of sex reform, and lively surveys (and some not so stimulating) were offered on a variety of sex-related topics.

It was under the heading of censorship that most of the issues touching on homosexuality cropped up. Various speakers, including Bertrand Russell, spoke of the suppression of *The Well of Loneliness*, which had occurred the year before. Related themes were developed. John Van Druten complained of the portrayal in the theatre of homosexuals as 'effeminate men, mincing and wilting' while serious discussion was tabooed. George Ives developed the analysis of 'The Taboo Attitude', and typically quoted extensively from his press cuttings. Though they have a period flavour, echoes can still be found today. He quoted from the *Evening News* (12 November 1920): 'There are certain forms of crime prosecutions which are never reported in the newspapers and of which most decent women are ignorant and would prefer to remain ignorant.' And the *Daily Express*, stable-mate of Radclyffe Hall's persecutor, had primly stated (5 September 1928): 'There are certain evils in the world which as they cannot be cured, must be endured, but in silence'.[21]

Some of the more enthusiastic members of the British Sexological Society, however, felt that there was too much silence on the subject of homosexuality. Cecil Reddie believed that the 'homogenic temperament and its concomitants' was somewhat avoided. And in that there were no specific papers, this was true. The tocsin had already been sounded earlier on this at the 1928 World Congress. Kurt Hiller, the German homosexual leader, had addressed an appeal to that congress 'on behalf of an oppressed human variety' (read for him by Hirschfeld) in which he had observed ominous signs that the left, traditional defenders of homosexual rights, were tempering their support in some sections of the socialist movement.[22] And 1929, as it turned out, whatever its inadequacies, was to be the high-water point. Two further congresses were held, in Vienna in 1930 and in Brno in 1932. But in 1933 the world movement was deeply disrupted by the Nazi onslaught in Germany and the triumph of reaction in the USSR. In this blizzard, the international campaign for homosexual rights turned out to be a frail barque which foundered almost without trace. The fundamental premise for the work of the World League for Sexual Reform was the possibility of convincing governments of the rationality of sex reform. Following the economic collapse of the world capitalist economy, the threat to the bourgeois democracies posed by fascism, and the reversals in the USSR, this pillar seemed less secure.

In Germany, Hirschfeld's Institute was among the first to suffer the impact of Nazi anti-intellectual tyranny. In May 1933 the premises were sacked. The archives, containing irreplaceable material (including the charts dealing with inter-sexual cases prepared for the 1913 Medical Congress), the library, and the records of the World League for Sexual Reform were removed, and burnt a few days later in a public ceremony. A bust of Hirschfeld was carried in a torch-light procession and thrown on to the pyre. Hirschfeld was himself luckily abroad at the time, but other homosexuals, such as Kurt Hiller, were less fortunate, and were interned in concentration camps. A year later, in the USSR, homosexuality again became a criminal offence.

In Britain, there were sharp echoes of these events. Dora Russell has recalled how a new authoritarianism entered into personal relationships in the 1930s; her own marriage to Bertrand collapsed in the rubble of bitterness and recrimination. And the remnants of feminist militancy faded into pressure-group conservatism and constitutionalism. The impact on what were, in any case, tiny reform organizations was at first limited, and Haire later recalled that the British section of the league continued and even increased its activity during the 1930s.[23] But with the world economic depression and the advance of fascism, sex reform no longer seemed a major issue. By the mid 1930s, when the old British Sexological Society was wound up, most of its original members were either dead or ageing rapidly. Moreover, the economic and social crisis posed political problems which the international sex-reform movement was unable to resolve. Dora Russell, in her autobiography, recalls that in the 1929 Congress:

> . . . the contributions were nearly all designed to inform and influence public opinion rather than to organize political action for the ends which were thought desirable . . . on the whole my learned colleagues contented themselves with describing the existing state of public knowledge and practice, exposing the inhumanity of the laws without envisaging any serious organization to change them.[24]

She was later to come to believe that the wide gap between cultural opinion and political activity was one of the factors which contributed to the inroads of reaction. This was a topic which was to split the world movement after Hirschfeld's death in 1935. The two remaining presidents were Dr J. Leunbach of Denmark and Norman Haire. Leunbach believed firmly that the league had gone wrong because of its failure to join the international workers' movement, to integrate the struggle for sex reform into the struggle against fascism and for socialism. Haire remained, and equally passionately, firmly apolitical. This split over strategy was fundamental, and in the rubble of the international movement could not be easily resolved. The two presidents therefore dissolved the World League for Sexual Reform, with the recommendation that national sections should remain in being where they could. In fact, by the late 1930s, only Haire's organization was formally extant. It was the thin, stretched line of continuity from the early reform hopes.

## 12
## Homosexuality and the Left

*'This too I know – and wise it were*
*If each could know the same –*
*That every prison that men build*
*Is built with bricks of shame,*
*And bound with bars lest Christ should see*
*How men their brothers maim.'*
– *Oscar Wilde*, The Ballad of Reading Gaol

The questions posed by the quarrel between Leunbach and Haire were fundamental. The early sex reformers, such as Carpenter, had taken it for granted that sex reform would only come about as part of a transition to a higher stage of social life in socialism. The interpretation of this socialism varied, and it was not until after the Bolshevik Revolution in 1917 that the stark issues of the nature of political power were clearly posed. But from the 1890s to the 1920s the most sympathetic supporters for sex reform in general, and homosexual reform in particular, had come from the left; and, as a corollary, most of the reformers were clearly men and women of the left. But the theoretical and practical problems that this connection raised had never been clearly explored. The socialism that Carpenter represented was based on a long utopian tradition, but in the new world of the twentieth century it was increasingly challenged.

One of the problems was that there was no fully worked-out theoretical position on women and sexuality in the socialist tradition. The starting-point for many socialists was, of course, the work of Marx and Engels, and Engels's *Origins of the Family* was the classical text. This, however, contained a number of implicit assumptions which have had a long resonance among Marxists.

First, there is a clear belief in the 'natural' biological basis of social roles. The sexual division of labour between men and women – with the women primarily responsible for child care – is unquestioned. It only assumes oppressive qualities, we must understand from Engels, with the development of private property, and he seems to believe that, under socialism, the family will embody a traditional division of labour, even though many of the family's previous functions will be socialized.

Secondly, as a corollary of this, there is an inevitable bias towards heterosexuality. Marx and Engels inherited from the utopian socialists a classically romantic belief in the all-embracing nature of true love between men and women: 'our sex love has a degree of intensity and duration which make both lovers feel that non-possession and separation are a great, if not the greatest, calamity'. This sex love has been distorted by commodity production but will flourish on a higher plane under socialism so that 'monogamy, instead of collapsing, [will] at last become a reality'.

Sexuality is seen as a single biological force, expressible in 'natural' ways, not as a diffuse and malleable entity, which is increasingly how we see it today. Homosexuality is consequently abhorred by Engels, its expressions seen as 'gross, unnatural vices', a symptom of the failure of sex love, and the degradation of women.[1] It would have been extraordinary in the early 1880s, when the exploration of homosexuality was still in its infancy, had Engels thought otherwise. It reveals, however, a failure to explore the social and historical determinants of sexual and emotional behaviour which underlines another key assumption. Engels assumes that the 'personal' is natural and given, and that once the constraints of a society dominated by the pursuit of profit are removed, private life would spontaneously adjust itself to a higher stage of civilization. There is no concept, that is, of the need for conscious struggle to transform interpersonal relations as part of the transformation necessary for the construction of a socialist society. This left the door open for later endless political confusions.

In practice, many European Marxists did work out positions which often encompassed warm support for sex reform. In the immediate wake of the Oscar Wilde trial, Edward Bernstein, a leading German Social Democrat (later to help split the Second International over 'revisionism') produced a materialist analysis of bourgeois sexual hypocrisy, which all the way through insisted that sexual mores should be seen in historical perspective rather than in absolute terms. This position remains an essential base for a materialist analysis. Further, Bernstein warned his fellow socialists that

> Although the subject of sex life might seem of low priority for the economic and political struggle of the Social Democracy, this nevertheless does not mean it is not obligatory to find a standard also for judging this side of social life, a standard based on a scientific approach and knowledge, rather than on more or less arbitrary moral concepts.

Other leading German Socialists, like Bebel and Kautsky, gave support to the Petition Campaign, and Hirschfeld was, of course, a supporter of the Social Democratic party (SPD). Bebel seems to have found Hirschfeld's campaign too apolitical, in fact, and in the early 1900s urged him to go further in mobilizing support. By 1912, Hirschfeld's Scientific Humanitarian Committee came out for a more consistently political commitment. An advertisement just before the 1912 election made the political point clear:

Third Sex: Consider This! In the Reichstag, on May 31, 1905, members of the Centre, the Conservatives, and the Economic Alliance spoke against you . . . but for you the orators of the Left! Agitate and vote accordingly![2]

This is posed as a tactical rather than a strategic alliance, but it reflected a real balance of opinion. The SPDers had given consistent support to the repeal of Paragraph 175 in the Reichstag from 1897 onwards, and after the split in the international workers' movement following the Russian Revolution, the revolutionary tradition, as embodied in the Communist Party, continued to do so, at least till 1930. In May 1928, in reply to a questionnaire, it stated 'the CP has taken a stand for the repeal of Para. 175 at every available opportunity'. Nevertheless, in the absence of a consistent socialist position on sexuality, it was easy to fall back into a simple moralism. A dialogue Edward Carpenter had with Robert Blatchford, editor of the socialist paper the *Clarion* in the early 1890s, illustrates the problem. Blatchford defended Carpenter, and urged readers to study his works on women. But when Carpenter wrote to Blatchford in late 1893 suggesting that he write on sexual matters, the latter replied: 'I am a radical but . . the whole subject is nasty to me.' And in a further letter he wrote: 'Now, you speak of writing things about sexual matters, and say that these are subjects which socialists must face. Perhaps you are right; but I cannot quite see with you.'

To justify this, Blatchford put forward arguments which still enjoy currency: first, that reform of sexual relations would follow industrial and economic change. If this is so, then, secondly, anything which inhibited economic change would also hinder sexual change. And as sex reform was unpopular, it would be best not to raise it at present. 'I think that the accomplishment of the industrial change will need all our energies and will consume all the years we are likely to live.' As a result, sex reform will, 'not concern us personally, but can only concern the next generation'.[3] Blatchford's position was not untypical for the period, and in his case went with an unholy worship of the family and the British imperial mission, but it rehearses all the common prejudices often heard on the left.

It was the cautious pragmatic approach rather than Carpenter's espousal of a 'cosmic consciousness' which made most impact. The Marxist philosopher, Belfort Bax, questioned whether 'morality has anything at all to do with a sexual act, committed by the mutual consent of two adult individuals, which is productive of no offspring, and which on the whole concerns the welfare of nobody but the parties themselves'.[4] This is the classically liberal argument for toleration, and it has been the most typical 'progressive' view on the left.

This was pre-eminently the case in Bolshevik Russia. Penal restrictions on homosexual acts were removed in 1918 side by side with the legalization of abortion and contraception, the liberalization of divorce and so forth. These were seen by Wilhelm Reich as the harbingers of sexual revolution brought in on the wings of the social. But, in actuality, it must be doubted whether these legal gains ever amounted to more than a formal acceptance of the most advanced bourgeois theories, given the enormous social backwardness of the Soviet population. Little was done positively to encourage social acceptance of homosexuality, and although throughout the 1920s Soviet laws were regarded as models for the rest of Europe, no theoretical advances were made. The article on homosexuality in the first edition of the *Great Soviet Encyclopedia* in 1930 followed Hirschfeld and, to a lesser extent, Freud. The biological stereotypes were written into their outlook.

Nevertheless, in terms of sexual policy, Russia was after 1918 far in advance of Germany and the Anglo-Saxon countries. For this reason, its achievements were exaggerated and its retreat from the 1930s ignored. The Communist Party of Great Britain was moreover only peripherally interested in women's issues such as birth control from the 1920s, and apparently not at all concerned with other issues of sex reform. Many of the British literary generation of the 1930s who flirted with Marxism – including W. H. Auden and Christopher Isherwood – were themselves homosexual, but their political significance was limited, and their Marxism broke under the strain of the 1930s. Most British socialists and libertarians either went on praising Soviet policy when there was nothing left to cheer for (as Alec Craig did in his book *Sex and Revolution* in 1934) or grimly closed their minds to the contradictions and continued defending the USSR as the first socialist country (as members of the British Communist Party did), and the only alternative to worse.

What is clear is that, from the 1930s, the organized left, instead of being the defenders of homosexuality increasingly saw it as a bourgeois deviation and decadence. There are two overlapping sources for this. The first is the Stalinist counter-revolution in the USSR in the 1930s, which subordinated all aspects of personal freedom to the priorities of production as determined by the ascen- dant bureaucracy. The strengthening of the family was seen as a necessary part of this, and with it went the revocation of most of the legal gains of the early revolutionary period. In March 1934, when homosexuality again became a criminal offence in the USSR, it was specifically defined as a product of 'decadence in the bourgeois sector of society' and a 'fascist perversion'. The apparent rampant homosexuality of the upper echelons of the Nazi Party in Germany was used as one element in justification. As we have seen, Hirschfeld's books had already been burnt by the Nazis, and almost simul- taneously with Stalin's clamp-down, the Röhm purge (the 'night of the long knives') inaugurated a new wave of terror against German homosexuals. The fascist counter-revolution of the 1930s took homo- sexuals as one of its categories of scapegoats.[5] But because of the central role of Stalinism in the world communist movement, there was no challenge to this sexual counter-revolution in the various communist parties. A belief in homosexuality as a bourgeois deca- dence survives in many of the Stalinist parties to this day.

The second source is closely intertwined with the first and stems from a particular interpretation of the psychoanalytic tradition. This sets up a norm of heterosexual 'genital sexuality' as the height of sexual relations, and homosexuality is seen as a falling from this. The work of Freud and his followers is the locus for much of this attitude. But there was also a reaction against social conditions in pre- fascist Germany. Juliet Mitchell has shown the way in which Wilhelm Reich's values were a reaction against the decadence of pre-Nazi Berlin:

> With chronic unemployment the mass of the people had little left to sell but their bodies. It is against this bourgeois decadence and working class wretchedness that the moral tone of Reich's sexual theories must be set – his predilection for hetero and healthy sexuality, his wish for men to be men and women, women.[6]

Unfortunately, few people seemed able to detach the accidental from the necessary and essential. The writing of Alec Craig, one of the leading British sex reformers, is a good example of the latter tendency. He was obviously 'sympathetic' in his own way to homosexuals, and opposed to legal penalties against them. But he retreats to a sort of low-level vulgar Freudianism to conclude that 'few would disagree that a great deal of homosexuality is a symptom of arrested or distorted development. Where this is so it is surely our duty to do what we can to correct this deviation from normality, and to do what we can to prevent its recurrence in other cases.'[7] And this conclusion is embedded in a eugenics framework in which, to preserve 'certain stocks' and 'certain racial characteristics', it would be necessary to discontinue conditions which encourage the setting up of homosexual fixations.

Members of the British Communist Party were not slow to defend Soviet retreats. One of its intellectuals, Ivor Montagu, undertook a vigorous defence of Soviet policy in Haire's *Journal of Sex Education* in 1949. He accused critics of the changes in Soviet sex attitudes of suffering from the ultimate sins, bourgeois leftism and intellectualism. 'It is no good transplanting as absolute, into alien conditions, standards and opinions that we have constructed in relation to quite different sets of conditions.' Abortion was acceptable in conditions of unemployment and bad social conditions as the lesser of two evils, he argued, but it meant something else in a society where everyone had work, and where increase of population meant increased productive capacity. Similarly, the Soviet reversal on homosexuality could be justified.

I remember libertarians in this country considering the reintroduction of restrictions in that quarter as a retrograde step. Maybe. But the remote regions of the USSR included tribal societies where homosexuality in the style of the Greek and Persian classic period (or for that matter of Oxford and Cambridge until recently) was an institution for inculcating every new generation with the conception of the superior nobility of the male and the relegation of the female to the darkness of the veil. Here the fight against homosexuality was . . . an indispensable part of the defeat of counter-revolution.

This apologia for Soviet policy implicitly accepted that homosexuality was a barbaric hangover or a bourgeois decadence. Not surprisingly, it went with an explicit worship of the great Soviet family, 'the cherished integral unit comprising society and helping to cement it'.[8] The liberation of human personality and potentiality that socialism had offered to its pioneers was buried in the uncritical acceptance of the degenerated Soviet state that existed in 1949. Thus, when reformers reassembled their energies in the 1940s and 1950s, they looked not to radical political movements for change, let alone to the self-activity of the people concerned, but to narrowly directed, pressure-group single-issue politics.

It need not have been. Though the great social and economic crises of the inter-war years posed awesome choices, the historic narrowing of socialism was not an inevitable response. It was a result of political decisions made, or not made, in Russia and in numerous socialist movements. It is only now, in new social and political conditions, that we have the opportunity to recover these wider possibilities of earlier socialist aspirations.

# 13

## Norman Haire and Sex Education

'Q: *Assuming that homosexuality consists of one man inserting his penis into the rectum of another, is this not exceedingly painful for the passive partner? . . .*

A: *You are mistaken, Madam, in assuming that homosexuality necessarily involves insertion of the penis into the rectum. Have you ever read* The Well of Loneliness *by Radclyffe Hall?*'
– *Norman Haire,* Journal of Sex Education, *December 1949–January 1950*

With the demise of a distinctive socialist contribution, the initiative returned to the liberal individualistic tradition – and to Norman Haire. Amid the ashes of the world movement, Haire managed to keep alive the British section of the World League for Sexual Reform to the edge of war, in 1939. Then followed eight years of inactivity. The war was largely responsible, but Haire's towering influence was also absent. He spent the war years in his native Australia. His own account records a breakdown of his health, but there were many who preferred to believe he was merely escaping the impact of war.

The Sex Education Society was revived in the autumn of 1947. The first season began with eight lectures, including one on adolescence by A. S. Neill, the progressive educationalist, and several by Haire on subjects including artificial insemination and impotence, frigidity and masturbation, and 'sexual aberrations'.[1] There was a scanty attendance at first, but by the third lecture over two hundred people had to be turned away. The Society had obviously touched a nerve in emergent Welfare State Britain. For the next meeting, Haire hired the larger Conway Hall in London. The society had strong lines of continuity with the pre-war organization, both in personnel (Haire himself as president, Professor J. C. Flugel as hon. secretary, and Dr Harold Avery as treasurer, were all veterans of the 1930s); and, in aims, close to those of the old World League: the furtherance of sex enlightenment of public opinion, and the support of relevant legislative measures. Homosexual reform was clearly part of its programme. Point 8 called for 'the establishment of a rational attitude towards sexually abnormal persons', and Point 9 for the reform of the law relating to sexual offences.

The main activity of the society was the sponsorship of public lectures, but Haire was always conscious of the need to reach a wider audience through a journal. This had been a preoccupation of the old league, and had been endlessly discussed at the 1929 Congress. The most widely accepted proposal there had been that the birth-control paper, *New Generation*, should act as the British voice of the league, but little came of it. In 1933 the league finally produced in Germany the first number of its own journal, *Sexus*. But before it could be distributed the Nazis took over, and practically the whole issue was tipped on the pyre. During the 1940s a magazine, *Marriage Hygiene*, edited by the Indian psychologist A. P. Pillay, transformed itself into the *International Journal of Sexology*, but Haire did not find this arrangement congenial. His differences with Pillay seem to have been both personal and theoretical. He was certainly scathing about Pillay's work.[2]

Partly as an alternative to Pillay's magazine, partly as the voice of the Sex Education Society, Haire finally produced the first issue of his own *Journal of Sex Education* in August 1948. This was formally independent of the society, but Haire was the latter's president and the former's editor. The journal printed many of the society's lectures and news of its activities. Both were part of a common endeavour. Above all, both fully reflected Haire's own basic position, that education and reform were organically linked, and education was a process which transcended political differences. 'We are neither Right nor Left, Conservative nor Radical, Communist nor Tory.' When a reader inquired in issue No. 5 whether sex reform was only possible in a Marxist society, Haire replied firmly that he did not believe so. The journal's primary purpose was 'to enlighten the ordinary intelligent adult' – and this was the starting-point for reform.

Although homosexual reform was only one part of the society and journal's agenda, to a large extent they could glide along new avenues of research. The first issue of the journal carried information about Alfred Kinsey's *Sexual Behaviour in the Human Male*, which had just been published, and succeeding issues reveal the penetration of Kinsey's research findings. For someone of Haire's experience, Kinsey's taxonomic conclusions could scarcely have come as a major surprise, for much of advanced opinion for a generation had been interested in a spectrum theory of sexuality which Kinsey's tables seemed to confirm and put on a statistical basis. But Kinsey's major impact was on public opinion – which raged in a torrent of discussion for the next decade over the validity of his findings – and, for the first time, sex reformers could break through to a wider public already aware of the latest ideas.³ The *Journal* sought to exploit and channel this new public, and it carried numerous useful references to homosexuality. No. 5, for instance, carried a piece on homosexuality in Germany by Rudolf Klimmer, showing how Paragraph 175 was still being used, and people still imprisoned under it, even in post-war 'liberal' Germany. Haire's comments were invariably sensible.

Many homosexual people responded eagerly. The December–January 1951/2 issue carried a long letter from a lesbian, very defiant and critical of the usual tone of most apologists. 'Do they *never* stand up for themselves?' She goes on:

> Homosexuals – and female homosexuals in particular – have a fair case. They should come out into the open with it and insist on pleading it before the general public – instead of apologising so humbly for themselves, and asking rather limply, if they can be cured.

She then rather spoilt her case by going on to say that lesbianism was preferable to heterosexual love because she could not bear 'unnatural' birth-control devices. Haire gently remonstrated with her for this, and for her stridency: 'It is much wiser to do what you can gradually and carefully, to alter public opinion, by removing prejudices, through a gradual process of re-education on sex problems in general, and the problem of homosexuality in particular.'⁴ He suggested she subscribe to the *Journal* and join the Sex Education Society.

Several other correspondents obviously felt that the *Journal* did not 'crusade' hard enough against the laws on homosexuality. In response, Haire argued that they did crusade, in their own way, through 'the education of public opinion about these matters', but he grumbled that not enough of these complainers were prepared to join the society. 'One of our oldest members died recently. He had no dependants and he left property worth over £20,000. Yet he never subscribed more than the minimum to either the Journal or the Society.'⁵

The *Journal* obviously answered an important need, both in educational, and personal terms. Hundreds of people wrote in from all over the world with their personal problems to a 'Dear Marje' type of column which Haire conducted with varying degrees of patience. When one unfortunate wrote in with a prolonged tale of his male contraception experiments, Haire tartly replied: 'You have been bombarding the Editor of this Journal with letters on this and other subjects for nearly 30 years, and this is positively the last occasion on which he will take the slightest notice of communications from you, on this or any other subject.'[6] Others were rather less frivolous. Men and women, particularly from Australia, wrote earnest letters about birth control, impotence, frigidity, unfaithfulness and so forth, as well as homosexuality.

Haire generally gave sound advice, though by the late 1940s an increased tetchiness is apparent in his tone. He was troubled for the last fifteen years of his life by diabetes, and towards the end suffered from serious heart trouble. The April/May issue of the *Journal* in 1950 recorded a serious breakdown in his health. This underlined the major weakness of the society and *Journal*: their close reliance on their founder's energies. Much of the work devolved on him, and there seems to have been little membership participation. It was very much a group of the 'enlightened' speaking *to* the population. Inevitably, then, the financial basis of the *Journal* was insecure. A Sinhalese student (who worried about her exhaustion after intercourse) won a sharp reprimand: 'You are not a subscriber to this Journal, and you do not offer to make any contribution towards the expenses of its production, but you expect us to devote a considerable amount of space to answering the question.'[7] This was a recurrent note.

But, despite these weaknesses, the society and the *Journal* had small-scale successes. The issue of February/March 1951, for instance, recorded the setting up of a Sex Education Society in Manchester. And it also had the important function of keeping its readership informed of moves and changes outside Britain. This was particularly relevant to the homosexual readership, which was probably disproportionately high (after all, there was no other vehicle for its views). The *Journal* carried a report in 1949 of a radio broadcast on homosexuality in New York which for the first time broke the taboo on the subject. Haire commented: 'Here in England, where no commercial stations exist, where the BBC has a monopoly, and where broadcasting suffers under the dead hand of the Churches, such a broadcast would, at the present time, be unthinkable.'[8] In fact, the American activity presaged a more significant shift, with the setting up of self-help homosexual-reform organizations in the United States. In Holland, too, there were significant developments which the *Journal* reported, with the foundation of the Dutch Cultural and Recreational Centre (COC). Under its auspices, an International Conference for Sexual Equality was held in Holland at Whitsun 1951.

It was supported by Jean Cocteau, Alfred Kinsey and some fifty participants from Switzerland, Scandinavia, Germany, Italy and Holland. It examined various aspects of homosexuality, and called on the United Nations to 'initiate steps towards granting status of human, social and legal equality to homosexual minorities throughout the world'. This was, in embryo, a revival of the old world movement, and in fact several other international meetings were held during the 1950s in which British reformers participated.[9]

Unfortunately, the Sex Education Society and the *Journal* were frail plants which failed to survive the demise of their founder. Haire died in 1952. No further issue of the *Journal* appeared. And the society was superseded by others, equally small-scale. Haire's role in keeping alive the issue of sex reform was almost entirely forgotten when a new kind of reform organization was launched in the late 1950s. It would be regrettable, nevertheless, if Norman Haire's importance was to be obscured. Above all, he represented a continuity with the pioneering sex reformers in a tradition which stretched back to the nineteenth century.

# 14
## Prelude to Reform

*In the last few years there has been much discussion of this question, and many authoritative men and women have given their views about the prevalence, nature, prevention, punishment, and cure of homosexuality. There have not, I think, been any among them who could say, as I do now: 'I am a homosexual'. – Peter Wildeblood*, Against the Law *(1955)*

Law reform came, at last, to England and Wales in 1967. When it arrived, mild and aetiolated, the walls shoring up society did not collapse. The British Empire had already declined; there was little love-making in the streets. Its impact was not on society at large, but on the individual lives of many homosexuals. For the political élite, it was as if a minor pimple had been removed from the body politic. By 1967 the heat had largely been dissipated from the question.

The change was the result of an evolution of attitudes which can be traced back to the 1950s and early 1960s. There were many factors involved. But what is most curious in retrospect is the self-contained nature of the change. Some liberal stalwarts of the 1930s sat on the worthy liberal committees and campaigns of the 1960s. There was, however, little evocation of pioneering names: sometimes of Havelock Ellis, certainly (a memorial society was formed in the 1960s), but rarely of Edward Carpenter, George Ives or Norman Haire. The pioneers were forgotten. Law reform came about because it was finally seen that the contradictions in the social position of male homosexuals were absurd. These contradictions exploded not so much through the work of ardent reformers, but because of their own inherent instability in the more relaxed social climate of post-war 'affluent' Britain. Law reform was a product of the long post-war boom in capitalist society. A narrow and limited achievement, it was not brought about by homosexuals campaigning for their own rights. Nevertheless it represented a tiny fissure in the walls. Through it the more radical forces that appeared after 1968 could begin to force their way. The cautious reformers wrought more than they thought – or sometimes cared for.

There was an ambiguous duality in the moral attitudes of the 1950s. On the one hand there was the heightened ideological emphasis on the joyous merits of a secure family life, the need to protect and enhance which was knitted into the fabric of the post-war Welfare State. In particular, the working-class family, largely through redistribution of its own income, apparently achieved a more solid economic stability in better health facilities, family allowances, National Insurance and the ideology of 'full employment'. All were to be undermined with the renewal of capitalist crises in the late 1960s, but in the 1950s they were seen as the basis for a stable, rationalized capitalist economy.[1]

This economic reorganization was accompanied by changes in the *pattern* of family life. Between the censuses of 1931 and 1951 the population of England and Wales increased by 9·5 per cent while the number of households increased by 28·2 per cent. By the 1950s, radical critics were lamenting the passing of the old working-class extended family, with its network of supportive relations, through affluence, consumerist values, advertising and the break-up of working-class communities. The nuclear family model – reduced to a core union of mother, father and young children living in their own homes on often new, sometimes anonymous housing estates in pockets of emotional warmth and consumption – was increasingly asserting itself as the dominant family pattern. This created strains of its own, so that by the 1960s sociologists were analysing and lamenting the crises of the family, the divorce rate, the youth problem and 'madness', but 'the family' was still a dominant model in ideology. Thus Gordon Westwood (Michael Schofield) wrote in his 1952 book, *Society and the Homosexual*, which sought to look sympathetically at the problems of homosexuals: 'Under ideal circumstances, the father should be an understanding, tolerant but virile and decisive male. The mother should have the gentleness, patience and passivity usually associated with womanhood.'[2]

This model, by its nature, must exclude homosexuals except as aberrations. So, not surprisingly, Westwood, partly no doubt as an adjustment to the climate of the times (later he was to play a more positive role) has to conclude that homosexuality is a 'disease' (pp. 8, 181), a 'severe mental sickness [which] usually requires long analytical psychotherapy' (p. 8), a 'mental disorder' (p. 172). This inevitable 'deviation from the norm' was underlined in the characteristic tendency of the 1950s to emphasize the polarity of the sexes, in sociology, psychology, films, advertising, clothes, cosmetics and work situations. The consumer revolution, the careful gearing of marketing through television and the press to the family – and now the working-class as well as middle-class family – as a fountain-head of consumption, underlined the exclusion of the 'deviant' as a misfit, an outcast.

On the other hand, there was a countervailing tendency, and this was to be found in the increased emphasis on sexuality and sexual pleasure which became apparent during the period. The media presentation of woman emphasized her physical characteristics; cosmetics and costume clothed her in glamour and sexual allure. In the 1950s this was still hamstrung by traditional bourgeois puritanism.[3] There was a new stress on the duty of the married couple to provide each other with sexual pleasure as a cement of the relationship. Marriage guidance counsellors found a new trade, and women's magazines began to advise tentatively on techniques of pleasure-giving. Not till the 1960s, with a vast increase in birth-control facilities and an apparently limitless vista of growing (if inflation-fuelled) prosperity, did the 'new hedonism' become a dominant ideological presence. But when it did the position of homosexuals looked very strange. If a David Hockney could be a luminary of the 'swinging London' scene, how to explain his (homo) sexual life-style? For most homosexual media stars of the period, the question was evaded, either in an ostensibly shining virginity and a glowing religiosity, or in nervous breakdown. But if sexual pleasure was a desirable goal, how could homosexuals be excluded? Especially as the Kinsey 'heterosexual homosexual rating' told everyone that most people had had some homosexual experiences at certain periods of their lives.

These questions were in the problematical future in the immediate post-war years, but the real contradictions were already becoming apparent. In the fifteen years following the outbreak of the Second World War, the number of indictable homosexual offences increased five-fold.[4] In 1938 there were 134 cases of sodomy and bestiality known to the police in England and Wales, in 1952, 670, and in 1954, 1,043. For indecent assault, the increase was from 822 cases in 1938 to 3,305 in 1953, while for 'gross indecency' (the Labouchère offence) the rise was from 316 in 1938 to 2,322 in 1955. The number of persons proceeded against in the same period rose from 719 to 2,504. There had been a steady rise in the figures during the 1930s, when, as Montgomery Hyde says, parts of what was still a 'largely submerged iceberg' began to surface. But the really dramatic rise took place in the late 1940s and early 1950s. Montgomery Hyde attributes this to an 'excess of zeal' on the part of the police, which does seem to have been undoubtedly the case. For the first time, the use of *agents provocateurs* seems to have become common in catching homosexuals, usually in public lavatories. But, as Wolfenden noted, by far the greater number of those convicted were discovered through other offences. The early 1950s saw a number of chain prosecutions, with the police often promising immunity to witnesses if they reported on other homosexuals. This was a feature of the most famous case, the Montagu–Wildeblood trial of 1954, when the chief prosecution witnesses, two airmen on whom the whole case hinged, were promised immunity if they turned Queen's Evidence. This case also illustrated the revival of another offence, that of 'conspiracy', which could go beyond the rules of evidence needed for conventional offences. As in the more widespread revival of 'conspiracy' charges in the early 1970s, the use of such charges was clearly political.

The stepping-up of the purge on homosexuals seems to have coincided with the appointment of Sir Theobald Mathew, an ardent Roman Catholic, as Director of Public Prosecutions in 1944. He was backed up by the Labour Home Secretary, Herbert Morrison, the son of a policeman and a stalwart of the Labour right. The flight to Russia of the two British spies, Guy Burgess and Donald Maclean, in 1951, both of whom were homosexuals, accentuated the tendency, and the Tory Home Secretary in the last Churchill government, Sir David Maxwell-Fyfe (later Lord Kilmuir), demonstrated that he was determined to clamp down on all homosexuals, whatever their political proclivities. The prosecutions reached a peak in late 1953 and 1954 after the appointment of a new Metropolitan Police Commissioner, Sir John Nott-Bower. One of the problems facing a new public moralism was the acute disparity in the rates of prosecutions as between different parts of the country, and in the punishments meted out. Maxwell-Fyfe bluntly ordered the Metropolitan magistrates to make sentences more uniform, and he underlined his obsessive concern in the House of Commons:

> Homosexuals, in general, are exhibitionists and proselytizers and a danger to others, especially the young. So long as I hold the office of Home Secretary I shall give no countenance to the view that they should not be prevented from being such a danger.[5]

But why, in 1954, should they be seen as such a danger? One reason was given in 1953 by a London Correspondent of the *Sydney Morning Telegraph*. He suggested that there was a plan, urged on the British government by the US government, to weed out homosexuals as security risks from prominent positions.

The disappearance of Burgess and Maclean undoubtedly caused a furore in inter-government circles. In the early 1950s, with the Korean War a searing memory and McCarthyism burning like a bush fire in the United States, homosexuals emerged to the fore as scapegoats and victims of the Cold War. The US State Department had already conducted a purge on homosexuals in its own echelons. A document on the 'Employment of Homosexuals and other Sex Perverts in Government' in 1950 concluded that 'There is no place in the United States Government for persons who violate the laws or the accepted standards of morality, or who otherwise bring disrepute to the Federal service by infamous or scandalous personal conduct.' It went on to speak of homosexuals being a 'security risk' by reason of their 'lack of emotional stability', the 'weakness of their moral fibre', their susceptibility to 'blandishments' and blackmail.[6] With such opinions endorsed at the highest levels in Washington, there can be little doubt that the US government was anxious for its British allies to fall into line.

There was more than a hint of contradiction and organized hypocrisy in British government response. Homosexuals there had always been in the British government, and at least one sat at the Cabinet table with Maxwell-Fyfe. Moreover, some of the closest aides of the prime minister, Winston Churchill, including Sir Edward Marsh, once his private secretary, were known to be homosexual. It obviously depended on whom you knew. During the war, in 1941, a young Member of Parliament, Sir Paul Latham, was driven out of public life following homosexual offences in the army; after attempted suicide, a broken marriage and social ostracism, he died a few years later, a broken man. In 1953, a Labour member, W. T. Field, similarly had his career ended, and during the 1950s there were several other cases, including Ian Harvey, a Tory Junior Minister, and Ian Horrabin, a Tory M.P. When the actor, Sir John Gielgud, was convicted on a trivial charge in 1953, there were outraged cries that he should surrender his new knighthood. (His theatrical audiences were more generous: on his first appearance after conviction he was given a resounding ovation.) But others, better connected, successfully evaded the net. Tom Driberg (later, briefly, Baron Bradwell) was a left-wing Labour M.P. and a close friend of Guy Burgess, whom he visited in Moscow. But he was also a former employee (as 'William Hickey', the *Daily Express* gossip columnist) of Lord Beaverbrook, the strongest character among press lords. According to A. J. P. Taylor, '. . . on another occasion, Tom was convicted at Bow Street. Lord Beaverbrook ensured that no mention of the case appeared in any newspaper. Thereafter everyone took Tom's homosexuality for granted.'[7] Not a murmur this time, from James Douglas or John Gordon, the *Sunday Express*'s men of all prejudices. Other homosexuals convicted in the 1950s – Rupert Croft-Cooke, Lord

Montagu, Michael Pitt-Rivers, Peter Wildeblood and countless obscure names – were less fortunate.

They were often socially prominent – Lord Montagu was heir to a long aristocratic tradition, Wildeblood was diplomatic correspondent of the *Daily Mail* – but politically nugatory. It appears that prosecutions were stage-managed more for their dramatic impact than for any real content. The purge did not prevent later scandals involving homosexual spies (for example, William Vassall in 1962). But it did, as the Oscar Wilde trial had done, sharpen that dividing-line between the 'normal' and the 'deviant', the 'respectable' and the 'outlaw'.

The Montagu–Wildeblood trial of 1954, which received sensational publicity on both sides of the Atlantic, illustrated the current mood. At an earlier trial, in late 1953, the jury had been unable to agree on a charge that Montagu, along with the film director, Kenneth Hume, had committed 'indecent assault' on two Boy Scouts. The Director of Public Prosecutions had ordered that he be retried in the next sessions. Michael Pitt-Rivers and Peter Wildeblood were arrested three weeks later. In addition to several specific charges of indecency, they were also charged with conspiracy with Montagu to commit the offences: a charge carefully designed to jeopardize Montagu's retrial. At the trial of all three in April 1954, the prosecution offered an amazing display of prejudice and malice – and a careful loading of the dice. A small party attended by all three was turned, in the prosecution's vivid imaginings, into a wild orgy; a meal of simple food and cider was turned into luxury food and champagne. Most revealing of all were the attempts made to suggest that the accused had breached the still impassable barriers between the classes and between the sexes. Wildeblood was asked about the social position of one of the witnesses.

It is a feature, is it not, that inverts or perverts seek their love associates in a different walk of life than their own?

I cannot accept that as a deduction. I have never heard any suggestion that that is the ordinary rule.

I mean, for instance, that McNally was infinitely – he is none the worse for it – but infinitely your social inferior?

That is absolute nonsense.

Well, perhaps that is not a very polite way of answering my question.[8]

The same determination to find corruption was revealed when Wildeblood was asked about one of his letters to McNally. Here the prosecution quoted directly from the Wilde trial, and spoke of it 'breathing unnatural passion in almost every line'. As in 1895, virtue triumphed. All three were convicted and imprisoned.

What emerged in this, as in other trials of the period, was the attempt to sustain a stereotype of male homosexuals as decadent, corrupt, effete and effeminate. And in this endeavour the state was aided by the popular press. During the Wildeblood trial the *Daily Mirror* published a photograph of the defendant which made him look extremely effeminate. On close inspection it is apparent that the print had been touched up, to make it look as if he was wearing lipstick. As Wildeblood himself said: 'I could hardly have chosen a profession in which being a homosexual was more of a handicap than it was in Fleet Street. Its morality was that of the saloon bar: every sexual excess was talked about and tolerated, provided it was "normal".'[9]

Throughout this period, much of the press acted as 'magnifiers of deviance', asserting what it took to be the proper values of its readership. Actually, in discussing homosexuality, the press in the 1950s was expressing a new-found freedom. As George Ives pointed out in 1929, scarcely even the word could be mentioned at earlier times. When, in 1952, the *Sunday Pictorial* published a series of articles on homosexuality – called, characteristically, 'Evil Men' – this was seen by its former editor, Hugh Cudlipp, as the end of the 'conspiracy of silence' on the subject. Silence might have been better than these particular articles, described as 'a sincere attempt to get to the root of a spreading fungus'. But even after this, the press's concern was less with homosexuality as such, or with homosexuals, than the shockability of its readers; interest was generally expressed only when events forced the subject on them. During most of 1957, for instance, the *Daily Mirror* (stablemate of that conspiracy breaker the *Sunday Pictorial*) never mentioned homosexuality at all. After the publication of the Wolfenden Report in September it devoted 963 column inches to the subject in two weeks. The following week, interest dropped to forty-three inches, and thereafter to practically nil.

The influence of the popular papers was no less vicious for being spasmodic. It had a manifold influence in reinforcing the homosexual stereotypes. It characteristically *objectified* homosexuals, turning them into less than human beings. Some of the characterizations of homosexuals in the 1950s and early 1960s were similarly de-humanizing. A description of the spy William Vassall noted his pale eyes, which 'flickered like a lizard's towards the domed ceiling . . . He listened unblinking, motionless as a newt.' Meanwhile, 'Burgess sits in Moscow like a patient toad awaiting his next victim.' Or there might be a suggestion of primitivistic goings-on. Four reporters of the *People* (20 March 1968) reported what they saw on Hampstead Heath: 'At least one hundred men cavorted among the bushes. Some were naked, some were partly dressed. They embraced. They kissed. They cuddled.'

So what? one might ask. But, for the popular press, it represented the anarchic forces beneath the thin veneer of civilization, a 'civilization' that the press believed it represented and aspired to defend. It attempted to adjudicate on the line between 'normal' and 'abnormal', so that conventional gender roles were reinforced by this stereotyping. As the 'Evil Men' article put it: 'Most people know there are such things – "pansies" – mincing, effeminate young men who call themselves queers. But simple decent folk regard them as freaks and rarities.' Male homosexuals are seen to work in the non-virile professions – 'Homosexuality is rife in the theatrical profession. Dress designers, hat makers, window dressers have a high percentage of homosexuals . . .' They have 'mincing ways', call 'each other girls' names openly', are 'painted perverts', wear women's clothes. Hence a fascination with sex-change operations; here the identity problem is resolved, and the 'body and mind' can be matched. They are still laughable, but the transsexual transcends the gender problem: he/she is wrenched into a deformed normality. The very act of changing sex is seen as legitimizing conventional gender roles.

Not all articles stereotyped quite so blatantly. In 1963 the *Sunday Pictorial* published an article on 'How to Spot a Homo' which seemed to suggest that all homosexuals wore sports jackets, smoked pipes and wore suède shoes. But whatever the subtlety of the stereotype, the media reinforced the moral consensus by caricaturing its sexual deviants. They were either corrupters – usually of youth – or carriers of contagion dangerously poisoning society; or they were potential or actual traitors – perhaps a 'Traitorous Tool of the Russians' as the *Daily Telegraph* unfortunately called Vassall. And this sort of hysteria was catching: it matched a Cold War fear of political collapse; and it complemented an internalized self-hatred that many homosexuals felt.

Donald Cory, writing in the 1950s, put it neatly: 'the worst effect of discrimination has been to make the homosexuals doubt themselves and share in the general contempt for sexual inverts'. This self-hatred went through the whole homosexual consciousness. A respondent of Gordon Westwood said:

We were persuaded to plead guilty and get off with a fine. The detective was clever and played on our fears and said it would go no further if we pleaded guilty. I shouldn't complain. I was guilty in mind if not in practice.[10]

The guilt stemmed, above all, from the need to lead a double life, to struggle constantly against the norms of a hostile society. The strain was often intense, so that being caught, and punished, was often a release. Wildeblood wrote after his prison sentence:

I was able, at last, to move out of a false position and take up a true one. There was no further need for pretence; I could discard the mask which had been such a burden to me all my life.[11]

The trial of Wildeblood and Montagu in fact proved a catalyst which revealed the inherent problems in the situation of homosexuals. Either the law had to be tightened up further, more rigorously and evenly applied, as Maxwell-Fyfe and other Tory luminaries, such as the ineffable Lord Winterton, wanted; or it had to be reformed. There were suggestions by 1954 that public opinion was not as mono-lithically hostile to reform as the popular press imagined. Wildeblood was surprised by the support he received from some of the people outside the court. And there were hints of change in attitudes within the Church. As early as 1952 the Church of England Moral Welfare Council had initiated a study of homosexuality. The committee had consisted of clergymen, doctors and lawyers, and their report in 1954, *The Problem of Homosexuality*, while not denying its 'sinful-ness', attempted to separate the ecclesiastical and legal aspects, and called for law reform. The Council and the Howard League for Penal Reform, supported by one or two Members of Parliament, such as Robert Boothby, pressed the Home Secretary to establish a Royal Commission to investigate the law. He stubbornly resisted. But pressure came to a head during the Montagu-Wildeblood trial, and shortly afterwards he finally announced the setting up of a Home Office departmental inquiry. The chairman was to be Sir John Wolfenden, vice-chancellor of Reading University, a man who, as he admitted, knew nothing of the subject. This was nonetheless the first step on the road to reform.

The publication of the Report of the Wolfenden Committee, three years later in September 1957, was a crucial moment in the evolution of liberal moral attitudes. The departmental committee had been appointed to consider:

(a) the law and practice relating to homosexual offences and the treatment of persons convicted of such offences by the courts; and

(b) the law and practice relating to offences against the criminal law in connection with prostitution and solicitation for immoral purposes, and to report what changes, if any, are in our opinion desirable.

The terms of reference thus lashed together, in nineteenth-century fashion, homosexuality and prostitution, but, in fact, its conclusion, by applying a single pragmatic criterion, finally separated them, both emotionally and legislatively.

The conclusions that the majority of the committee came to stemmed from its definition of the function of the criminal law. Its purpose, they argued, was to preserve public order and decency, and to protect the weak from exploitation. It was *not* to impose a particular pattern of moral behaviour. It followed that there were areas of life which were no concern of the criminal law, even though they might be of *moral* concern to individuals and society. They therefore concluded that homosexuality in private could be decriminalized, just as prostitution as such was not illegal. But the logic of their position was that penalties for public displays of sexuality should be strengthened. Thus, with regard to prostitution, the committee recommended that the maximum penalties for 'street offences' be increased, and other restrictions imposed on the prostitutes themselves rather than on their clients:

> ... the simple fact is that prostitutes do parade themselves more habitually and openly than their prospective customers, and do by their continual presence affront the sense of decency of the ordinary citizen. In doing so they create a nuisance which in our view, the law is entitled to recognize and deal with.[12]

The same logic was pursued with regard to homosexuality. It should not be legitimized or even made fully lawful.

> We do not think it would be expedient at the present time to reduce in any way the penalties attaching to homosexual importuning. It is important that the limited modification of the law which we propose should not be interpreted as an indication that the law can be indifferent to other forms of homosexual behaviour, or as a general licence to adult homosexuals to behave as they please.[13]

What was proposed was that offences which were difficult to discover and troublesome (and politically embarrassing) to prosecute should be removed from the statute book, the better to preserve public decency. The law should cease to be the 'guardian of morality' and become a more effective upholder of order. The chief recommendations were therefore that consensual homosexual behaviour between adults (i.e. of men over twenty-one) should be decriminalized; that those under twenty-one should be prosecuted only with the sanction of the Director of Public Prosecutions or the Attorney-General; that maximum penalties should be revised; that buggery should be reclassified as a misdemeanour; and that, except for indecent assaults, the prosecution of any offence more than twelve months old should be barred.

It is often said that the Wolfenden Report represented the final acceptance of a sickness theory of homosexuality. This is not strictly the case. It represented rather a widespread acceptance, by a representative section of ruling-class opinion, of homosexuality as an unfortunate condition. They remained agnostic on the causes or nature of homosexuality. Hence their final two recommendations:

(xvii) That prisoners desirous of having oestrogen treatment be permitted to do so . . .

(xviii) That research be instituted into the aetiology of homosexuality and the effects of various forms of treatment.

Limited and conservative as the proposals were, they caused a whirlwind of controversy. The editor of a well-known medical periodical was quoted as saying: 'I am afraid I should hate to be mixed up in any way with the Wolfenden Report. As the Editor of a medical journal I want to keep quite clear of Wolfenden and his unsavoury crowd.'[14] The 'unsavoury crowd' had included two M.P.s, two O.B.E.s, two C.B.E.s, two clergymen, the Marquess of Lothian and other worthies.

In terms of logic, the modest conclusions were irrefutable, and even the popular press was prepared to discuss the possibility of reform. It was estimated that 4 per cent of the male prison population were there for homosexual offences; the proposals would have reduced the numbers by half; hardly a revolution. It is revealing that in the next ten years of debate the only strong *intellectual* current against the Wolfenden conclusions came from the legal right. Lord Devlin in his 1959 Maccabean lectures attempted to refute the utilitarian notion that the criminal law should have no concern with morality, but even he supported reform in 1967. (No one, of course, attempted to put a more radical view which fundamentally challenged the Wolfenden problematic.) It was essentially prejudice and ignorance and timidity that held back the immediate application of the proposals.

## 15
## Law Reform

*'It is not so much public opinion as public officials that need educating' -- Oscar Wilde to George Ives (1898)*

It was as a challenge to timidity that the Homosexual Law Reform Society was founded in the spring of 1958. The year following the appearance of the Wolfenden Report had seen a crushing unwillingness on the part of the government to act. The Tories had a substantial parliamentary majority, but much of it consisted of backswoodsmen, interested in nothing more than the moral *status quo*. Their Home Secretary, R. A. Butler – who made a long career and a political philosophy out of pursuing the 'art of the possible' – was himself probably not unsympathetic, but he made it clear that the government would not act on homosexual reform until public opinion had shifted. (He showed rather more haste with regard to prostitution, rushing through the Street Offences Act of 1959, which pushed prostitution off the street while it punished the women and ignored their clients, in line with Wolfenden recommendations.) Conservative complacency and hypocrisy was approaching its apogee in the forthcoming election year, and no humanitarian reforms could be expected. There were actually disturbing signs of a further clampdown; a number of 'chain prosecutions' in the spring of 1958 revealed that the law still had a vicious tail.

The initiative in establishing a reform organization was taken by two former college friends, both middle-class professionals: A. E. Dyson, then a young academic in the University of Wales (later an organizer of the right-wing *Black Papers* on education), and a clergyman, the Rev. Andrew Hallidie Smith. They approached a number of distinguished public figures, and a letter appeared in *The Times* on 7 March 1958 which contained thirty-three signatures stating that the existing law no longer accorded either with liberal or Christian opinion and calling for reform. The signatories included the former Labour prime minister, Lord Attlee, the Bishops of Birmingham and Exeter, the philosophers A. J. Ayer and Isaiah Berlin, Julian Huxley, Sir Robert Boothby, J. B. Priestley, Jacquetta Hawkes, Bertrand Russell and Barbara Wootton. A month later a further letter in similar terms appeared, this time signed by fifteen 'eminent' married women. Many of these signatories – described at the time as the 'pick of the lilac establishment' – became founder members of the Honorary Committee of the new society, which was formally launched in May.[1]

Hallidie Smith was the society's first secretary, and Dyson became vice-chairman. The chairman until 1964 was Kenneth Walker, a distinguished sexologist, who as medical secretary of the British Social Biology Council was already sponsoring the first Kinsey-type research in England on male homosexuals then being carried out by Gordon Westwood/Michael Schofield (a mere hundred people, however, compared to Kinsey's far bigger sample). Walker was succeeded on his death in 1964 by C. H. Rolph (Cecil R. Hewitt). The Honorary Committee was the respectable public front, the guarantee of establishment toleration, but the actual work was done by a small inner core of volunteers, including the founders and several others who quickly responded to the call. Among these was A. E. G. (Edgar) Wright, a young barrister and journalist who as Antony Grey was later to play a major role in the society's activities. Many of the 'volunteers' were themselves homosexual, but this was neither explicitly nor implicitly made clear. Some 'risks' were, of course, being taken, given the then existing state of the law. Most of the society's early work was conducted at the home of two people living together in a homosexual relationship which might well have received unwelcome police attention. Not until the autumn of 1958 were enough funds gathered to pay for an office (a shabby, overcrowded place at 32 Shaftesbury Avenue, London, where it remained throughout the campaign), and a secretary, Hallidie Smith.

But the society was clearly not intended as a self-help homosexual grouping, and throughout the next eight years it maintained an air of well-drilled respectability. It early on burnt its fingers. When the Wolfenden proposals were first discussed in the House of Commons, in November 1958, the society had enthusiastically circulated a leaflet, 'Homosexuality and the Law', to all Members of Parliament. Simultaneously, and from another source, Peter Wildeblood's *Against the Law* and Eustace Chesser's *Live and Let Live* were distributed. There was an immediate outcry from the more entrenched reactionaries that the House was being subjected to pressure from 'a rich and powerful lobby of perverts'. The society hastily drew in its horns, advised by the M.P.s on the committee, particularly Kenneth Robinson, to avoid any early direct approaches. It therefore settled down to what Antony Grey later called 'the long haul' of educating public opinion on the need for reform.

It was, as Grey put it, 'a strenuous and sometimes disconcerting experience'.[2] It was a back-breaking job, of speaking at innumerable small meetings, organizing debates in student unions, of lobbying and writing to M.P.s and local politicians, penning endless letters to the press, distributing occasional literature, writing and sending out copies of *Spectrum* (the society's newsletter), *Man and Society* (an associated journal) and leaflets; constant travelling, begging for financial contributions, coping with the occasional hysteria in the press, dealing with the homosexual caller, with threats of suicide, despair . . . The job was often not helped by an honorary committee whose contributions came from their names rather than any campaigning ability, so that they were often a dead weight on the work of the secretary and his volunteer helpers.

The Homosexual Law Reform Society went fully public on 12 May 1960, the second anniversary of its foundation, when it held its first public meeting, at Caxton Hall, Westminster. The meeting was addressed by what was to become a familiar mix of liberals and clergymen – Mrs Anne Allen, a magistrate and popular Sunday 'problem' journalist, the Bishop of Exeter, Kingsley Martin, editor of the *New Statesman*, Dr L. Neustatter, a psychiatrist. There was little unity of approach, except for a shared recognition of the outdatedness of the law, but the speeches induced a great enthusiasm in the hall. It overflowed with over 1,000 people present, most of them, one would guess, homosexual.

Such enthusiasm was heartening, but it also posed problems in determining the right approach to campaigning. The society had made a deliberate decision to direct its primary work *not* at the homosexual community but at progressive public opinion, and ultimately, even more narrowly, at amenable M.P.s and other prominent figures – educating, in Wilde's formulation, 'public officials' rather than public opinion. The result was inevitably that the society was forced into a position of embattled neutrality, not openly committed to homosexuality as a way of life, but not obviously an objective organization either. There was also some ambiguity, at least publicly, in the society's attitude towards sex. The Rev. Timothy Beaumont, described at the time as a 'new-look clergyman', a supporter of reform and later president of the Albany Trust, gave as his opinion that, 'God has called homosexuals among others to chastity and to use their energies in other channels . . .'[3] It was that careful 'among others' which betrayed the cautious liberalism, the placing of homosexuals as one among other 'problem' groups. And some of the advertising adopted by the society revealed the same judicious blend of reformism and opportunism.

Homosexual Law Reform
Is *Vital*
For reasons of
    Justice – Security – Public Health.

Unfortunately, the falling in with current fads and fantasies about national security and public welfare did nothing to challenge prejudice. Both the society and its sister charity, the Albany Trust, were worried at being drawn too deeply into wide-ranging controversy. In 1963 Douglas Plummer published his book *Queer People*, a breezy canter through the subject, and in it thanked the society for its help. Antony Grey noted in a review that the society 'is of course in no way responsible for any of the views which are expressed in *Queer People*'.[4] The society was torn between its genuine desire to improve the lot of homosexuals, and its acute – perhaps over-acute – assessment of what 'public opinion' would take. Inevitably, it veered in the direction of caution.

The Homosexual Law Reform Society was essentially a classical middle-class single-issue pressure group of a type which flourished in the 1960s. Socially, its membership was overwhelmingly professional middle class, with what seems to have been a preponderance of lawyers, clergymen and medical men. Politically, it was middle of the road, veering perhaps towards the Labour Party, basically because a Labour majority was most likely to change the law, but careful at the same time never to alienate influential Liberal and Conservative figures. Publicly it kept a non-political stand. *Man and Society*, the journal of the Albany Trust from 1961, reflected its concern with 'progressive' opinion, which in essence was centrist liberal opinion. It was fiercely anti-Marxist editorially, and basically worked within a framework of traditional liberal utilitarianism. Issue No. 1 in the spring of 1961 made clear its adherence to the idea of *negative* freedom, and quoted freely from Sir Isaiah Berlin. A. E. G. Wright, in an article on 'Law and Morality', began with a quote from John Stuart Mill, the great apostle of moderate liberalism. The tendency was well in line with the Wolfenden proposals – the idea, above all, that the state should not interfere in individual matters where these matters were no concern of the wider society. But, on the crucial issue of the merits or not of homosexuality, liberal utilitarianism necessarily remained silent.

Within this framework, *Man and Society* attracted a wide range of writers, Members of Parliament, prominent penal reformers (among them Lord Longford, then regarded as a liberal, Martin

Ennals of the National Council for Civil Liberties), literary figures (Iris Murdoch, Angus Wilson), medical men, psychologists. The ability amassed was impressive, though on the whole the names were the ones one would have expected. The relatively narrow base of the society meant that its financial position was always precarious. At the peak of its activities in 1965–7 it employed seven full-time employees, but it still relied heavily on extra voluntary help. The result was that Grey, full-time secretary from 1964, often had to spend a good half of his time worrying about finances. At the end of 1963 there were 1,055 subscribing supporters of the trust, but many more had lapsed. Subscriptions were the only regular source of income. A special appeal in early 1964 raised £3,000, enough to keep a full-time secretary and office for a year; but £1,350 of the total was actually given by seven people, and the remaining donors gave an average of £7 each. Income for the year to 5 April 1965 was £7,003, and to April 1966, £6,453. This was scarcely enough to maintain a healthy campaign.[5]

It was to help ensure a steady income that the Albany Trust had been founded in 1958 as the charity arm of the organization. Through the trust gifts and endowments could be channelled to help the cause. Its journal, *Man and Society*, consciously sought to widen the basis of its role, giving coverage to abortion-law reform and other progressive sex reforms, and holding more 'philosophical' public meetings than the society attempted. It sponsored, for instance, a series of six winter talks in London in 1963–4. Effectively, the trust and the society were two aspects of a single organization, and their work was complementary.

While *Man and Society* acted as a 'theoretical journal', *Spectrum* was the regular newsletter, keeping members in touch with ongoing campaigns, providing useful statistics, quotes from parliamentary speeches, appeals for money and so on. It made a more regular appearance than the magazine, which during the crucial period 1966–9 did not appear at all. The society also published a series of leaflets and pamphlets. The first edition of *Some Questions and Answers about Homosexuality* went out of print at the end of 1964 with 10,000 copies sold or distributed. Other pamphlets included *Homosexuality and the Law*, the report of its first public meeting, *The Homosexual and Venereal Disease* and *Christian Society and the Homosexual*. They were sober and carefully written essays, designed to calm fears and advance reform. Even so, they aroused some alarm. The VD pamphlet was particularly objected to because some thought it would give the impression that homosexuals spread disease.

After 1964 the pressure increased and changed its form. The return of a Labour government opened up the possibility of a move towards reform, and this led to a reshaping of the whole campaign. The society had never, in any case, had wide support in the country. Several local committees for Homosexual Law Reform had been established to back up the national work, but of these only the North-Western Committee, based in the Manchester area, had any firm roots. These committees were useful in organizing local opinion and advancing public education, but their work was obviously secondary in pressuring Parliament. From 1964 the society essentially subordinated itself to its parliamentary supporters, particularly Lord Arran in the Lords and Leo Abse in the Commons. Grey, who now came into his own as an agile lobbyist with friends in the Labour establishment, later described the 'discreet' methods of lobbying that were adopted: 'We were largely guided in what we did by the advice and requests of our chief Parliamentary sponsors . . . we endeavoured to carry out, to the best of our ability, what they required of us.'[6] In the short run, in terms of achieving a limited change of the law, the result was sound. But in terms of the longer-run need to challenge and transform attitudes, it proved a bankrupt policy.

The mid 1960s was the golden age of liberal-humanitarian reforms, and of single-issue campaigns, mostly of long standing, to achieve them: the abolition of capital punishment and abortion-law reform and divorce-law reform as well as homosexual law reform. And this was a European phenomenon. Of the major countries of Western Europe, only France, under the authoritarian Gaullist régime, showed a different trend; there, in particular, the codes relating to homosexuality and 'public decency' were sharply tightened. The simultaneous changes throughout the West were no accident. The 1960s saw the climax of the long period of economic expansion and affluence. Under its impact, puritan moral codes began to crumble. The result was often squalid. But the disintegration of one form of bourgeois morality threw a spotlight on some of its most absurd corners. The contradictions of the legal situation of homosexuals had already been exposed by Wolfenden. With an increased emphasis on sexual pleasure and a rising divorce rate, it became impossible for the Churches to argue that homosexuality was more of a threat to the family than, say, adultery, which was not a legal offence.

Some of the more radical Christian sects went further. The Quakers produced a pamphlet, *Towards a Quaker View of Sex*, which was for the period a model of good sense in its attitude to homosexuality, throwing the last vestiges of sin into the dustbin of history. There was also a new tendency in psychology which tended to echo the Wolfenden vision of homosexuality as an unfortunate condition which nevertheless should, for the sake of social decency, be accepted. D. J. West's Pelican book, *Homosexuality* (various editions from 1955) was influential in this. Intrepid radical journalists, on radio and television and in ink, began to explore the homosexual sub-culture, and found it strange but scarcely outrageous (see Bryan Magee's *One in Twenty* for the *locus classicus*).[7] Radio and television were able to introduce homosexuals – usually absurdly stereotyped – into their programmes. The BBC radio comedy show *Round the Horne* even utilized parylaree, the homosexual argot, for some of its regular humour. Films, too, began selfconsciously to adopt 'sympathetic' positions. The trials of Oscar Wilde were celebrated in two simultaneous films in the early 1960s, while Dirk Bogarde jeopardized his glamorous film career to appear in *Victim*, the archetypal liberal 'pity' film of the period, which effectively endorsed the Wolfenden positions. Five hundred copies of the first issue of *Man and Society* were distributed at the première of this film. The audience, some of whom found the film a little too sympathetic, did not have their tolerance greatly challenged. Issue No. 1 had endorsed Kenneth Robinson's position that homosexuality was a 'disability, a deviation from the norm'.

All of this fitted neatly into the changing political climate. The major political groupings all entered the 1960s with a new commitment to 'modernizing' British capitalism. In practice, this meant patching up the creaky mechanism of an already decaying industrial society, but in the rhetoric of the 'white-hot technological revolution' it seemed as if the millennium of ever-expanding wealth was imminent. For some of the 'revisionists' in the Labour Party, this was the basis for their transmutation of socialism. If the old problems of poverty and inequality were no longer major ones, then the only real scope for change lay in the 'personal' issues previously ignored. 'Conscience' issues thus became central to the politics of people like Roy Jenkins and Anthony Crosland and other Labourites. This was one pressure towards reform. It fitted in, not entirely incongruously, with another type of liberalism, endorsed by figures such as Lord Arran, the eccentric Liberal peer who steered reform through the House of Lords, or Enoch Powell, an evangelist of the *laissez faire* right, who saw the issue as one of individual liberty, however much they may have personally abhorred homosexual behaviour. But perhaps a more important force came from the pragmatic ideology endorsed by the Wilson leadership of the Labour Party, with wide cross-bench support (though Wilson himself was not very keen on reform). This was essentially a negative, utilitarian position: the law obviously did not work, so the best thing to do was change it. This deliberately avoided the question of merit while maximizing support. As Professor Richards wrote: 'A feature of the Parliamentary debates on this subject is that the fundamental moral issue was consistently avoided.' As a result, the task, as the parliamentary reformers saw it, 'was to arouse Christian compassion, not Christian controversy. Their tactic was to keep public and parliamentary debate as rational and moderate as possible because of the danger that an upsurge of emotion and prejudice would ruin the chance of success.'[8]

Antony Grey and the Homosexual Law Reform Society saw clearly the merits of this approach, and it fitted, in any case, into their instinctive philosophic positions. Here the society was able to push at a door that was already beginning to creak open, and thus began to act, in effect, as a secretariat to the parliamentary reformers, supplying information, researching details, doing routine clerical work like parliamentary whipping, and preparing lists of M.P.s and peers favourable to reform.[9] At the same time, the society stressed the autonomy of homosexual law reform. It argued, rightly, that the law could be changed without society collapsing. And it argued, wrongly, that reform had no wider implications. It thus ignored the whole issue of sexuality and the significance of sex-roles socialization, but in so doing it was merely underlining the inevitable adaptation to parliamentary politics.

The reformers had clearly won the arguments from the start. No national body was active against the Bill, though individual members of the Boy Scouts, the Church of Scotland, the medical profession and so forth were vocal; and public opinion was divided, but not too violently. An opinion poll in July 1966 indicated that 44 per cent were opposed to change, 39 per cent approved, while 17 per cent were don't knows.[10] Reform pressure therefore proceeded steadily, hindered by the oddities of the parliamentary time-table and the lack of outright government support until the last few months.

June 1960: Kenneth Robinson, Labour M.P., urged early action on Wolfenden; defeated.
March 1962: Leo Abse, Labour M.P., proposed a mild Bill, to alleviate worst excesses under the existing law; defeated.
July 1964: New Director of Public Prosecutions issued instructions that all cases were to be referred to him before prosecution;

numbers of prosecutions brought actually increased.

May 1965: Lord Arran raised the issue in the House of Lords; a Bill providing for the decriminalization of consensual adult homosexual relations was introduced.

October 1965: Lord Arran's Bill passed in House of Lords.

February 1966: Humphry Berkeley introduced Bill in Commons. Passed first and second readings. Fell because of election in March. The Election returned a Labour majority of 100.

April 1966: Arran reintroduced his Bill in Lords. Passed in June. Abse then introduced an identical Bill in Commons; approved by 244 votes to 100 on first reading.

December 1966: Abse's Bill passed second reading by 194 M.P.s to 84.

April 1967: Abse's Bill passed through committee stage.

3 July 1967: Passed third reading, by 99 votes to 14.

27 July 1967: The Bill given Royal Assent and passed into law.

The Sexual Offences Act 1967 decriminalized male homosexual activities in private for adults over the age of twenty-one. But its restrictions were harsh from the start. It applied only to England and Wales, by-passing Scotland and Northern Ireland. It did not apply to the merchant navy, nor to the armed forces. It tightened up the law with regard to offences with 'minors' and to male importuning. And it absurdly restricted the meaning of 'private': for the sake of the Act, 'public' was defined as meaning not only a public lavatory but anywhere where a third person was likely to be present. Nor, as a later judicial ruling made clear, was homosexuality as such legalized. All that had effectively happened was that a difficult-to-sustain legal remedy had been removed from the statute book. Lord Arran, chief architect of the Act, made his position clear: 'I ask those who have, as it were, been in bondage and for whom the prison doors are now open to show their thanks by comporting themselves quietly and with dignity.'[11] This was hardly a trumpet-call to freedom. And in the next few years the number of prosecutions actually increased.

It is clear that though the Homosexual Law Reform Society publicly expressed warm gratitude to Arran and Abse for their work, they themselves were largely ignored. Neither Arran (who was not even a member of the society's Honorary Committee) nor Abse ever invited the society to a drafting conference with the parliamentary draftsmen who drew up the Bill, with the result that where the Act differed from the Wolfenden proposals it was in a more restrictive manner.[12] The parliamentary reformers often failed to see the significance of certain concessions they made to get the Bill through. In Parliament, the opposition had been dominated by former officers in the armed services, and it was their pressure on not unsusceptible parliamentary reformers which led to the exclusion of the armed services. The merchant navy was excluded from the provisions after high pressure from the employers and the National Union of Seamen. In each case the opponents of the Bill were most successful on purely utilitarian grounds – such as, for example, the questions of discipline in the armed services. 'Pragmatism' could easily become a double-edged weapon. A particularly grave weakness foreseen by the society was over conspiracy charges. Twice Lady Wootton, at the society's request, tabled amendments to ensure that conspiracy charges should not be brought against people committing, seeking to commit or facilitate homosexual acts; each time she failed, with the result that, within a few years, charges of 'conspiracy to corrupt public morals' were successfully brought against the 'underground' paper *IT* (*International Times*) for carrying homosexual contact advertisements, and unsuccessfully against *Oz*. Later in the 1970s they were used against a new wave of homosexual magazines.

On summing up the impact of the campaign, Grey has said: 'The Society's chief contribution had been made before the debates of 1965 began, in creating the climate of opinion in which they could be held at all.'[13] The Society, certainly, contributed much more than any previous reforming organization to the achievement of a mild measure of reform; and Antony Grey in particular was in practical terms a more successful reformer than any of his predecessors. But in evading the central question – of the desirability or not of homosexual relations – the society finally subordinated itself to parliamentary tactics and pragmatic manoeuvrings. The result was a deeply unsatisfactory law. There was an obvious need for a new campaign to extend its provisions. But support for the society dropped away drastically. By the end of 1967, of all local groupings only the North-Western Committee survived in any strength. Nationally, with the effective repeal of the Labouchère amendment, the limited aims of most adult professional-class homosexuals were satisfied. The Homosexual Law Reform Society had exhausted itself in achieving this, and had no real perspectives for the future.

But despite its reluctance to appeal directly to the homosexual community, the work of the society did, almost despite itself, act as a stimulus to homosexual self-organization. This tendency was accentuated by the changes in the law. Towards the end of the 1960s Michael Schofield was asked:

'Has the law reform here changed much in people's lives?'

'No. It has changed things only a little. But I think it was vital and it opens the door to serious change in the future.'[14]

Paradoxically, there were signs of this change among lesbians, who were not affected by change in the law, as well as among male homosexuals. Charlotte Wolff, the distinguished psychiatrist and herself lesbian, noted in her book *Love Between Women* (1971) that lesbianism had been neglected, so that no 'authoritative book wholly devoted to the subject has been published to date'. There were one or two texts that lesbians could read, but these were still generally overwhelmingly negative. Anthony Storr put a representative position when he baldly stated that 'lesbians do not know what they are really missing'.[15] Not surprisingly, lesbians interviewed by Dr Wolff found Radclyffe Hall more self-supportive. The so-called 'permissive' society had its impact on the lives of many lesbians, but this was often distorted by the double standard that pervaded the liberalism of the 1960s. As Elizabeth Wilson described it: 'This then was our place in the permissive society – to make our friends feel liberated and progressive by "accepting" us, without their having to feel any challenge to their own sexual identity.' This 'liberalism' also pervaded the homosexual world itself, reinforcing stereotyped role-playing and relationships. This came out in the most commercially successful stage and film portrayal of lesbian relationships, *The Killing of Sister George*, Frank Marcus's drama about a fading radio soap-opera star and her young female lover. Parts of the movie version were filmed in The Gateways, the best-known lesbian club. The hysteria and exaggeration in the film had a real counterpart in life, where lesbians struggled to lead their lives in a social world pervaded by hypocrisy.

We *said* it was O.K. for everyone to do their own thing; you could sleep with who you wanted and you shouldn't be jealous; a good relationship was an open relationship. You shouldn't make moral judgements about sexual behaviour – an extreme of liberalism that clashed violently with the wish to 'succeed' as a stable lesbian couple, and often led to hysterical exaggerations of feeling.[16]

This is describing essentially a middle-class milieu, and most of the pressure for change in public attitudes in lesbianism came from professional women, including academics, journalists, physicians. It was in their lives – economically independent and sexually circumscribed – that the contradictions were made most explicit. But the lives of most lesbians, working class and probably married, were isolated, without even the opportunity to meet partners and form relationships, however distorted, in the small sub-culture. The early lesbian organizations, such as the Minorities Research Group and Kenric, inevitably saw their main function as alleviating loneliness.

The Minorities Research Group had been founded in 1963 by Esmé Langley and Diana Chapman. At first they counselled isolated lesbians in a private flat and began social gatherings in pubs. These were soon abandoned, however, and from 1965 the publication of a magazine, *Arena Three*, was the chief focus of the group's work. During the 1960s discreet advertisements in progressive journals like the *New Statesman* widened its circulation, but it was no substitute for supportive social gatherings. Several of the original members of the group were disturbed by the abandonment of social meetings, and established a new group, Kenric (the name derived from Kensington and Richmond, the areas of London where most of the founders lived). This brought together lesbians in private homes, and once a month at a club. Kenric was, and remained into the 1970s, a very cautious and conservative grouping, with a relatively small membership (about 500), which kept members in touch with each other through a monthly newsletter. This, as Charlotte Wolff delicately put it, reflected its 'circumspect and useful activities'. There was a high degree of discretion.

> No surname of any of the members is given, and Christian names together with phone numbers are the only indications as to where and when certain social or other events are taking place. This measure shows great fear of public opinion. A similarly furtive attitude was also recognisable during the interviews. I often had to assure my subjects of complete secrecy before they would give an account of their emotional autobiography. Almost all of them spoke to me of their terror of being recognised as lesbians, and of the subterfuges they had to take in order to hide the fact.[17]

This fear of public opinion, and the deep internalization of guilt and secrecy, had a corrosive effect on people's lives. The existence of support groups, however conservative and tiny, has therefore had an important impact. As a result of these many found that their sense of identity and self-esteem had been immeasurably strengthened.

This was an important first step. It would take the re-emergence of the women's movement and the development of the Gay Liberation Movement in the 1970s to carry the issue further.

For men, at least superficially, there were more obvious signs of a breaking of the ice-pack in the late 1960s. London, in particular, saw the appearance of a new type of gay club, supplementing the older established clubs and pubs which had for a long time acted as sexual market-places as well as social centres. Peter Wildeblood described a typical club of the early 1950s, its contours shaped by the harsh winds outside.

> The clubs where they congregated usually consisted of one room, with a bar and a piano. They were extraordinarily quiet and well-behaved. The clubs closed at 11 o'clock, and most of the men did not go there primarily to drink, but to relax in an atmosphere where it was not necessary to keep up pretences.[18]

Discretion, however, was the rule, as clubs could easily be raided and reputations ruined. By the 1960s there was a slightly more relaxed atmosphere, with the growth of discothèque-type clubs with pop music and dancing (as long as the men did not touch each other). There was often a close integration between the swinging scene and the homosexual world. Many of the youths who worked or shopped in the trendy boutiques of Carnaby Street or the King's Road, Chelsea, might be seen, in the height of fashion, at the new gay bars in the evenings.[19] The magazines that began to appear at the very end of the 1960s, such as *Timm*, *Spartacus* or *Jeremy*, reflected this new affluence and a muted openness, though there were subtle differences in emphasis. *Spartacus*, edited from Brighton by John D. Stanford, had a mixture of features on the gay scene, jokey poems, contact ads ('Trading Post'), correspondence about sex problems, a travel service with package tours to Holland and Denmark, helpful articles on the law or venereal disease, and an occasional moralism: 'Soliciting in public lavatories is perhaps the greatest blight on the homophile community.'[20] But the mainstay was the slightly risqué, discreetly naked pics that were the chief protein of the audience. After a court case in 1971, the magazine collapsed amid much recrimination, and Stanford retired to Amsterdam, where he began a highly successful and lucrative guide to the international gay world.

*Jeremy*, which folded before *Spartacus*, was trendier (published from the Carnaby Street area) and glossier. The boys in the photographs were younger, and there was more emphasis on high fashion.

Articles wove a web of excitement around new clothes, travel and sexual success. There were special offers of flimsy underpants, *Jeremy* 'fundies', and support badges ('Get down to it with Jeremy!'). Stills from 'gay' movies, such as Fellini's *Satyricon* or the film of Gore Vidal's *Myra Breckinridge*, were featured. There was an agony column ('Hangups'), which revealed less than liberated views: a married man who confessed to homosexual feelings was told to consult his doctor. Overwhelmingly, the magazine was, like *Spartacus*, male-orientated and it was geared to a special type of male: young, pretty, fashionable, affluent (or those who fancied the same). Inevitably it ignored the vast majority of homosexuals who were none of these things. It reflected more than anything the initial penetration in the homosexual sub-culture of the consumer values of the wider society.

Those who remained in the reform movement after 1967 realized that the social situation of homosexuals remained deeply unsatis-factory. In June 1967 the North-Western Homosexual Reform Committee decided to suggest formally to the Albany Trust that it should take on the sponsorship of some kind of club movement on the lines of the Dutch COC (Cultuur-en Ontspanningscentrum, or Centre for Culture and Recreation). Antony Grey was less than enthusiastic in response, feeling the time was not yet ripe. In any case, he felt that what was needed was 'social integration' not a new 'ghetto'.[21] But this ignored precisely the specific social circumstances and isolation of most homosexuals. The North-Western Committee, the predecessor of the Campaign for Homosexual Equality, had always been the most radical of the Homosexual Law Reform Society's support groups. Founded in October 1964, it was initially run from a miner's cottage, in Atherton, Lancashire, 'amid a fanfare of local publicity and a complete absence of public hostility of any kind'. Under the leadership of the secretary, Allan Horsfall, a Labour Councillor in Nelson, it had a far clearer awareness of what was necessary than the London organization. From the start the majority of the membership was homosexual, and some of them were not ashamed to proclaim it. They were also more prepared than the national leaders to break with conventional opinions. At a meeting in June 1967 they recorded their view that homosexuality was not a medical problem, and that the role to be played by social workers in making the homosexual condition more tolerable was limited. What was needed was not more social workers but more social facilities.[22]

This was not exactly on a par with how the Albany Trust saw its role in the post-reform period. The trust veered increasingly towards becoming an educational and 'counselling' organization, and towards the training of 'experts' to do this. There was certainly a need for supportive help. The publicity given to the issue of homosexuality in the mid 1960s revealed a vast pit of misery and isolation. An article by Montgomery Hyde in a Sunday newspaper in 1965 had brought a torrent of letters asking for help, many from working-class homosexuals. And the numbers, of both sexes, seeking help from the trust rose sharply – from 150 in 1966 to 500 in 1969. The trust's case-work was largely conducted by Doreen Cordell, a well-meaning social worker, but Montgomery Hyde summed up the representative response: 'The need for cultivating or inculcating discretion in the homosexual is perhaps the most valuable service which the psychiatrist or psychotherapist can render.'[23] This subordination to existing value structures did not offer a very hopeful road ahead. The case-load, the encouragement of research at universities, and the sponsoring of the First International Symposium on Gender Identity in July 1969, was the chief work of the Albany Trust in the late 1960s. It was useful, but it did not meet the real needs of homosexuals at the time.

But, at this stage, the North-Western Committee found its resources too flimsy to take over a leading role. Its modest proposals to establish a series of non-profit-making clubs – 'Esquire Clubs' – were denounced by Lord Arran and Leo Abse, who complained bitterly to Grey that this was not what they had intended.[24] Grey and his committee appear to have been too anxious not to alienate any of its old supporters at this stage, with the result that they now became a definite drag on any further moves forward. When Antony Grey (described as 'the harried, overworked director of the Albany Trust') was interviewed in the late 1960s, he gave as his opinion that 'It's still inconceivable that such a group as the [American, and mildly reformist] Mattachine Society could exist here. I'd say it won't happen for at least five years.'[25]

Events were to prove him wildly wrong.

*Part Five*

# THE GAY LIBERATION MOVEMENT

# 16
## The Gay Liberation Front, 1970–72

*'We've been playing an act for a long time, so we're consummate actors. Now we can begin to be, and it'll be a good show!'* – Carl Wittman, A Gay Manifesto *(1970)*

*'Say it loud, we're gay and we're proud'*
*'Two, four, six, eight, gay is just as good as straight'*
*'Three, five, seven, nine, lesbians are mighty fine'*
– Gay Liberation Front slogans

The early 1970s mark the turning-point in the evolution of a homosexual consciousness. The homophile organizations that tiptoed through the liberal 1960s were superseded in the 1970s by a new type of movement which stressed openness, defiance, pride, identity – and, above all, self-activity.

Last time it was done by an elite, who did it by stealth. They didn't have demonstrations in Trafalgar Square. This time it has to be done by us, brothers and sisters.[1]

Of this new movement, the Gay Liberation Front (GLF), which sprang up in London in the autumn of 1970, was the most typical and dynamic representative. By the middle of the decade, though the name lingered on, the GLF had become a nostalgic memory for most of its participants, and a bogeyman for its opponents. But for a time it seemed to many homosexuals that a new day was dawning, ushering in an era of spontaneity, openness and liberation: 'There was, I believe, a general belief among the people who made up the gay movement that we were at the beginning of an historic wave; we were on the crest and it was about to surge forward.'[2]

Although the promise was illusory and only a minority of gay people were directly affected even in the early days, the effect of the movement that the GLF triggered off was deep *and* liberating. It extended the vista for homosexuals in such a way that the homosexual identity, and society's attitudes towards homosexuality, could never be quite the same again. Which is why this chapter concentrates on the Gay Liberation Front, short-lived as it was, and in particular the London grouping, for in its 'rise and fall' is writ in microcosm the history of a particular, and special, type of movement.

The GLF from the first defined itself as a 'revolutionary organiza-tion'. What was new about this was the consequential stress on homosexuality as a political issue. With this came a new emphasis on the oppression of gay people, a belief that the taboo against homosexuality was so deeply embodied in Western civilization (the 'Judaeo-Christian culture') that only a revolutionary overthrow of its structures could truly liberate the homosexual. Furthermore, this could not be done by others *for* the homosexual, but only by homo-sexuals themselves, acting openly and together. The choice of name, Gay Liberation Front, carries in each word the peculiar flavour of the period, its militancy, its millenarian hopes and its radical aspirations. And it carries, too, the movement's inspiration in a particular Ameri-can political development.

The gay liberation movement developed in the United States out of the cauldron of revolutionary hopes released in and around the nodal year of 1968. For radicalized youth, and for jaded, middle-aged revolutionaries, 1968 lit a beacon of hope that the idea of revolution had not died in the West. The May events in Paris, the Tet offensive of the Vietnamese against American imperialism, the world-wide revulsion against the excesses of American foreign policy, the enforced abdication of President Johnson, the 'Prague Spring' in Czechoslovakia, the new wave of student militancy in universities across the world, from Britain and Western Europe to Japan; all this, and the 'revolution of the spirit', symbolized in the 'youth move-ment' by rock music, mass open-air concerts (prefiguring, as Richard Gott suggested in a moment of ecstacy, the communalism of the socialist future), the new freedom and openness about sex: for many it seemed as if the structures of capitalism were already crumbling beneath the new music and being consigned to the junk-yard of his-tory.

Even by the end of the year a more sombre assessment had to be made. Russian tanks in Czechoslovakia and the election of Richard Nixon to the US presidency showed that reaction was not dead, and the long post-war boom that was the material basis for the new youth culture was showing signs of acute instability, bringing with it a new conservatism. But a large part of a generation had been radicalized by 1968, and for the next half-decade the amorphous phenomenon known as 'The Movement' was the carrier of radical ideas in the United States. GLF, which crystallized in America in 1969, immediately identified itself as part of the 'The Movement', claiming solidarity with other oppressed groups, and totally rejecting

– at least on a verbal level – compromise with bourgeois society. 'Choosing homosexuality is in itself an act of rebellion, a revolutionary stance.'[3] The choice of the name thus represented a conscious association with other self-defined revolutionary struggles, and particularly the struggles of oppressed nationalities in Asia and Africa, and the blacks in America. 'Black power' was the model for 'gay power', however misleading the comparison. In the London GLF the catch-phrase, 'This is a Gay Liberation *Front*' (with the displaced stress somehow symbolic), was sufficient to still all liberal dissenters who might feel the movement to be too radical or confrontationist. The name was the surest touchstone of GLF's radical intent.

But 'The Movement' was not just – or perhaps at this stage was only very little – about external political change. It was supremely about personal liberation. The Women's Liberation movement, which sprang up parallel with 'The Movement', indicated that profound changes in the nature of sex roles and sexual attitudes were on the agenda, and provided an inspiration for the gay movement, both in method ('consciousness raising' became an important part of the gay movement in the United States and Britain) and in ideas. Gays, like ethnic minorities and women, began to reject the stereotypes that society thrust on them: 'Chick equals nigger equals queer.' Militant homosexuals intended to smash the caricatures and to 'become themselves'.

But if the political tone came from the amorphous radical movement, its style and emotional flavour came from an association with the counter-culture.

A major dynamic of rising gay lib sentiment is the hip revolution within the gay community. Emphasis on love, dropping out, being honest, expressing yourself through hair and clothes, and smoking dope are all attributes of this.

There was little in the original American or British counter-culture that indicated any rejection of stereotypes of women and gays. Thus the San Francisco Diggers:

Our men are tough. They have style, guile, balls, imagination and autonomy. Our women are soft, skilled, fuck like angels, radiate children, scent and colours, like the crazy bells that mark our time.[4]

But many saw the counter-culture, with its alluring mirage of an 'alternative society', growing up within the (prosperous and fertile) womb of the old, as the violet path of peace and love and liberation. Radical influences transformed the American gay movement – and, in turn, parallel movements in Britain and elsewhere. There had long been an association between political radicalism and homophile organizations in the United States (as earlier in Britain). The first major post-war society, the Mattachine Society, had its roots in the 'Bachelors for Wallace' group founded iń California in 1948, who supported the Progressive Party candidate, Henry Wallace, for President, and later regrouped in the early post-war peace movement. Other societies had developed during the 1950s and 1960s, including One Inc., the lesbian organization Daughters of Bilitis, the Society for Individual Rights, many of which grew in the fertile soil of California. (As Carl Wittman said, 'San Francisco is a refugee camp for homosexuals.') In 1968, the annual meeting of the North American Conference of Homophile Organizations had formally adopted the slogan 'Gay is good', and by early 1969 there were some 150 homophile groups active in the United States. But most of these were of a liberal, be-suited, reformist type, more radical than the British Homosexual Law Reform Society certainly, but not confrontationist and not in any sense constituting a mass movement of homosexuals. But 1969 saw the simultaneous emergence of more radical groups in both California and New York, though it was in New York that the crystallizing event occurred.

In June 1969 the police raided a popular homosexual haunt – the Stonewall Inn in Christopher Street, a regular gay beat. This was a regular occurrence, but this time the reaction was different – the homosexuals fought back: 'The result was a kind of liberation, as the gay brigade emerged from the bars, back rooms, and bedrooms of the Village and became street people.' The 'Stonewall riot' was, as Dennis Altman has put it, the Boston tea-party of the gay movement: it was the first time that homosexuals had openly fought back – and in a language and style that evoked 'the revolution'. The New York Gay Liberation Front was born in the immediate aftermath of this event. And as its founding statement put it:

'We reject society's attempt to impose sexual roles and definitions of our nature. We are stepping out of these roles and simplistic myths. WE ARE GOING TO BE WHO WE ARE . . . Babylon has forced us to commit ourselves to one thing – revolution.'[5]

The next few years saw a turbulence of ideas in the United States and a penetration of the new movement abroad. In June 1970, when I read about the Christopher Street Gay Pride march in New York, I remember feeling that *that* could never happen in London – and a good thing too. But by November of that year I was enthusiastically attending meetings of the London GLF and feeling that my whole outlook and life were being transformed. Simultaneously, similar gay liberationist organizations sprang up in other Western nations. In France, where a small revolutionary movement had developed in the wake of the 1968 events, but soon died, the Front Homosexuel d'Action Révolutionnaire (FHAR) was founded in March 1971. In Italy FUORI had a small but active presence in Rome and Turin. Germany, Belgium and Holland as well as Canada, Australia and New Zealand, soon had similar movements. Each drew its inspiration and rhetoric from the American example, but all could call on roots in the specific problems of their own cultures.

It was the transmission of the American model which spurred on the formation of the London GLF. There was no single precipitating occasion like Stonewall. It was founded in the autumn of 1970 by two young men who had met in the United States during the summer: Aubrey Walter, a graduate, in his early twenties with a background of political work on the New Left, and Bob Mellors, a nineteen-year-old sociology student at the London School of Economics. They had been enthused by what was happening in the United States and were determined to try to get a similar movement going in Britain. The first meeting, at the London School of Economics, consisted of nine people, some of whom had already been involved in the American movement, but within a month meetings were being attended by about two hundred people, women and men. By early 1971, when the GLF was forced to leave the London School of Economics (to meet first in 'Middle Earth', a cellar in Covent Garden, and then in All Saint's parish hall, Notting Hill Gate) between four hundred and five hundred people were coming to the weekly meetings. Despite these haphazard beginnings, it was immediately apparent that GLF had touched a vital nerve in the gay community, and so the enthusiasm generated created its own momentum.

The British Gay Liberation Front, in the American fashion, saw itself as a 'people's movement', a radicalized mass movement of homosexuals fighting for their own freedom. It rejected traditional organization and leaders, and this inevitably involved a rejection of the existing homophile organizations. The Albany Trust, practically moribund by 1970, was despised as an establishment body (ironically,

Antony Grey attended early meetings of the London GLF, and spoke frequently; and it was he who suggested the occasion for the first demonstration, but he was widely distrusted and soon withdrew). The Committee for Homosexual Equality (as it was still called) was sneered at for holding its meetings under an assumed name, for its bureaucratic tendencies and for its declining to 'come out'. As the poet and activist Laurence Collinson put it, 'CHE is an organization; GLF is a way of life.'[6] Behind this was the real belief that existing organizations were unwilling to recognize the deep-seated nature of homosexual oppression. Prosecutions of men after 1967 had, as we have seen, increased, not diminished. There were real pressures on the largely male homosexual sub-culture from police harassment, while the Albany Trust, in particular, did little to build alternatives. But, above all, there were the subtle but pernicious pressures that derived from the surviving liberalism of the 1960s – what Christopher Isherwood called 'annihilation by blandness'. The GLF recognized three external types of oppression: persecution (largely legal, but also physical in the phenomenon of 'queer-bashing'); discrimination (in jobs, in housing, in cases involving child custody, in meetings, in displaying signs of affection in public); and thirdly, 'liberal tolerance'. As a gay liberationist pamphlet, *With Downcast Gays*, put it, 'the liberal "we" invariably excludes the very minority whose integration is being urged'.[7] Increasingly this super-cilious 'acceptance' came from the media, the psychiatric and medical professions – but in its generosity it reaffirmed its superiority. But there was a fourth, more dangerous form of oppression – self-oppression, the internalization of guilt, of self-hatred, of the values of the oppressors. The existing organizations, in asking (some said begging) the oppressor for acceptance, were revealing their own self-oppression. GLF, in its confused but dynamic way, set out to expunge this oppression. The appropriation of the word 'gay' was a prime symbol of the aim. The word had been used by homosexuals in the United States at least since the 1950s, but in Britain, though it was known, it tended to have an upper-class connotation. It was associated with the classier clubs, all mirrors and pillars, rather than with the typical 'queer' pub or 'cottage'. 'Queer' was the universally used word, the definition of the oppressor, and the term symbolizing the accepted oppression. 'Gay' was a word chosen by homosexuals themselves – it represented the new mood among gay men and women.

Inevitably GLF in its early days drew its support from those who had already been touched by the New Left or the counter-culture. It had a high proportion of artists, drop-outs, social-security claimants and the young (the typical age range was twenty-five to thirty-five) – that is, those who had least to lose by being defiantly open. But it also had a high percentage of new professional people, of students, teachers and sociologists (who provided much of the drafting and linguistic skills). Some liberals dissatisfied by existing organizations were early attenders, but there was also an immediate response from the sub-culture – and it was from this quarter that much of the energy derived. There were more men than women, as became typical in gay organizations (perhaps a ratio of 5 to 1), but certain women played a key role. Inevitably, most of the supporters were middle class, though often marginally or first-generation middle class; but there were few working-class gays.

What united this disparate fledgling movement was the simple excitement of being open, and what is striking in retrospect is the unexceptionable nature of many of the slogans put forward. Demands that all discrimination and oppression should end marched hand in hand with the demand that gay people should be free to kiss and hold hands in public.[8] But to put them forward at all in 1970 demanded a transformation of attitudes and seemed like an act of revolution. In the GLF this change revolved around three basic concepts: first, the idea of 'coming-out', of being open about one's homosexuality, of rejecting the shame and guilt and the enforced 'double life', of asserting 'gay pride' and 'gay anger' around the cry, 'out of the closets, into the streets.' Secondly, the idea of 'coming together', of solidarity and strength coming through collective endeavour, and of the mass confrontation of oppression. And thirdly, and centrally, the identification of the roots of oppression in the concept of sexism, and of exploring the means to extirpate it.

'Coming out' was the first and most obvious change. It was a touchstone of involvement in GLF that you should come out – to your friends, to your family, to your employers. You were encouraged to wear badges (GLF sold 8,000 in the first year), asserting your homosexuality, with slogans declaring 'Gay Liberation Front', 'Gay Power', 'Gay is Good', and later 'Lesbians Ignite', 'Avenge Oscar Wilde', 'How dare you presume I am heterosexual', and with prominent logos from the butterfly or clenched fist of the early badges to the pink triangle (commemorating homosexual victims of the Nazi concentration camps) and the purple lambda of later badges. Gay liberationists, men and women, held hands in public, kissed each other in Underground trains or on the streets, encouraged their comrades to come 'out of the closets', danced together at straight discos, demonstrated together, zapped public meetings, held openly homosexual dances and events. And coming out, the casting away of the generations of accumulated self-hatred and fear, *was* a tremendous liberation.

> Because of GLF, a great many people have been freed of their hang-ups to find themselves proud to be exactly as they are. And GLF ideas are slowly but surely getting to those people who are not even in the movement . . . they, too, are realizing they have a lot to be proud of.

Gay pride replaced self-oppression. 'I think Gay Pride is simply feeling that Gayness is good, that Gayness has as much potential for happiness and self-fulfilment as straightness has for straights.'[9] And with this assertion of self, of pride and anger, came a desire to demonstrate it publicly, to directly confront and challenge the oppressor.

The first GLF demonstration was a manufactured event, deliberately designed to encapsulate the élan and tap the movement's rising spirit. As the first issue of the GLF paper, *Come Together*, headed its report, 'We're Coming Out Proud'. Ostensibly in protest at the prosecution of the Young Liberal leader, Louis Eakes, for alleged importuning on Highbury Fields in London, the event on 27 November 1970 was in reality a demonstration of gay pride. Some 150 'beautiful gay people' paraded by torchlight across Highbury Fields, much to the bemusement of a few journalists and nocturnal walkers.[10]

Coming out had three distinct aspects: first of all it involved coming out to yourself, recognizing your own homosexual personality and needs; secondly, it involved coming out to other homosexuals, expressing those needs in the gay community and in relationships; but thirdly, and most crucially, it meant coming out to other people, declaring, even asserting, your sexual identity to all comers. This could be done on a personal level, but most satisfyingly it could, through GLF, be done collectively. Solidarity and strength through collective action underlined the new sense of well-being. And it promised a new community, a real community where one could *be*, as opposed to the traditional sub-culture where one had to *pretend*. Coming together meant not only an attack on the straight world, but also, most passionately in the early days, anger directed at the gay ghetto.

> The cottage is the coffin – come out and live.

The meat market smells! Drink up and leave the racketeering bars. Pull the flush in the cottage. Have a revolution in your life.[11]

GLF, in its heyday, rejected the values of the ghetto, its objectification of people, 'seeing other human beings in terms of the superficial alone – face, body, clothes'; its emphasis on looking right, the 'piss elegance' which 'reflects the materialism of western society'. And it challenged the exploitativeness of the traditional gay commercial scene.

The Gateways has made thousands of pounds out of women who come to the club (precisely how much money and publicity was gained from *The Killing of Sister George*?) . . . We are not sick and don't like people who condescendingly treat us as such – especially when they are making a living off us.[12]

The Gateways was zapped on 20 February 1971 by a small group of GLF women and men. The police were called and several men and women arrested (one eventually to be deported). But the point was made: GLF represented something different from the traditional gay scene.

The first two years of gay liberation were punctuated by a series of similar confrontations with gay commercial establishments and pubs that refused service.

Several of us took newssheets to the William IV on Friday evening . . . They threw us out, so we distributed the sheets outside. They, and the brewery, live off gay people. They rip us off, they despise us and they want to make sure we stay down because we're easier to exploit that way.[13]

There was a bitter feeling that even the increased visibility of gay people made them more exploitable. In the early autumn of 1971 there was a confrontation with some trendy but 'straight' pubs in Notting Hill Gate, to which GLF supporters would go after the weekly meeting, because the landlords had refused to serve them. There were several militant demonstrations and sit-ins at two pubs, the Colville and the Chepstow, during which the police were called, though no arrests were made.[14] In the end the point was taken: the pubs did agree to serve. Within a few years the Chepstow was gladly allowing its premises to be used for gay meetings; and the space for gay people in London was widened a little.

The problem was how to build the gay alternative, free of 'rip-off' pressures. The first answer was to create a new atmosphere where people could meet, free of the traditional cruisey 'meat-market' atmosphere of gay meeting-places. An all-gay discotheque was held at the London School of Economics on 4 December 1971, the first such event outside the closeted atmosphere of a private club. Women and men there were encouraged to touch, kiss and dance with each other, breaking the unspoken taboo (and legal threats) which had prevented this before. In the next few months, attempts were made to hold a regular Friday-night disco, but at first there was constant police harassment. At the Prince of Wales pub in Hampstead Road, London, the police raided the first publicly advertised gay disco, ostensibly searching for drugs, and frisked many of the men as they left. One policeman was heard to say that, 'We're showing the flag.' Another pub was warned by the police that it could be in breach of the peace by holding a gay disco and was frightened off. It was only by repeated effort that the right to hold such a disco was accepted.

On a grander scale there was a series of big dances, open to all, 'people's dances' as GLF fondly called them, where gays and straights (the more liberated) were encouraged to mingle and dance, where clothes were freaky, the light show a whirlwind of psychedelic colours, the atmosphere heady. The *People* newspaper noted the first dance at the Kensington Town Hall: 'It's all happening at the old Town Hall', and observed that seven hundred homosexuals were present and five hundred turned away; while some of the people there actually wore dark suits, collars and ties.[15] Throughout 1971 the GLF dances became freakier, the clothes more way-out, the atmosphere increasingly counter-cultural. After one dance in Camden Town Hall, a more 'radical' fringe refused to clear the hall at midnight and shouted at the harassed staff – with clenched-fist salute – 'Revolution now!', 'Power to the people!' It was unlikely that the revolution would break out in a public dance hall, but the excitement of public spectacle had its own intoxicating momentum. GLF wanted to create its own political style. 'Dances *are* political' was a frequent comment in the early days; politics had to come down to the nitty-gritty of everyday life, and, in a world hostile to homosexuality, creating one's own scene was a 'political act'.

So was street theatre. The Theatre Workshop of GLF was one of its early dynamic centres, and in its street shows it could make an effective and dramatic political point.

On February 4th, some members of Women's Liberation were on trial at Bow Street for their liberation of the Miss World Meat Market. Street theatre went along to tell it like it was. We held a 'Miss Trial' competition outside the court, but halfway through the performance, police hassle became the threat of real arrest and we split to a room in the court with sisters and brothers from GLF and WL. We got a big response from the press and the public, including tomatoes from the Covent Garden people and, as the Man from Auntie said, 'Can't remember when I've enjoyed a demo so much'.

As one of the GLF founders put it:

We want to give GLF demos a different role to straight demos. We want to have fun as well. We want our revolution to be enjoyable.[16]

During spring and summer there was the opportunity for more enjoyable gay demos – including 'gay-ins', or 'gay days' as they came to be known – picnics and celebrations of gayness in public parks.

Gay Days seem to me to provide a perfect fusion of self-liberation and external campaigning. They are a celebration of our growing love for one another, and an enjoyment of our new-found freedom. At the same time they look outwards. We do our thing in the public parks. We show our gay pride to the world, and most importantly, to our gay sisters and brothers who have not yet joined us.

Gay days were held both in middle-class areas, such as Primrose Hill, and in working-class areas like Finsbury Park, Battersea Park and Victoria Park, Hackney. Sometimes the atmosphere was heavy and hostile, but there was invariably an upbeat feeling.[17]

The biggest celebrations of all were in gay pride weeks. These had been celebrated in the United States since 1970, the climax being the Christopher Street March, commemorating Stonewall at the end of June. In 1971, GLF held a march at the end of August through London (28 August), but in 1972 there was a full-scale gay pride week at the right time, the end of June, culminating in a march through London to Hyde Park on 1 July. Some 2,000 women and men marched down Oxford Street, a number puny by American standards, but shouting gay pride slogans, demonstrating 'gay love', popping balloons, distributing leaflets, blowing kisses, and climaxing in a picnic in Hyde Park. Gays were out of the closets – and very definitely on the streets.

But what were they there for? The politics of GLF were very vague in the early days, yet what came to shape its contours, and differentiate it from the older homophile groups, was its recognition of the existence of sexism: 'Women and gay people are both victims of the cultural and ideological phenomenon known as sexism. This is manifested in our culture as male supremacy and heterosexual chauvinism.'[18]

The notion of sexism had been developed in the American women's movement and taken up within British feminism, but at first there was little linkage with the oppression of gays. None of the seminal women's texts in the United States or Britain had discussed lesbianism, let alone homosexuality in general, at any great length, the subject being confined to footnotes in Germaine Greer's *The Female Eunuch* and Kate Millett's *Sexual Politics*. But it was from the more radical feminist analyses that most of the ideological concepts of gay liberation came. *Come Together*, 3, reproduced Martha Shelley's article 'Stepin Fetchit Woman' which had placed lesbianism firmly at the centre of women's struggles: 'Lesbianism is one road to freedom – freedom from oppression by men'; and *Come Together*, 5, had carried the male equivalent of this argument in Steve Danski's 'Hey Man', which placed the struggle against sexism, and its expression in maleness, at the heart of gay liberation:

All men are male supremacists.
Gay men are no exception to the maxim.

Consequently, gay liberation could be the first step in the 'cultural de-manning of man'. This concept was taken up enthusiastically by leading elements in GLF and achieved its clearest statement in the London GLF *Manifesto*, written by a mixed collective of men and women in early 1971. This located homosexual oppression in the gender-role system of society which affixed stereotyped roles to men and women, and made outcasts of gay women and men.

The oppression of gay people starts in the most basic unit of society, the family, consisting of the man in charge, a slave as his wife, and their children on whom they force themselves as the ideal models. The very form of the family works against homosexuality.

This exclusion of homosexuals pervades the whole of society and its basic institutions, and is so deep that only a revolution could change things: 'reform cannot change the deep-down attitude of straight people that homosexuality is at best inferior to their own way of life, at worst a sickening perversion'.[19] And these feelings were reflected in the lives of gay people themselves, whose lives were embodiments of sexism: in compulsive monogamy, the youth cult ('ageism'), in role stereotyping in gay relationships – where one partner would ape the husband, the other the wife – in discrimination within the gay community itself (the despising of 'femme' homosexuals and transvestites, the derogatory use of phrases like 'screaming queen' to put down people, the fear of pedophiles and of having a bad name, the urge towards respectability). Gay people had internalized these sexist values so successfully that most were not even aware of them.

The oppression of homosexuals was thus defined essentially as a cultural phenomenon, pervading all aspects of society. But, historically and practically, it was directly related to the oppression of women whose economic, social and cultural subordination was the mainstay of sexism. This suggested that the strategic aim of gay liberation should be a link-up with feminism. It was this concept that added intellectual content to the essentially emotional force of coming out and coming together. But it also posed the most acute problems in terms of political direction for the young movement.

GLF declared itself to be on the side of all oppressed peoples, and in a vague way seemed to be aiming towards a new sort of revolutionary approach, linking the personal and internal with the external and traditional politics. The period 1970–72 was one of massive class confrontations as the Conservative Heath government sought to impose its 'silent revolution' while breaking the strength of the labour movement through the Industrial Relations Act. London GLF members participated in the huge marches against the Bill in December 1970 and January 1971, under their own banner: 'Gay People are on the March!' The march organizers were obviously less than enthused, and in the January march GLF and its extrovert banner was consigned to the rear of the 100,000-strong column. Sexist comments were rife – especially jokes speculating about the sexual orientation of 'Sailor Heath' – but it was a necessary part of taking the struggle into the organized labour movement. As class conflict reached a peak in mid 1972, GLF was again present, manning the picket outside Pentonville Jail in solidarity with the dockers jailed for defying the Industrial Relations Act, and taking its turn on the vigil outside the United States Embassy in protest over the Vietnam War ('Militant homosexuals against the male chauvinist pig Nixon'). GLF added its own distinctive colour to the political ritual:

> Theme for Gay Vigil at Grosvenor Square on Thursday, 27 June, is BALLOONS – BRING BALLOONS – FROCKS – AND LOVE.[20]

A typical week in the life of GLF in the summer of 1972 reveals an intoxicating mixture of the political and social: the Vietnam vigil and the Pentonville picket went cheek-by-cheek with an 'End of Season Dance' at Fulham Town Hall, a gay day on Clapham Common, a disco in a pub in Putney, a meeting of South London lesbian liberation, plus the regular meetings of the GLF functional groups: the Counter-Psychiatry Group, the Church Research Group, the Youth Education Group, the Action Group, and the various consciousness-raising groups. Gay politics had a way of becoming a new way of life, mingling the radical political stance with the personal exploration (sometimes so earnestly that people complained they never had time for simple sex).

Besides the wider political events, there were, of course, the specifically gay-orientated demonstrations. The London Counter-Psychiatry Group, formed early in 1971 to challenge the assumptions and pretentions of the psychiatric profession (and consciously seeing itself as part of the anti-psychiatry movement that took as its mentor men like R. D. Laing and David Cooper), was most active in this regard. It organized a Harley Street demonstration in the spring of 1971, much to the bemusement of the consultants there and the few passers-by, and a continuing campaign against David Reuben's blatantly sexist book *Everything You Always Wanted to Know About Sex: but were afraid to ask* – a multi-million American best-seller, which managed to malign both homosexuals (homosexuals apparently liked food and degradation) and women in a flip and obviously saleable way. The publishers naturally ignored the objections and *The Times* failed to publish a letter of protest organized by the Counter-Psychiatry Group and signed by a number of well-known liberal reformers[21] – which shows how little people do care to know about sex where money is involved. But, again, it helped to define a homosexual consciousness against those who would undermine it.

These were straightforward enough issues, but on the central issue of sexism the problem was less clear-cut. If that was what was at the heart of homosexual oppression, then it had to be tackled in a more conscious way. But, from the early days even, the position of women in the GLF was problematic. Both GLF women and men had supported the feminist demonstrations on International Women's Day in February 1971 and 1973, and there was constant verbal acknowledgement of the significance of sexism. But beneath this there were extreme tensions developing. GLF was a movement whose sheer newness and apparent daring and zest unified a host of disparate tendencies, but as the initial impetus and enthusiasm exhausted itself, the contradictory elements began to resume their centripetal tendencies. This was reflected in the weekly meetings: always chaotic, zooming from topic to topic, wary of 'super-stars' and leaders but easily swayed by a gifted verbalizer, who would shoot in the empyrean, glisten and then fade, often never to be seen again. Terrified of 'organization' and chairmanship, but tyrannized by its own lack of structure, GLF had always been like a pantomime horse, pulling in two different directions at once.

In the early days this had been exhilarating, as new ideas were exchanged and enthusiasm and comradeship generated. Speakers were always careful to address one another, as in old labour movement meetings, as 'sister' or 'brother'; meetings were celebrations of gayness rather than business occasions. GLF wandered on its way, directed haphazardly by the weekly meetings. But there were practical problems. GLF rejected the idea of 'membership': it was a movement or it was nothing. But it needed an office, and obtained one, in the basement of the *Peace News* building in 5 Caledonian Road, near King's Cross. Who was to pay for it and who was to control it? Money, typewriters and equipment were often ripped off in the name of brotherly love, and no general meeting could stop this, or even control it for sustained periods. GLF had a perpetual identity crisis, with consecutive 'think-ins' to define and re-define involvement, with little success. From early 1971 most of the creative work came out of the small functional groupings, concerned with the *Manifesto*, putting together the journal *Come Together*, discussing psychiatry, Christianity and Jewishness, supporting night workers or youth, planning action and street theatre. But inherent in these were a host of different approaches to gay liberation. These strains were already apparent by the late summer of 1971, when splits developed in the media workshop over the future of *Come Together*: how was it to relate to the revolutionary movement generally; what should its attitudes to the gay world be, especially that outside the privileged confines of London?[22] One symptom of the strain was the establishment of sub-GLFs within London itself – in Camden, West London,

South London, East London, all with different interests and biases, all attempting, with varying degrees of success, to root themselves in the gay community. From the middle of 1971, four major splits developed which were fatally to affect GLF's cohesiveness: between the women and the men; between the activists and the feminists; between the socialists and the counter-culture; and, most damagingly, between the dreams of the GLF and the real possibilities of 1972. These were not successive or even exclusive developments, and there was a much greater confusion than any simple categorization indicates. But they developed out of real contradictions within the GLF.

Although in a minority, certain women had played a major part in GLF from the start. Women participated in most of the important activities, and in drawing up the *Manifesto*. But there were real per- sonal difficulties and problems of political orientation. Many women felt that the atmosphere of meetings was overwhelmingly male. Men who were accustomed to dominating meetings had little sympathy for the problems of women unused to public speaking, and many women felt that sexist attitudes were as prevalent among men in the gay movement as outside. By early 1972, after a think-in on the subject, the women in London GLF decided to withdraw and set up an autonomous organization. They gave three reasons: the drain on their energy caused by the endless fight against the men's sexism; the unradical nature of GLF politics generally; and the need to provide a 'viable alternative to the exploitative "straight" gay ghetto'.[23] This did not, in fact, mean a final break as women and men continued to work together in various functional groupings, but it was indicative. One factor which made a break easier was that it became increasingly possible for gay women to raise the question of lesbianism in the Women's Liberation movement. At the Skegness Women's Liberation Conference of 16–17 October 1971, women from GLF had success- fully raised the issue of sexuality and had overturned the Maoist leadership of the National Co-ordination Committee on the ques- tion.[24] It would be another three years before the movement as a whole adopted as its sixth demand: 'The end to all discrimination against lesbians and the right to define our own sexuality.' But the dialogue with the women's movement was on-going, and the primacy of association with a largely male gay movement disappeared. There were continuing problems which did not remove the need for autono- mous lesbian organizations. But the point remained that there seemed little possibility of lesbian issues being taken up seriously in the GLF.

This underlines a second point: that though united by a term, 'homosexuality', and by an emotional solidarity in the movement, there were fundamentally divergent approaches between the men and the women, stemming from the simple fact that lesbians were women and gay males were men. On one level there was obviously an important material basis for this divergence in the fact that, generally speaking, most gay men were relatively privileged economically compared to most lesbians. (For instance, the ratio of men's pay to women's was still roughly 2 to 1, as it had been for a hundred years. This meant that most gay men, without dependents, were well off, and lesbians correspondingly were not.) But stemming from this were the complex and different historical developments of attitudes towards male and female homosexuals – sub-cultural and legal. The long-term interests of both might be identical – the obliteration of sexism – but the immediate needs were different. Women were not centrally interested in lowering the age of consent or with 'cottaging', and it was in fact to prove very difficult for any single organization to combine successfully the necessarily disparate approaches.

This touched on the second major split developing in GLF – between those (chiefly gay men) who wanted GLF to evolve in the direction of the New York Gay Activist Alliance, which had early split off from the GLF and which stressed the primacy of gay issues, and those who could loosely be termed feminists. No one disagreed that emphasis had to be placed on fighting specific examples of homosexual oppression, but the danger threatened that GLF would become just a more militant reformist organization and would abandon any more radical pretensions. In practice, the argument revolved around the question of action and organization. The 'gay activists' stressed the need for a tighter organizational structure, for clear-cut aims, for greater stress on the media, and on understandable propaganda:

> Gay activists are not apologetic about their homosexuality, so they can be more militant and defiant. But they refuse to think politically. Gay activism is generally for men, often hostile to women. It wants rights for gay people as they are; it does not challenge butch or femme stereotypes, or examine new ways of relating.[25]

There was, perhaps, a need for this type of organization, but GLF stressed, above all, 'new ways of relating'. This was the core of the early emphasis on the role of consciousness-raising groups, small groups of (usually) men who would discuss sexism, relationships, sexual hang-ups, and attempt to leap to a broader knowledge by generalizing personal experience. And this stress lay behind the experiments in commune building, groups of men (and sometimes women) living together without predetermined or received roles, often sharing bedrooms, with strict taboos against pair-bonding and individualism. The *Manifesto* laid great stress on this 'new life-style':

> Our gay communes and collectives must not be mere convenient living arrangements, or worse, just extensions of the gay ghetto. They must be a form of consciousness-raising (i.e. raising or increasing our awareness of our real oppression) and of gay liberation activity, a new focal point for members of the gay community.[26]

Several gay communes were established in various parts of London, often in squats of unoccupied houses. There were frequent clashes; in working-class Brixton windows were broken; in counter-cultural Notting Hill the police tried to evict. They were often unstable entities, riven by personal jealousies despite the ideologies, divided by questions of who should do the work, beset by a constant stream of visitors looking for 'crash pads', temporary stopping-off places. As a transitional phase in exploring new relationships, they were often personally liberating, and they seemed to offer in embryo an alternative to the nuclear family. But they were also utopian. If they set out to be something more than temporary ways of living together, they came up against iron laws about property, about how to live and work together harmoniously and uncompetitively within a hostile economic and social environment. They also conflicted severely with the emotional structuring of most members. The need for pair-bonding might well have been a result of bourgeois conditioning – but to say that did not will the need away. Nevertheless communal experiments did emphasize an important dichotomy – that between 'personal' liberation on the one hand and political action on the other. Rarely did the two meet.

This was at the heart of the third split, within the ranks of those who had been most influenced by feminist ideas. Those with a socialist or neo-Marxist background stressed the need to take the gay liberation and feminist struggles into the labour movement, the trade unions and left groupings, identifying the common enemy as a male chauvinist capitalist ruling class. They wanted to extend traditional socialist analyses beyond the purely economic and to lay the base for a mass anti-sexist socialist movement. Counter-poised against this tendency were those who had been most influenced by the counter-culture: these stressed the liberating effects of drugs and communal sharing, of defiant openness about appearance, were into make-up and drag, and were less concerned with doing things collectively than with being something individually. All types of people who came into contact with GLF were affected by the counter-culture – in appearance, in the frequent use of soft drugs, in the adoption of a sort of hip mid-Atlantic dialect (the constant use of the interjectory 'like' was another badge of liberation; and other words such as 'rip-off' for stealing, and 'bread' for money, slipped easily into common speech). Within this general framework there was a loose political tendency which called itself 'radical feminism' or, later, 'radical queenery' or 'faggotry'.

This extended the logic of early arguments, such as those of Martha Shelley and Steve Danski, which saw the primary contradiction in society as one between men and women; hence it was 'maleness' that had to be wiped out. 'Male homosexuality could be the first attempt at the non-assertion of cultural manhood . . .' The bible of this grouping was Shulamith Firestone's *The Dialectic of Sex* (1970), which located the true dialectic of history in conflict between the sexes and looked forward to women being liberated from childbirth. The logic of this position was for gay men to subordinate themselves entirely to women's struggles, to 'relinquish all power' to women, to give them a veto in the movement, and for men to give up their 'male privileges'. One way of doing this was to embrace political drag, to dress in women's clothing without, as in the traditional drag scene, apeing female glamour. So you would see hairy men walking arm-in-arm down the street in pretty dresses and with rich make-up: the aim was not so much to pretend to be a woman as to reject being a man and so invite personal abuse. This had its interesting personal effects, but as a political gesture it was almost entirely useless. Many women in the movement were horrified at the heaviness of these self-defined anti-sexist men, while the men were alienated by their overbearing evangelist fervour.[27]

There was a streak of pure voluntarism in the movement, stemming from the belief that simply willing a change would speedily bring it about; and, beyond this, a real anti-intellectualism which rejected any form of directing or analytical reason in favour of 'letting it all hang out'. This might liberate many individuals from their personal hang-ups; it might release personal energies hitherto repressed. But its chief result was to turn many gay people inwards, to make them politically passive. Moreover, 'dropping out' could never be more than a minority activity. The problem of capitalist society is that people are imprisoned in their roles; it is usually only the privileged few who 'drop out'. A mass movement could never be built on such a basis.[28]

Nevertheless, it was a strong if ultimately divisive force in the London GLF by 1972. These conflicts of approach were already implicit by the summer of 1971, but came to crisis in the early summer of 1972. The gay pride week at the end of June 1972 marked the climax to the GLF's energy and activity, but it was a hysterical rather than a real unity. The conflicts within the ranks came to a head during gay pride week itself, and revolved around how the marchers should dress or behave. It was high tide, and within months GLF had fragmented completely. Various types of activity continued throughout 1972 and 1973, but by the end of 1973 even the GLF office had closed. Small GLFs existed in South London and outside London, especially in Lancaster and Leeds, and later Bradford, and these generated much local energy. Remnants of communes struggled on for a while in Notting Hill Gate (where the Colville Houses commune was the locus of the radical queens), and in Bethnal Green, where the 'Bethnal Rouge' commune had a bookshop in the old Agitprop offices. But the spirit had collapsed as rapidly as it had risen. From mid 1972, it is safe to say, the main activities of gay liberation went on – but no longer specifically within the organizational form of GLF.

To begin to grasp the reasons for this, we have to understand the fourth split – between what GLF claimed to be, and what it actually was, between itself and the homosexual world outside. GLF itself was based on the illusion that there was a mass force of revolutionized homosexuals willing and able to follow its lead; it was an illusion born of euphoria which turned out to be sadly wrong. There were, and are, structural factors in the social situation of homosexuals which make it very difficult to build a large-scale movement. There is, first of all, the central fact that homosexuals are not visibly different from their heterosexual parents, friends and colleagues. It is possible, therefore, for homosexuals to 'pass' for straight, whereas it is not possible for women to pass for men, or blacks for white. And the hostile pressures are such that it is easier for most homosexuals to pretend to be heterosexual than to risk the opprobrium that still attends coming out.

On the other hand, and paradoxically, the very real success of GLF made it less necessary to become politically active as a homosexual in order to achieve more than a seared double-life. Many of the early demands of GLF – for example, 'that gay people be free to kiss and hold hands in public, as are heterosexuals' – were not formally accepted, of course, but as gay people in coming out did them, and the heavens did not fall in, so it became easier for gay people to be more open in their sexuality. The essence of GLF was to change consciousness. But once it had begun to change it – and without a revolution! – it seemed less necessary to build the sort of radical movement that GLF claimed as essential to carry it through. GLF's revolutionary rhetoric masked a unity that was located around reformist aims, ones which could be attained within the framework of liberal bourgeois society. Furthermore, although it would have been heresy to say so at the time, it turned out that homosexuality was not a stable basis on which to build a large-scale movement; a host of conflicting class, cultural, sexual, political and social allegiances tugged in increasingly divergent directions and were to create diverse entities in the gay liberation movement as it developed. But, as the problems became more apparent, so the tone of GLF became even less attractive. It was not helpful in building a new type of homosexual movement to be told that you *must* wear political drag, must break with your family, must not enter monogamous relationships. Some, or even all of these demands may have been right in the abstract, but they ignored the actual socialization and cultural experiences that male and female homosexuals had, in their diversity, undergone. The increasing isolation of GLF from the gay community in mid 1972 led to an increasing tone of hysterical heresy-hunting, as the 'radical queens', by this time the dominant elements, lashed out at any reformist tendencies, attacking, for instance, the founders of *Spare Rib* for selling out the feminist cause, and physically attacking members of the GLF office collective and sellers of *Gay News*.

But behind these factors specific to the homosexual experience were wider changes in the political situation which made millenarianism decreasingly relevant. GLF had early on observed the threats posed by the revival of the evangelical anti-sex crusade epitomized by the Festival of Light, Mrs Mary Whitehouse's censorship campaigns and Lord Longford's anti-pornography crusade. It had effectively zapped the inaugural meeting of the Festival of Light,[29] and was involved in 'Operation Rupert', the counter-cultural response against its implications. But there were also signs of a toughened response to radical groupings by the state machinery. The prosecution of the *Little Red School Book* and the trials of the editors of *Oz* (one of whom was a supporter of GLF) suggested a cultural backlash; while the trials of alleged members of the 'Angry Brigade' (one woman among the defendants – indicted, detained, tried and found innocent – had been prominent in GLF) indicated a harsh clampdown on the political fringe.

GLF was vulnerable to the change of climate. It had been the last major product of late 1960s euphoria; it collapsed as that euphoria died. It had already exhausted itself in the United States by 1971, and events in such other major capitalist countries as Australia were to follow a similar pattern. The years 1972–3 saw the demise in Britain of the underground, the old counter-culture. Magazines such as *IT*, *Ink*, *Oz*, even the more political *7 Days*, collapsed, their role probably exhausted – and, if not, their funds usually were. The political realities of the period 1972–4 – with the growth of the 'strong state', developing economic problems and a move towards mass class confrontations – made the utopian hopes of 'The Movement' seem redundant – even naïve. John Shane's film *Come Together*, which looks at the early months of GLF, has an interview with a leading activist, Warren Hague, who was placed against a carefully composed background of books: Laing, Cooper, Marcuse. The 'politics of experience', the 'dialectics of liberation' that they represented, and which was expressed in the radical revival of the late 1960s and reflected in aspects of GLF, had secured its purpose by the early 1970s. New attitudes and responses were needed for the new class realities.

But, despite these cautionary comments, the influence of GLF should not be under-estimated. On at least three levels its impact was deep: on the individual, on the gay community and in political debate. For many individuals it provided the possibility for at least partial individual liberation. They asserted their homosexuality, got rid of personal hang-ups caused by social pressures, developed relationships and new life patterns. The individualism which weakened GLF as a movement was for many people its greatest achievement.

For the gay community it had an immensely stimulating effect in ways that are still being realized. GLF did not cause the changes that have taken place, but it suggested that they might be possible. That was its historic function. Finally, GLF helped make homosexuality a political issue in the broadest sense. In terms of legislative change, the effect so far has been nugatory; but in terms of homosexuals' ability to conceptualize their social position, the change has been immense – and it is this which portends most for the future. The historic wave that GLF seemed to promise has not surged forward; but the undercurrents have had a deep effect on many gay people's lives.

# 17
## A Gay Community?

*'The Gay Community is the tip of the iceberg. It is that part of Gayness which can be seen and identified'* – Come Out Fighting (*Los Angeles gay liberation paper*)

The Gay Liberation Front at first aroused intense fear and panic among many homosexuals. The general secretary of the (then) Committee for Homosexual Equality (CHE), reflecting a general feeling in his organization, denounced in the *Guardian* newspaper the GLF's 'extreme Marxist analysis', its 'unrepresentative' nature, its 'weird-looking' members, and concluded by suggesting that if people wanted something more 'level-headed', they should write to CHE – care of an anonymous box number in London WC1.[1] This fear of rocking the boat, of over-militancy, of alienating necessary respectable support, was to become a recurrent theme. For a while the London CHE office even refused to stock GLF literature. By 1972, however, there was a goodly spread of gay organizations of various types throughout the country, the more active and interesting successfully reflecting GLF's underlying philosophy of self-reliance and self-organization. The real theme of gay liberation during the 1970s is the growth of this self-help principle, and, paradoxically, though this new stress emanated from GLF, it was the reformist bodies such as the Committee (Campaign from 1971) for Homosexual Equality which were to prove the real beneficiaries.

At grass-roots level the metropolitan stress on sectarian perfection inevitably lost much of its meaning. In most of the British Isles, especially in Scotland and Ireland, the fundamental principle to establish was the right to organize at all. The gay organizations that did spring up therefore reflected local needs and bias and a wide political and class variation. In December 1971, a section across the British Isles would have revealed something like this.[2] In Birmingham, a Gay Action group reported a host of activities, including leafletting, involvement in a television programme, letters to booksellers about the Reuben book *Everything You Always Wanted to Know About Sex*, a film night at the Arts Lab, where 108 people turned up; a Christmas dance; coming out at straight dances; and a sticker campaign. More sedately, Cambridge CHE, which met every Thursday, had a list of invited speakers, was planning film shows, strategy and planning meetings, and was aiming for a gay dance in the spring. Cardiff GLF was also pursuing the anti-Reuben campaign, with leaflets (1,100 distributed) and street theatre, and went on a march against unemployment with a banner and eight people. Chiltern CHE were a little less active; founded at the end of 1970, they had fifty members, a number of organized coffee evenings, and also had tape records of recent radio and TV programmes played to them. Hull University had a sexual liberation society, which held a forum on homosexuality; Leeds CHE was 'feeling our way'; members were planning to go to see *Twelfth Night* and *Lulu*. In London, the London organizer of CHE, Roger Baker, reported on the establishment of its counselling arm, Friend; while London GLF laid a wreath at the Cenotaph on Remembrance Sunday, 'In memory of the countless thousands of homosexuals branded with the Pink Triangle of homosexuality who died in the gas chambers . . .' And in Manchester, where CHE had its headquarters, activity was developing at the university, and women were particularly active.

In Scotland the situation was different and much more difficult. The 1967 Act had excluded Scotland and Northern Ireland, and the 1885 Act and the anti-buggery provisions were still on the Statute Book (though, in practice, the police in Scotland rarely prosecuted cases where they would not be prosecuted in England and Wales). The Scottish Minorities Group (SMG) had been founded by five people in 1969 to begin a fight against this situation, but its growth was at first slow. By January 1971 it had only twenty-eight paid-up members; though this rose to 200 by 1972. The social situation was not very propitious. 'It's hard to describe the social scene in Central Scotland. Very hard.' To combat this, the group organized COBWEB, a Saturday-night social which offered 'warmth and friendliness'; and a social emphasis was among its aims, along with campaigning and befriending. Though small, it was an enterprising group, organizing a 600-strong teach-in on Homosexuality in Edinburgh (8 March 1973) which recieved a good press reaction; and in December 1974 it was host to the first International Gay Rights Congress, also held in Edinburgh. In terms of campaigns for law reform, it was closely linked with CHE.

But if the situation was difficult in Scotland, it was nearly impossible in Ireland. The political division of the island, the dominance of Roman Catholic ideology in the South and among many republicans in the North, the near civil-war situation in the North itself, militated against any deeply rooted organization. After a visit by Antony Grey in 1969, the Elmwood Association had been founded in the

North, essentially to counsel homosexuals, but this petered out in
1970. After 1972 several organizations, influenced by gay liberation
ideas, sprang up in Belfast, and later Dublin; first a Gay Liberation
Society in Belfast, then the Union for Sexual Freedom in Ireland
(USFI), and later, after a split, the Irish Gay Rights Association, with
support in Dublin. Up to the mid 1970s their role was limited to
providing support and a social milieu, though a Gay Rights Conference was held and USFI supported the Campaign for Homosexual
Equality and the Scottish Minorities Group in their campaign for
further law reform.[3]

What all these disparate organizations had in common was an
allegiance to the belief that homosexuals themselves could best respond to specific problems and special needs. Inevitably this rash
of new organizations left the established Albany Trust organization
stranded. In 1970 the old Homosexual Reform Society transformed
itself into the Sexual Law Reform Society, which in 1972 produced
a useful report on lowering the age of consent to fourteen. Its respectable past gave it an ear in the press and Parliament, which
the grass-roots movement at first lacked. Moreover, from 1974
the trust benefited from a £30,000 government grant. But, in the
early 1970s, its crisis of identity and direction reached a climax.
In the autumn of 1971 it even for a time handed over its counselling
work to the Rev. Michael Butler of the Samaritans, while promising
to pursue a policy of public education in its place. But, later the
same year, it also gave up its new director, Michael de-la-Noy,
who had succeeded Grey. De-la-Noy complained to the *Sunday
Times* (7 November 1971) that the 'general liberals' who had helped
previously seemed no longer to be around, while homosexuals
themselves seemed unwilling to help. This was deeply ironical,
considering the ferment of activity in the gay world, but it did under-
line the trust's isolation from the homosexual community. Nor
was Antony Grey any more successful in making the National
Federation of Homophile Organizations (of which he was president)
any more viable. Mooted in summer 1970 to coordinate activities on a
national scale, this had finally been established in October 1971 with
most British gay organizations (apart from the GLF) as members.
By 1973 deep disillusion had set in. The Scottish Minorities Group,
and then the Campaign for Homosexual Equality, pulled out with
some acrimony. The SMG chairman wrote:

> SMG agrees that we need to meet together. But do we really
> need a 20-page constitution, a sliding scale set of fees, joint

group or individual membership, another executive committee and another round of annual general meetings and elections to achieve this?[4]

The Albany Trust remained torn between the desire to do something, and its perennial fear of offending too many people if it did it. Unfortunately, the Campaign for Homosexual Equality, which was by 1972 the largest British gay organization, never seemed capable of taking full advantage of the new opportunities. It had developed out of the old North-Western Committee, and when it re-established itself as an independent organization in mid 1969 under the title of the Committee for Homosexual Equality, it recognized the need for a more ambitious programme than that of the old Homosexual Law Reform Society, that is, one extending beyond law reform.

By the end of 1969 there were a hundred members, and the committee decided to encourage local groups. By the end of 1970 there were 500 members in fifteen local groups; by the end of 1971, 1,800 members; and by the close of 1972, 2,800 members, in sixty local groups, though only between 6 and 8 per cent of these totals were women.[5] Though still small in absolute terms, it was a spectacular increase for a British homophile group, and undoubtedly the chief stimulus came from the GLF. The committee was always careful to distinguish itself from the GLF, and to stress its non-political stance. 'We do not believe that prejudice against homosexuals has anything to do with capitalism or the class struggle.'

But there were early signs of what could be achieved in terms of enthusiastic engagement when London GLF gave its support to the committee's campaign to establish an 'Esquire Club' in Burnley. The plan to set up a chain of 'Esquire Clubs' had been in abeyance since 1969, but in 1971 apparently suitable premises were found in Burnley. The committee organized a public meeting in Burnley and a contingent from GLF attended. The result was a dramatic example of coming out. When a member of GLF asked the gay people there to stand up, over half the audience did so. The impact was muted on the town, which never saw an 'Esquire Club' (nor, indeed, did anywhere else); but this type of public solidarity was vital in building up a new homosexual consciousness.[6]

Under this sort of encouragement, the committee made a radical change in its structure. In a new constitution adopted in the spring of 1971, it changed its name to the *Campaign* for Homosexual Equality (though the identifying initials CHE of course remained the same) and vested constitutional power in the membership rather than, as previously, in the executive committee. It also took up new office premises in Manchester and employed its first full-time general secretary, Paul Temperton, a former market researcher in his early twenties. But there was an acute schizophrenia built into the campaign organization from the start. At the same time as it formally became a grass-roots organization, so it expanded its list of honorary vice-presidents to include even more respectable, weight-carrying names. An investigation into the 'structure' of the London CHE in 1971 by an inevitable 'working party' produced a document enticingly called 'People not Paper'. This, however, in place of the democratization hinted at, proposed a new structure with a chairman 'from the highest possible echelons of society' to inspire the whole organization and *three* deputy chairmen (for an organization of less than 500).[7] The Campaign for Homosexual Equality became notoriously concerned with 'structure', revising its constitution in 1971 and 1974, with new proposals in 1976, and displayed a constant preoccupation with *how* to do things rather than *what* to do. Panaceas came and went. In 1972 the national CHE flirted with a 'Policy, Programme, Budgeting System' (PPBS for short) which was to be applied to the objectives of CHE. The *CHE Bulletin* proudly boasted that it had been used by the Department of Education and Science and the Milton Keynes new city corporation. It was never heard of again.[8]

Even its apparently uncontroversial adherence to law reform and the building up of social facilities had its problems. The advancement of further changes in the law was always a central plank, and in July 1975, after much cogitation, a draft Bill sponsored by the CHE, SMG and USFI was launched. This proposed that the age of consent be reduced to sixteen; that the new law should apply to Scotland and Northern Ireland; that homosexual acts between members of the armed services should be legalized; that 'privacy' and 'consent' be more sensibly defined; that the offence of 'gross indecency' should be abolished; that a new importuning offence be introduced for heterosexuals; and that homosexual magazines should have the same freedom to publish as heterosexual ones. Obviously sensible as this was, it *was* chiefly a campaign for gay men. The CHE claimed to be an organization for women and men, and, indeed, in the period after the launching of the draft Bill, the chairperson was a woman, Glenys Parry. But to put an undue emphasis on legal reform unnecessarily unbalanced the energies of the organization. It demanded certain lobbying abilities that were at odds with CHE's other ambitions. The carrot dangled before the CHE lobbyists by 'sympathetic' Members of Parliament was to play for minor legislative modifications as a first step, but it was essential for the unity and enthusiasm of CHE that it should have a coherent and wide-ranging campaign. This was particularly so after the second annual conference, held at Malvern in May 1974, which signalled a formal coalescence between the separate strands represented by GLF and CHE, and CHE's formal commitment to a policy of militant reformism. As *Gay News* put it at the time, the theme of Malvern was 'Don't ask – demand!' And euphoric veteran gay liberationists were heard to say that it was just like 'the old days of GLF'.

Certainly, the conference was a key event in concentrating ambitions and hopes: out of it came not only the new enthusiasm for legal reform, but plans for an international conference in Edinburgh; a new and urgent recognition of the need to recruit gay women; and, inevitably, a lengthy debate on the organization's 'future structure'. When the delegates sang a final 'We shall overcome', many felt that at last a *national* campaign had got off the ground. A year later, at the annual conference in Sheffield, the enthusiasm was still there; the meeting was bigger still (with over 1,000 delegates) and the social scene better than ever, but little seemed to have been achieved. And by the 1976 conference a definite sense of deadlock was in the air.[9] Somewhere there was a layer of genuine activists, anxious to *do* things to change attitudes. But initiatives like the CHE Activists Register, launched in 1973, almost immediately disappeared without trace, swamped in the inertia of the mass of the membership. When genuine emergencies cropped up, as in 1976 when several people were sacked from their jobs because of their open homosexuality, CHE seemed incapable of reacting with any agility.

The abilities needed to draft excellent model Bills were not the same as those needed for rapid support action. And CHE seemed unable to retain the engaged involvement of a sufficient number of politically committed individuals. The uncertainty of grasp of the elected leadership was reflected in the rapid turnover of membership of the executive committee and the brief tenures of the appointed general secretaries. Howarth Penny was appointed general secretary in October 1973 amid a great fanfare; he was forced to resign in December 1974 after disagreements over his function and the role of the national office. The new general secretary, Alan Clarke, appointed in February 1975, was sacked in April 1976 after similar problems. There was a conflict between the need for orderly administration and active campaigning, between publicity-seeking and respectability.

These problems were compounded by the social bias at the base of

CHE. Most people joined CHE, after all, because they were lonely or isolated, because they wanted to meet people and build up relationships. CHE encouraged this by its recruitment literature – CHE is 'the biggest gay club in the country' – and the existence of a national organization inevitably made it a focus for interest and inquiries. In the 1975 report members were warned that eventually the CHE office might have 15,000 incoming letters and 12,000 telephone calls.[10] But there was a constant complaint from the more activist members that CHE was too social. The campaign became increasingly adept at organizing social functions. Some were disasters, such as the CHE travel service ('Join the CHET-set'). Others brought together gay people around common interests. Most successful of all were the discothèques and dances that CHE began to organize, in London and elsewhere. Many people were prepared to lavish energies on organizing these; less on more militantly reformist actions.

Inevitably the stress on social activities increased the difficulties of women in the organization. Gay men wanted to meet other men; lesbians other women. In the predominantly male atmosphere of CHE, women often felt deeply alienated, especially as there was little grasp of the specific needs of lesbians. The lesbian magazine *Sappho* called the Sheffield conference 'an example of the oppression of lesbians within the gay movement'. There was no crèche, no organizational provision for a women's caucus, little interest in women's motions.[11] After the Malvern and Sheffield annual conferences, where anti-sexist talk was much to the fore, there was a token integration of women into the top structures of CHE. Five women sat on the executive council in 1975–6. But by the end of 1976 only one remained: the rest had left through alienation, boredom, exhaustion or political disagreement. Beyond this was the question which was rarely posed, let alone confronted by CHE: of what, in the short term, the men and women had in common in a single organization like the campaign.

If CHE aimed to be an umbrella organization, then there was obvious room for a variety of groups, male and female, social and political, cultural and activist, beneath its generous shade. But if it was a unitary organization, as it claimed to be, then it had to forge aims that united and involved its membership. The campaign attempted this – with its sex-education campaign, its youth activities, its (usually belated) support of particular cases, its slowly developing trade-union activities. All of these were essential, but by their nature they were low-key, specialized campaigns, and not often successfully executed. The only campaign that promised to arouse national attention was over law reform – and that was of little direct interest to women. At the 1976 annual conference in Southanpton, out of some seven hundred people present, fewer than fifty were women.

That many activist women were prepared to involve themselves in CHE at all is an indication of the paucity of lesbian alternatives. For many committed lesbians, the Women's Liberation movement offered a counter-pole of attraction to the gay movement, especially as some women's groups moved towards a separatist position which rejected any cooperation with men. This became the position of the London Women's Liberation Workshop which for a period refused even to answer phone-calls from men. For many previously heterosexual women in the movement, lesbianism became a valid politicosexual identity. 'What is a lesbian? A lesbian is the rage of all women condensed to the point of explosion.' Nevertheless there remained ambiguities in the attitude of many in the Women's Liberation movement, and its existence did not remove the need for autonomous lesbian organizations, both for supportive activity and political discussion.[12] The largest grouping of lesbians was around the magazine *Sappho*. The magazine itself, founded in early 1972, after the demise of *Arena Three*, was a grass-roots production, designed more to keep its subscribers in touch with each other's preoccupations than to advance political perspectives. It published poems, short stories and articles on the gay movement as well as letters, and by November 1976 it had a mailing-list of about seven hundred, including some people and organizations abroad. Its dominating force was Jackie Forster, a dynamic speaker with a distinct populist tendency, and *Sappho* became the focus for regular weekly meetings of lesbians, usually at the Chepstow pub in Notting Hill Gate, where there would often be a guest speaker and discussion; and frequent discos. *Sappho* lacked the political dynamic that had brought many women together in the early GLF, but it performed a key function in keeping many isolated lesbians in touch.

But apart from this no consistent national focus existed for lesbian organization. There was, however, a great deal of more specialized activity in various groups. One of the most energetic was the Action for Lesbian Parents group which campaigned in 1976 on the issue of custody of children, and which engaged the support of the ardently feminist MP Maureen Colquhoun.[13] More directly political was the Lesbian Left group which held regular meetings from 1976, and was composed of various revolutionary left tendencies, and the 'Wages due Lesbian' campaign which had grown out of the 'Wages for Housework' campaign. The Third National Lesbian Conference in Bristol (28–9 February 1976) underlined many of the possibilities, and also the acute contradictions in lesbian self-activity. Over five hundred women attended the conference, and on the Saturday they had marched to the Queen Victoria Statue on College Green to say 'We exist'. Workshops were held on coming out, lesbian wives and mothers, abortion, bisexuality, orgasm, wages for housewives and lesbian publications. But when it came to strategy, there were deep differences. Should lesbians, for instance, support abortion? Should they support the 'Wages for Housework' campaign? Were all women potentially lesbian, or were lesbians only a fixed minority? Significantly, although a general feeling of sisterhood was reported as prevailing throughout the weekend, only on the Sunday was any practical unity forged, on the specific question of how to respond to attacks on women by men such as had taken place at a disco the previous evening. The most potent maker of unity in action was external oppression, and this was as true for women as for gay men.[14]

While the national gay organizations seemed to lack a coherent direction, bumping and grinding along winding tracks like old steam trains, the smaller organizations, with specific, variously defined tasks, were more successful, and from 1972 there was a blossoming of these. Some were sponsored by the Campaign for Homosexual Equality, such as the August Trust, founded in August 1974 by a small group of homosexuals who felt there was an urgent need to provide congenial accommodation for elderly gays. By August 1976 the trust had collected £1,000 in donations, but had been refused official charity status, and its future was problematical.[15]

Broader in scale, but reflecting a similar desire to help the isolated or unhappy homosexual, was Friend, which grew up as CHE's counselling arm. Founded in April 1971 as 'Task Force', this was relaunched as Friend ('Fellowship for the Relief of the Isolated and Emotionally in Need and Distress') at the end of 1971. It became a national counselling and 'befriending' organization for people with problems related to their sexual orientation, but was also a community-orientated organization rather than the cadre of trained and 'professional' counsellors that the Albany Trust had traditionally favoured. Friend was given a firm foundation in 1975 when the London Borough of Islington and the Home Office jointly awarded it £40,000 under the Urban Aid Grant scheme. This enabled it to secure permanent premises in London and to extend its work nationally.[16]

A number of other counselling services developed in the mid 1970s, some of them intended as money-spinners, others as politico-religious bodies (the Festival of Light set up its own organization to help benighted homosexuals to find Jesus). But the most radical community-based support organization was London Icebreakers, a telephone service for isolated homosexuals set up in spring 1973. Icebreakers had its roots in the old Counter-Psychiatry Group of the London GLF, and from that tradition came the perception that it was not homosexuality that was the problem, but society's attitude towards it.

Icebreakers began with the principle that what most isolated, unhappy or even desperate homosexuals wanted was not 'expert advice', but the simple affirmation of their identity and sexual orientation. Icebreakers made a point of telling their callers that they were themselves homosexual, and that this was a source of pride, not shame. The phone number (01-274 9590, 7.30–10.30 p.m. every night of the year), was widely advertised through stickers, advertisements in the gay and alternative press, and an occasional article in the orthodox press, and there was an immediate response. Icebreakers received some 4,000 to 5,000 calls a year, about one in six of which were from women. One in ten of the callers was married; one in twenty calls were from transvestites, while a small number was transsexual. The callers covered the gamut of sexual tastes, class position and age range (from eleven to seventy). 'Problems' varied from loneliness to difficulties of youth and age, of relationships and of being married and gay, of being religious and gay. What most callers had in common was a sense of isolation – either physical or in their inability to speak of their problems to family or friends. An ongoing contact with Icebreakers provided a lifeline out of this loneliness.

To complement the telephone service and provide a more personal forum than the telephone could offer, a regular Sunday-afternoon social gathering for men and women was begun, and this proved enormously successful, with sometimes thirty or forty people coming to the homes of individual Icebreakers. Later a similar fortnightly meeting especially for lesbians was started. At these meetings callers could discuss their particular problems, find they were not so particular and began to build up personal links of friendship and support. Icebreakers as an organization kept itself deliberately small (with a collective of about thirty people) since it was anxious to remain both democratic and community-based.

Despite its straightforward approach, Icebreakers aroused a great deal of controversy, especially in its rejection of the role of specialist counsellors. The Albany Trust in particular (which was devoting a large part of its Urban Aid Grant of £30,000 to training counsellors) was outraged, and sharply attacked Icebreakers for being 'silly' in its attitude to experts.[17] But at stake there was a whole philosophy of homosexual politics. The Albany Trust remained wedded to a position of what it called 'supportive neutrality' in its attitudes to homosexuals, whereas the gay liberation organizations were increasingly committed to *positive* espousal of gayness.

Organizations such as Friend and Icebreakers were based on certain assumptions about the existence or possibility of a gay community growing up within the confines of the dominant culture. Icebreakers in theory went beyond that, in stating clearly its adherence to a wider political position, that gay liberation proper could only come with the breakdown of rigid gender division and the transition to a new society. But, in practice, it had no alternative except to continue to induct individuals into a community within existing society. The most characteristic achievement of the gay-liberation movement from 1972 was the astonishing expansion of this community. Gay groups sprang up in an amazing range of places. By 1976 all the major political parties had gay groups within them, acting both as support groups and as focuses for political pressure for reform. The Liberal Party led the way on this in the early 1970s, and in 1976 was poised to begin an education campaign on homosexuality in its ranks when the enforced resignation of Jeremy Thorpe, after months of rumours associating him with a homosexual relationship (which was denied), made the moment seem inopportune.

The Labour Movement bred the Gay Labour Group in 1975, which did some helpful propaganda work, but reflected in its tidily bureaucratic organization and concern for procedure the less enticing traits of its party. A small group of Conservatives followed suit in 1976, inspired by Ian Harvey. By 1976 the Communist Party and the smaller revolutionary groupuscules to its left were also beginning to explore the causes of homosexual oppression, and recognized gay groups within them. A number of gay groups were established, too, in trade unions, mainly white-collar unions in the public sector, and these promised to be important focuses for future agitation in the field of job discrimination and in taking gay liberation debates into the labour movement. Gay groups also sprang up among several professional groups – 'gay teachers', 'gay social workers', 'gay medics and dentists.' In universities and colleges, too, it became a little easier and more pleasurable to be openly gay after the National Union of Students adopted a gay rights position and sponsored a number of 'Gaysocs' throughout the country. And in the theatre, a professional small gay theatre troupe, 'Gay Sweatshop', was set up in 1975. It had a successful lunch-time theatre season in London's West End, and then toured Britain with its own plays, particularly the coming-out plays *Mr X* and *Indiscreet*. Gay Sweatshop, and the Bradford-centred 'General Will' troupe, were able to take fairly basic gay liberation positions (of coming out, solidarity and support) into various largely gay gatherings, and to encourage the new type of gay consciousness.

The most recalcitrant areas were inevitably the religious, but even here there was some permeation. A Jewish gay group organized a conference in London in 1972 on the position of Jewish homosexuals and held regular support meetings.[18] There was predictably little give from the Jewish authorities. Christian denominations proved a little more flexible. The Quakers, as ever, proved more liberal as an organization, and with David Blamires's *Homosexuality from the Inside* published a sensible essay influenced by gay liberation ideas. The Church of England set up a working party in 1975 to explore further its attitude. In terms of gay self-organization, the impact of gay liberation was less than in the United States where the Rev. Troy Perry, author of *The Lord is my Shepherd and He knows I'm Gay* (1972), became a media personality in the wake of his establishment of gay Metropolitan Community Churches. In London, an affiliate, the Fellowship of Christ the Liberator, was set up, with its own church (in Earls Court) and a similar brand of sentimental piety. Other, more broadly based Christian gay groups – Quest, Open Church, Reach – sprang up, with varying emphases; and in the spring of 1976 an ecumenical, Gay Christian Movement was launched with a more 'radical' and 'democratic' approach. Within six months this achieved a membership of some two hundred and a mailing list of over six hundred, including a number of church dignitaries. The aim of all these organizations was obviously to demonstrate that homosexuality was not incompatible with central Christian teachings, but this commitment came into sharp conflict with nearly 2,000 years of Christian prejudice, and there was an uphill struggle. An anonymous contributor to *Crockford's Clerical Directory* in 1976 denounced, in uncompromisingly old fashioned terms, the flaunting of homosexual behaviour, and this was patently still the majority opinion.[19]

The spread of the gay community was not, obviously, without its considerable hazards, but none of the old barriers seemed to be any longer entirely insurmountable. Not only did the homosexual world expand, but access to it was immensely eased. John Stanford's *Spartacus Gay Guide* had a host of imitators, while the establishment of Gay Switchboards in London and elsewhere to provide instant information over the telephone was an immense success. The London Gay Switchboard, founded early in 1974 in the old GLF office in Caledonian Road, received over 20,000 calls (most for information about gay meetings and places, but sometimes for legal help, sometimes for support) in the first year. By 1975 some sixty volunteers manned the switchboard twenty-four hours a day, and received some thousand calls a week.[20]

But perhaps the most dramatic expression of the expansion of the gay community after 1972 was the appearance of a new gay press. Magazines with a specialized sexual flavour (usually carrying pictures of naked boys) had long been a feature of the sub-culture, but the early magazines that tried to go public – such as *Jeremy* and *Spartacus* – were premature. The potential audience was there, but it could not easily be tapped. The impact of gay liberation was to make that audience more visible, and to ease the channels of communication. GLF's magazine *Come Together* was an early attempt to express the new aspirations of the gay community, but it never properly found a tone which could express its ambitions. Beginning as a duplicated four pages, it eventually became a decently designed paper and ran to sixteen irregular issues. But the mood and content changed from issue to issue, as different people with changing ideas put their hands to the task. The Campaign for Homosexual Equality set up a magazine working party in 1971, and this eventually produced a magazine, *Lunch*, which made a fairly regular appearance until 1974. Lacking GLF's radicalism of tone, it was too eclectic to attract many people outside CHE (or even, indeed, inside), but following a drab start it carried a number of useful articles.

After 1972, these early experiments produced three different types of paper. The first were the specialized gay liberation papers, either reflecting political leanings or local interests (Birmingham GLF's *Glad Rag*, Bradford GLF's *Graft*, or various CHE newsletters, culminating in its own paper, *Out*). *Gay Marxist*, a movable feast of a journal which appeared in five issues (1972–4), was the best of the early political papers, but in its excessive eclecticism – produced by a different collective each issue, and carrying articles that were not only non-Marxist but anti-socialist and even semi-reactionary – it underlined the complexities of the positions it was trying to develop. *Gay Left*, which appeared from 1975, cautiously attempted a more coherent approach, and built up a steady circulation.

The second type of paper was the frankly pin-up type: *Jeffrey*, *Line-up*, *Quorum*, *Man to Man*, *Play Guy*, *Q International* and many others, most of which were expensive and full of glossy pictures of non-erectile men, with articles, stories, comments, advice and letters in the spaces between. Despite high cover costs, and the big potential market, few of these achieved any lasting success. Most disappeared after a year or two, but this did not stop new ones springing up immediately in their wakes.

More successful were the attempts to establish gay *news*papers, and *Gay News*, founded in 1972, was here the pathmaker and market leader. Its evolution is the most striking illustration of the type of gay community that was emerging. *Gay News* was first mooted towards the end of 1971 by a mixed collective from GLF and CHE. The aim, as the editorial collective stated it, was to go beyond the sectarianism of earlier publications and appeal to the 'whole of the gay community'. By June 1972 it was ready to launch itself as a regular fortnightly paper. In the early days it was clearly one of the heirs to the ambivalent GLF heritage, stressing its collective nature and communal approach: 'We talk, and always will be doing, about the Gay News collective . . . No one person is in a position of greater authority than any other.'[21]

Where *Gay News* differed from the more radical GLF tendencies, was in its conception of the community that should be approached. The paper had no ambitions to transform the homosexual consciousness in any way, but rather sought to tap the consciousness that existed. Its approach was essentially populist: a form of consciousness whose essential feature is not so much to transform as to *reflect* opinions as they are perceived by the populist. In the early days with a fairly small circulation, *Gay News* spasmodically indulged in more or less daring stunts. The first issues carried as a regular feature photographs of 'Hets of the Month', usually media people of dubious sexuality. Issue No. 8, reporting on the Longford Pornography Commission, had a mocked-up picture of Longford and the religious pop singer, Cliff Richard, nakedly inter-twined, with organs showing. In Issue No. 14, the most controversial of all, the front page featured two naked young boys, and produced an outcry.

In the early days the paper was not only for the gay movement but *of* that community, reflecting in its articles and tone the movement's myriad contradictions. This was partly necessity. At first the paper could not afford a professional distributor, and most of the big newsagents, such as W. H. Smith's, refused to stock it. Distribution was, therefore, as the paper regularly put it, by 'us, you and a prayer book', and it had a string of street and pub sellers who felt part of the enterprise. *Gay News* was also largely written by the collective (none of whom were at first professionals), and by the readers, and sometimes it had an endearingly amateurish quality. By the end of the first year, however, the complexion of the paper was subtly changing. A number of professional journalists began to join or write for it. The result was, perhaps, not better articles but a better surface gloss. The collective editorial structure broke down, and within the year Denis Lemon, the strongest personality, emerged as sole editor, with a conventional staff, 'features editor', 'news editor', 'art director' and so on, beneath him. And, perhaps most significantly, by the end of the year *Gay News* ceased to appeal to its readers for funds. Having discovered its community, it could begin to survive independently within it.

The success of its contact advertisenemts – 'Love knoweth no Laws' – illustrates a major reason for its taking off. *Gay News* was born in the wake of the House of Lords ruling in the *IT* case, which upheld the conviction precisely on the grounds of publishing contact ads. It was a nervous editorial collective that brought out the first issues. In fact *Gay News* did have some early brushes with the law. Lemon was arrested at one point for 'obstruction' while taking photographs of police harassment around the Earls Court gay bars; and several times *Gay News* was among papers seized in obscene publications raids. But it was never seized for its contact ads, partly because the paper was careful to disclaim any sexual intent for them. Nevertheless, the advertisements provided an easy entry for people all over the country into some sort of homosexual community. For the isolated subscriber, the plain brown envelope every fortnight might be a lifeline; for the more 'out' gay, the paper was a vehicle of communication with the multitude of activities going on in the gay world. As Roger Baker put it: '*Gay News* is the best thing that has happened for the gay world in this country.'[22]

Most readers believed this to be true, and this gave the paper its *raison d'être* and élan. *Gay News* provided some of the uplift of the parish magazine or local community paper, finding an ingenious gay line on a multitude of topics.

Within four years *Gay News* had evolved into a major bulwark of the gay community. With a circulation of over 20,000 ('The world's largest circulation newspaper for homosexuals'), thirty-six pages full of news, comment, letters and features, three regular pages of contact ads, and its own regular, four-page, densely packed, gay guide supplement, it reflected admirably the way the gay scene had changed over the decade. It was no longer completely furtive and underground. It was open, variegated, multi-dimensional, pleasure orientated. Access need no longer be restricted to those with arcane knowledge;

entry was immediate, via the pages of *Gay News*, now on sale in numerous bookshops and newsagents, distributed by Moore Harness, sold at last by W. H. Smith's.

But papers such as *Gay News* did not just reflect passively an emerging gay community, they also helped to mould it. The most popular articles generally displayed a traditional gay magazine concern with cooking, show-biz, films, fashion, star-gazing and pop music. Inherent in these articles were certain assumptions about the type of audience both possible and necessary, affluent, upwardly mobile, sexually relaxed, but apolitical, non-party and male. *Gay News* made a point of carrying a 'Women's personal' contact column, and featured several able women writers, but its basic allegiance was to the male homosexual world, from which, overwhelmingly, came most of its readership. But *Gay News* was no longer just speaking to a community; it was speaking to, and helping to create, a market. This had been inherent in its development from the start. The first anniversary issue of *Gay News* made the necessary juxtapositions: 'Advertising was up, classified were toned down to the right level, and in all, *Gay News* was starting to shape into something well worth 10p.'[23]

By 1977 *Gay News* was plump with advertisements: films, books, cosmetics, services. It had helped create a new visibility for the gay world, and in so doing had helped to make it profitable to service the new, expanded, 'out' sub-culture.

Two complementary tendencies were clearly observable by the mid 1970s: first the gradual merging of the gay movement and the commercial homosexual sub-culture into a new, more open and diverse culture – the 'ghetto is coming out'; secondly, the gradual, conditional integration of homosexuality into the mainstream heterosexual culture. Neither was unproblematical and without contradictions, but they represented the central thrust of the ever-changing relationship of homosexuality to British bourgeois society.

America, as usual, was the pathmaker. David Fernbach summed up a developing sense of disillusion at the diminishing distance between the ideals of gay liberation and the reality of the new situation, as first revealed in the United States:

After four years of 'gay liberation', Gay Pride Week in Los Angeles nowadays involves a motorcade of decorated floats, each sponsored by a bar, baths, porn house or other 'gay community organization' . . . What has so far passed for Gay

Liberation, beneath its rhetoric, has almost always been simply
gay liberation, capitalist style.[24]

As the socialist journal, *Gay Left*, put it in 1976, 'increasingly the gay
world is moulded and defined explicitly by the values of capitalism'.
The situation was not straightforward. The 'benefits' of the changes
were unevenly spread, both geographically (London and other
large towns were obviously far in advance of the rest of the country)
and socially (where the male, middle-class or upwardly mobile
gay was likely to benefit more than the small-town working-class
man or woman). Women, even in the mid 1970s, had little opportunity
even to explore the ambiguities of the commercial gay sub-culture
outside London and a few other cities (and even there the lesbian sub-
culture was infinitely smaller than the male). Women and men
throughout the country still suffered agonies of loneliness and self-
doubt as they came to an expression of their homosexual needs,
often in complete, frightened isolation from families and friends. But
the barriers were now lower, access into the sub-culture was easier,
if not automatic. Provided there was no counter-revolution like the
one which happened in Germany in the 1930s, it seemed likely that
the walls would get lower still. But:

... the changes have occurred often at the expense of any genuine release from the pressures of a competitive, commercialised
and sexist scene. We have been offered an improved situation only
if we surrender to it completely. The gay subculture is riven with
clashes and illusions. The women tend to be split off from the
men, butch men from fem, leather queers from drag queens, and
so on. Many of these attitudes are themselves reflections of
heterosexual values; others of the pervasive cash nexus.
    In this gay world it is all too easy for people to lose their
individualities, sex becomes the aim of life; individuals become
things.[25]

There were obviously countervailing tendencies, in individual
lives, in small gay liberation groupings and in the growth of gay
social centres (as in various parts of London, Bradford, Manchester,
among other places) offering a non-commercial community centre
for meetings, social gatherings and entertainment. The latter were
always bedevilled by shortage of money, and usually wrecked by
political in-fighting, but they did demonstrate the persistence of an
alternative value system. But outside these, the closer integration of

the movement and the traditional scene indicated what was the most striking development of the 1970s: the massive growth of the homosexual sub-culture.

By definition a sub-culture survives *within* a dominant culture, and although there were overlaps, and indeed striking affinities, the homosexual sub-culture remained *separate*. For what is striking is not so much the breakdown of differences between heterosexuality and homosexuality as the confirmation of their separateness, while, simultaneously, their values began to overlap. Homosexuality was increasingly acceptable, but only so long as it did not cross certain unmarked frontiers. The vast majority of homosexuals indeed seemed reluctant to cross these frontiers themselves.

Two specific areas of gender or sexual expression illustrate this very clearly: first, the questions of transvestism and transsexuality; and secondly the issue of pedophilia, or adult sexual attraction to children. The first raised starkly the question of gender identity which is at the heart of any analysis of homosexual oppression. For, if gender identity is socially ascribed on the basis of cultural assumptions, and not inherent in individuals by nature of their biological appearance, then transvestites and transsexuals are obviously people on whom society has been unable to impose its conventional gender expectations. There is an obvious affinity in the causes of social hostility to both homosexuality and transvestism, and this was generally recognized in the early gay liberation movement. Political drag became for a while, as we have seen, a central mode of action. Sometimes it could lead (as it was designed to) to genuine identity confusions. Take the case of Rachel and Edith, two American transvestites. Rachel was genetically male, but emotionally and politically a transvestite. She called herself a lesbian. Her legal wife was Edith, genetically female. She also called herself a lesbian, because of her relationship with Rachel.[26] This was what one American paper called 'Gender fuck and its delights'.

Few transvestites and even fewer transsexuals had much of these delights – confronted as they were by public contempt and police harassment (usually for 'disturbing the peace'). Cross-dressing is often a peculiarly isolated mode of behaviour, and it was partly to assist isolated people that the Beaumont Society was founded in the 1960s. For a long while this cultivated a pipe-smoking respectable image, stressing vehemently that it had little to do with homosexuality. The gay liberation movement from 1970 seemed to have a stimulating effect even on this staid body, and membership increased somewhat. From the early 1970s there was also a transsexual organization in

Britain, a British cell of the American Transsexual Action Organization, but this seems to have been small. Essentially, there were four different layers of awareness: first, there were those who just liked cross-dressing occasionally (such as drag artistes); secondly, there was the privatized and often isolated transvestite or potential transsexual (represented, if at all, in the Beaumont Society); thirdly, there was a minority of politicized people, generally active on the fringes of the gay movement, some of whom might be genuinely transvestites, while others were political transvestites; but fourthly, there were those who felt the need to change their external gender appearance to accord with what they saw as their true identity. Ultimately, this became a medical question, putting decisions in a most radical way into the hands of an often unsympathetic profession. Here the isolation was most acute, and the possibilities of social pressure sharpest. Both within and without the gay movement, their positions were deeply ambiguous. (Women, for instance, were often deeply hostile to the elaborate dresses of male transvestites, feeling they were aping the most stereotyped features of femininity.) Partly to talk through such problems, a national TV/TS Conference was held in Leeds in March 1974, with the support of the Beaumont Society. Over a hundred people attended and there was, according to attenders, a valuable exchange of views, some attempt even being made to assess the political implications of cross-dressing.[27] But, perhaps inevitably, there was little interest demonstrated in the gay movement as a whole. It was too close to the caricature of the homosexual as a 'screaming queen' or 'diesel dyke'.

Even more controversial and divisive was the question of pedophilia. Although the most emotive of issues, it was one which centrally and radically raised the issue of the meaning and implications of sexuality. But it also had the disadvantage for the gay movement that it threatened to confirm the persistent stereotype of the male homosexual as a 'child molester'. As a result, the movement generally sought carefully to distance itself from the issue. Recognition of the centrality of childhood and the needs of children had been present in post-1968 radicalism, and had found its way into early GLF ideology. The GLF gave its usual generous support to the Schools Action Union, a militant organization of schoolchildren, backed the short-lived magazine *Children's Rights* in 1972, campaigned against the prosecutions of *Oz* (for the schoolchildren's issue) and the *Little Red Schoolbook*. But the latter, generally a harmless and useful manual for children, illustrated the difficulties of how to define sexual contact between adults and children in a non-emotive or moralistic way. In its section on this, the *Little Red School-book* stressed, rightly, that rape or violence were rare in such contacts, but fell into the stereotyped reaction by talking of 'child molesting' and 'dirty old men': 'they're just men who have nobody to sleep with'; and 'if you see or meet a man like this, don't panic, go and tell your teacher or your parents about it'.[28]

But the issue of childhood sexuality and of pedophile relationships posed massive problems both of sexual theory and of social practice. If an encounter between child and adult was consensual and mutually pleasurable, in what way could or should it be deemed harmful? This led on to questions of what constituted harm, what was consent, at what age could a child consent, at what age should a child be regarded as free from parental control, by what criteria should an adult sexually attracted to children be judged responsible? These were real questions which had to be faced if any rational approach was to emerge, but too often they were swept aside in a tide of revulsion.

A number of organizations in and around the gay movement made some effort to confront these after 1972 on various levels. Parents Enquiry, established in South London in 1972 by Rose Robertson, attempted to cope with some of the problems of young homosexuals, particularly in their relationships with their parents. Her suburban middle-class respectability gave her a special cachet, and with a series of helpers she was able to help many young people to adjust to their situation by giving advice, holding informal gather-ings, mediating with parents and the authorities.[29] More radical and controversial were two pedophile self-help organizations which appeared towards the end of 1974: PAL (originally standing for Pedophile Action for Liberation) and PIE (Pedophile Information Exchange). Their initial stimulus was the hostility they felt to be direc-ted at their sexual predilections within the gay movement itself, but they both intended to act as a self-help focus for heterosexual as well as homosexual pedophiles, giving mutual support to one another, exchanging views and ideas and encouraging research. The sort of gut reaction such moves could provoke was illustrated by a *Sunday People* 'exposé' of PAL, significantly in the Spring Bank Holiday issue in 1975. It was headed 'An Inquiry that will Shock every Mum and Dad', and then, in its boldest type, 'The Vilest Men in Britain'.[30] Despite the extreme hyperbole and efforts of the paper and of Members of Parliament, no criminal charges were brought, since no illegal deeds were proved. But it produced a scare reaction in parts of the gay movement, especially as CHE had been gratuitously dragged in by the newspaper.

Neither of the pedophile groups could say 'do it' as the early gay liberation movement had done, because of the legal situation. Their most hopeful path lay in public education and in encouraging debate about the sexual issues involved. PIE led the way in this regard, engaging in polemics in various gay and non-gay journals, conducting questionnaires among its membership (about two hundred strong) and submitting evidence to the Criminal Law Revision Committee, which was investigating sexual offences.[31] PIE's evidence, which advocated formal abolition of the age of consent while retaining non-criminal provisions to safeguard the interests of the child against violence, set the tone for its contribution. Although openly a grouping of men and women sexually attracted to children (and thus always under the threat of police investigation), the delicacy of its position dictated that its method was the classical liberal one of investigation and public debate. Significantly, the axes of the social taboo had shifted from homosexuality to conceptually disparate forms of sexual variation. For most homosexuals this was a massive relief, and little enthusiasm was demonstrated for new crusades on wider issues of sexuality.

The social climate in the wider world was itself ambivalent and contradictory. An opinion survey conducted for *Gay News* in 1975 (and published in *Gay News*, Nos. 83–5) revealed apparently a more tolerant attitude than had prevailed in the 1960s. With regard to law reform most respondents felt that the post-1967 situation was just right. Few wanted to make male homosexuality illegal again; but few also wanted to make the law more liberal. Some 40 per cent (of the random sample of 1,930 adults) felt that homosexuals should be able to live together openly, but 53 per cent were opposed to gay marriages. And 45 per cent believed that there should be a partial ban on the employment of homosexuals in certain professions: especially medicine and teaching. Stereotypes of homosexual behaviour persisted. Most people still assumed an affinity between homosexuality and 'effeminacy' in males, though, partly because of the revolution in women's clothing, there was less emphasis on the 'masculine' appearance of lesbians. But lesbianism itself was still scarcely recognized in comparison with male homosexuality. Homosexuality was still seen as a largely male, middle- or upper-class phenomenon, and there was a widespread ignorance of bisexuality and transvestism.

The media reflected many of these contradictory attitudes. The *Sunday Mirror*, successor of that *Sunday Pictorial* which had blazed a not particularly enlightened trail in the 1950s, heralded 'The Gay

Explosion' in a special feature article (27 March 1977) and spoke of 'this astonishing revolution'. Its two-page spread looked at a gay clergyman, Roland Jeffrey, Secretary of Friend (though it failed to provide the organization's address or telephone number), and the comedian Graham Chapman, and gave a generally favourable and positive, if vague, picture of what was changing. Unfortunately it totally ignored lesbianism, thus compounding the image of homosexuality as a largely male phenomenon. The *Sunday Mirror*, as a mass-circulation paper, in fact lagged behind the 'quality' press in recognizing the presence of the gay movement. Papers like the *Guardian*, and even the arch-Conservative *Daily Telegraph*, had for some time been using the word 'gay' in headlines, sometimes even without the quotation marks (though the *Guardian* gagged at pedophilia, and the *Daily Telegraph* hinted that a tightening of the 1967 Act might not be a bad thing).

It was in the literary and show-business world that homosexuality became most tolerated. Writers such as Robin Maugham and Angus Wilson came out. Pop stars like Elton John declared their 'bisexuality'. Yet an ambivalence remained. Several feature films portrayed homosexuality more or less positively, though the audience's gasp when Peter Finch kissed his male lover in John Schlesinger's film *Sunday, Bloody Sunday* was audible. The BBC featured a male gay couple in its serial, *The Crezz*, in late 1976, but almost inevitably the characters were highly stereotyped, and the episode in which they featured was called 'Bent Doubles'. The BBC had shown even less bravado with regard to Quentin Crisp's memoir, *The Naked Civil Servant*, and turned down the rights. Thames Television instead made a widely acclaimed and prize-winning television film, which encouraged a wide discussion (and made Crisp into a media star in his own right). Audiences still gave hoots of laughter to limp-wristed caricatures; Kenneth Tynan still preferred to call homosexuals 'queer'; attempts to make genuinely community-based feature films (such as the long-planned *Night Hawks*) limped along because of lack of money; and television and radio refused to rush *too* far ahead of public opinion. An edition of the radio programme *So You Think You've Got Problems* which positively discussed lesbianism was arbitrarily banned by the controller of Radio 4 early in 1977. Christopher Isherwood might get full media coverage when his autobiography was published (including the ultimate establishment accolade of a Foyle's Literary Luncheon), but the average life of homosexuals was covered only sporadically, if at all. Much had changed; much still remained to be done.

This was clearest with regard to the role of the state, through the law and police activity, which still articulated and held together the oppression of homosexuality. Police action varied enormously. In some areas 'liberal' chief constables made conciliatory noises towards local gay groups; in others, they seem to have strengthened their 'vice squads'. Traditional methods of police harassment, including futile raids on public lavatories, raids on baths and saunas (in one raid in Notting Hill, London, there were two coachloads of police for a tiny sauna; see *Gay News*, 112, 10–13 February 1977) and the use of *agents provocateurs* continued. In one cottaging case in Southampton (reported in *Gay News*, 106), the prosecuting counsel told the jury that: 'If you find the defendant innocent as charged you will in fact be saying that both the police officers invented their evidence to convict him.' The defendant was nevertheless found innocent.

Police activity was often dictated more by local pressures and a police reading of public opinion than by national policy. But at the level of the state there was little progress in the way of reform. When the Labour government introduced a measure to consolidate the law on sexual matters in Scotland in late 1976, it would have been a simple step to exclude the clauses relating to homosexual offences, but such an obvious and simple move to liberalize the law in Scotland was defeated, in an apparently uncaring House of Commons, by 37 votes to 27. During 1976 there was a considerable debate about the age of consent for male homosexuals. Not only the traditionally liberal National Council for Civil Liberties but also the staid Royal College of Psychologists favoured reducing the age to sixteen. But no immediate action followed. The government referred the whole matter of sexual law, including rape and homosexuality, to its Criminal Law Revision Committee (due to report in 1977). But however positive its reports may be, it is likely that it will be several years before any advocated changes are translated into law (it took ten years from Wolfenden to 1967).

During the early part of 1977 it in fact seemed probable that the most worrying legal threat to the position of homosexuals would come from another quarter. *Gay News*, 96, had published a poem by Professor James Kirkup on 'The Love that Dares to Speak its Name'. Mrs Mary Whitehouse launched a prosecution against *Gay News* because it 'unlawfully and wickedly published a blasphemous libel, namely an obscene poem and illustration vilifying Christ in his life and in his crucifixion'. It seemed that the long line of reformers since Ellis and Carpenter had laboured in vain when such medieval hangovers could so easily be trundled out again. The incident underlined the need for vigilance in safeguarding the advances that had been made, as well as foresight in planning the changes still to be undertaken. *Gay News* launched an appeal fund, and many elements in the gay movement rallied around to defend the paper, whatever they thought of its politics. *Gay News* was an important symbol of the changes that had taken place. Its defence was an essential part of homosexual politics.

The gay liberation movement had advanced the theory that homosexuals were an oppressed minority within capitalist society. The evolution of the movement as it moved into the late 1970s had been based on the assumption that this minority could, through its own activity, gradually be absorbed and integrated into society without too much disruption. Events seemed to prove this right up to a point. But there were, it now became apparent, deep pockets of resistance. Men were still imprisoned, humiliated and segregated for sex with other males under twenty-one; men and women still lost their jobs for being too openly gay; homosexuals still found it difficult to find and set up homes in partnership; homosexual parents still had to struggle to retain custody of their children.[32] In many parts of the country it was still difficult to be openly homosexual. There were continuing private and public reticences, a fear of being regarded as homosexual. Guilt, evasions, a sense of inadequacy and isolation persisted among many homosexuals; inevitably, for all had grown up into families which, by their very nature, seemed to invalidate their experience. There were still few traces of a real community where gay women and men could meet each other without stereotyping, competitiveness, sexism or age discrimination. There was a highly uneven integration of homosexuals into society. On the one hand, there were the achievements: the new, relative openness, the expanded and more lavish sub-culture; on the other, there was deeply ingrained sexism, fear of sexual freedom, religious and social norms antipathetic to homosexuality. Sexual mores were in a state of flux.

In this situation, gay people could no longer rely on others to change things for them. Whether the situation was to get worse, or better, the choice was now in their hands. And that suggested to many that what was needed was not a more conservative policy of accommodation but a more vigorous radical alternative.

# 18
## Old Ways, New Departures

*'Liberation' is an historical and not a mental act, and is brought about by historical conditions* – Karl Marx and Friedrich Engels, The German Ideology (*1846*)

The changes of the past twenty years have transformed the possibilities for living openly homosexual lives. But, as with all change, their impact has been contradictory.

The transformation of the situation of homosexuals has been a product of a wider change in capitalist social relations, and in particular the complex developments which have led to the progressive relaxation of the grip of the state on sexual morality. Western capitalism no longer demands that sexuality be harnessed solely to the reproduction of labour power, and a thousand exotic blossoms have flourished. Herbert Marcuse, a prophet of the counter-culture of the late 1960s, described this transformation as no more than 'repressive desublimation', the granting of token concessions in order to secure more surely the underlying loyalty of individuals to the *status quo*. But we cannot ignore the real gains that have been realized. In particular, it has been possible for homosexuals to take advantage of the new historical situation to begin to transform their own consciousness and the circumstances of their lives. The gay liberation movement has been one consequence of this, and contained within it has been a radical critique of the forms of sexuality, both past and contemporary.

The trouble is that no sooner did gay liberation arise than it seemed (as Marcuse forecast) to be quietly absorbed into the new values of consumer capitalism. In Britain by the mid 1970s there were only tendencies in this direction, but America appeared already to have reached this culmination. Gay pride week in San Francisco in 1976 witnessed a march, two miles long, of 90,000 people, but this was 'a celebration rather than a protest; a circus or Mardi Gras rather than a political rally'.[1] The oppositional force of the gay liberation movement apparently lost its power as it became clear that its minimal demands – for limited openness, better social facilities and small changes in the legal situation – if not already universally conceded were now historically possible. And, simultaneously, the greater openness of the homosexual world, and its obvious desire for more of the benefits of the consumer society, made it possible for commercial interests to begin to service the gay world, and with easy profit. The apotheosis of this in London was reached with the opening of the Bang discothèque in the West End, early in 1976. A big cavern of a place, used for straight discos the rest of the week, on Monday evenings it became a hugely successful and fashionable gay meeting-place: reasonably cheap for its gay clientele, and conveniently lucrative for its owners, the Rank Organization. On an infinitely more lavish scale than most traditional gay clubs could afford, it seemed to demonstrate that big could be better. It was not so much that homosexuals were being exploited. The really significant factor was that both homosexuals and the professional entertainment business had found a common linkage, their warm embrace being to mutual advantage.

But these developments make it more, rather than less, necessary to develop a radical critique of contemporary sexual mores. Sexuality had been set free, but everywhere it was in chains. There was a dim recognition of this even within the gay liberation movement itself, but most groupings were tied by an unbreakable umbilical cord to the *status quo*. A gay group that worked within the Conservative Party could hardly be surprised if it made little impact on a leadership committed to the defence of traditional morality and the family. Gay Christians could not be surprised if a millennium of tradition came between them and gay liberation. If you commit yourself to working within deeply traditionalist organizations, you should not be astonished at the meagreness of your achievements.

At the heart of most gay activism was an assumption that homosexuals were a separate, minority group, participating in the general value systems of the wider society but simultaneously struggling for the right to a separate if equal existence. Most concepts of homosexual oppression began (and ended) with this belief, and it dictated the sort of accommodation that inevitably resulted. But implicit in and necessary to gay liberation was a wider theory: that what oppressed homosexuals was not so much a dominant heterosexual majority as the supremacy of an exclusive heterosexual norm, enshrined in custom and ideology, perpetuated in the family, upheld by Church and state, which stunted everyone's (and particularly the majority's) sexual possibilities.

If this were true, then a much more radical approach was both desirable and necessary, for it suggested that a real 'liberation' – which would end not only sexual oppression, but also the commercial exploitation of sex – could not be achieved by an act of will here and now, but could only be realized in a long, and necessarily complex and revolutionary, process of social change.

Inevitably it was the socialist groupings within the gay liberation movement that appreciated this most clearly. It was striking that after the effective demise of GLF in 1972 there was a spontaneous springing up of small Marxist discussion groups in various parts of the country. In London, a Gay Marxist Study Group met from the autumn of 1972, exploring both the classical texts of Marxism (to develop a method) and the works of early socialists on sexual questions (Engels, Lenin, Kollontai). Three National Gay Marxist Conferences were held between 1973 and early 1974, and a discussion bulletin, *Gay Marxist*, provided an important forum. Unfortunately, beyond the formal linkage of the name, there was little theoretical or practical unity. Some wanted a gay Marxist movement to be launched, to rekindle the dying embers of GLF; others, particularly in the London Group, preferred a low-key approach, with the ultimate aim of involving the socialist groupuscules in a dialogue on the issue. The tendency finally collapsed in the spring of 1974.

*Gay Left*, the socialist journal launched in the autumn of 1975, developed from a small group of men who had earlier been involved in gay Marxist discussions.[2] Its aim, as it stated in its first collective statement, was to work towards a Marxist analysis of homosexual oppression, and to encourage an understanding of the links between the struggle against sexual oppression and the struggle for socialism. The journal found an enthusiastic if not uncritical response, and by its third issue had a print order of 3,000 copies, with a number of copies distributed in the United States, Canada and Australia. The issues raised by the journal, and the response, proved that there was an important layer, both in the gay movement and among feminists generally, which was prepared seriously to examine the problems of sexual liberation.

A number of individuals felt that the best way to raise the issues of sexuality on the left was by direct involvement in one or other of the self-defined revolutionary groups. The Communist Party in particular saw an accession of strength from various socialist feminists, some of whom had previously been active in the gay liberation movement. The groups to its left, especially the International Marxist Group and the International Socialists, held various internal discussions on the gay issue from the early 1970s, and in 1976 both the Communist Party and the International Socialists formally adopted positions supporting gay rights, while the International Marxist Group began an internal education process on sexism.[3] Even the

*Newsline*, newspaper of the ultra-sectarian Workers' Revolutionary Party, saw fit to send a reporter to the 1976 annual conference of the Campaign for Homosexual Equality. The gay liberation movement, like the women's movement, successfully posed a number of central issues – on the role of the family, on the nature of sexuality, on the role of personal relations – which any revolutionary group had to confront. By 1976, it was clear that the response offered by a self-declared revolutionary group to the challenges of the sexual liberation movements was a good yardstick by which to measure its openness and radical intent.

The sort of difficulties encountered can be seen in the history of the gay group in the International Socialists, which in 1977 became the Socialist Workers Party. Before the 1970s the only hint of any policy on homosexuality came in an article originally published in response to the Wolfenden Report by 'C. Dallas'. She wrote that, in a socialist society, 'homosexuality would disappear naturally. If nature then produced an abnormality, which it might do in a small number of cases, medical treatment would take good care of it.'[4] This was hardly encouraging for people influenced by gay liberation. In 1972, Don Milligan, an International Socialist as well as a member of the Lancaster GLF, convened a meeting of homosexuals in the International Socialists to attempt to put pressure on the leadership to open itself to the new ideas and forces. Over the next two years the group struggled on, refused official recognition, until most of its members left the organization in disgust or despair. A pamphlet by Milligan, *The Politics of Homosexuality*, was given scarcely any publicity in the organization's press, while the gay group (unlike the IS History Group, or IS Brass Band) was refused an official listing in the weekly paper, *Socialist Worker*, and had to make do with a classified advertisement under the anodyne heading of 'Gay Socialist Group'.

Three levels of argument were advanced. The first was the danger of putting off potential working-class support by seeming to embrace 'fringe elements'. Inevitably, this ignored the fact that there was by no means universal hostility towards homosexuality among working-class people, while, obviously, most gays were themselves working class. The second argument overlapped with this: the belief that gay liberation was essentially a *petit bourgeois* concern. Most of its early advocates were indeed middle class in status, education and income (if not origins). But so, of course, was most of the leadership of the left groups. And gay liberation was of central concern to working-class homosexuals, who had least opportunity of escaping stereotyping roles, least access to social facilities and were most subject to state harassment. The third argument was, in some ways, the most interesting of all: 'IS does not take a position on what you describe as "sexism", and also contrary to your opinion we have not found the issue to cause any concern among the working class members of IS.' This implied not only that an absence was conclusive (ignoring the vital connecting fact that a socialist consciousness was also absent), but that a revolutionary group had no responsibility for leadership.

By spring 1976, after a series of internal upheavals, a new policy of support was adopted, a gay group was finally recognized, and a small addition made to the International Socialists' statement of aims. But it had been a long struggle, and in the process a number of socialists had found their beliefs firmly challenged. This sort of stubborn reluctance to confront new social forces was symptomatic of a wider inability on the left to extend out of the small-group mentality. But it was to have grave consequences on the attitude of homosexual socialists. The gay liberation movement was, in any case, not predisposed towards socialist analyses, given the disastrous impact of the anti-homosexual measures of the USSR and many of its allies (especially Cuba) and the position in China (where homosexuality did not officially exist). The fact that Marxists could theoretically explain (not justify) these attitudes was vitiated by their own inability to confront the issues of homosexual freedom on their own ground.

A further consequence of the need to struggle even for basic rights within a socialist grouping was that the effort needed for this elementary task exhausted the possibilities of widening the debate. The result was that the positions of both the Communist Party and the International Socialists were essentially civil-rights positions: that is, support for basic democratic rights and for law reform. Yet there was no real debate on sexual divisions within capitalism and the arbitrariness of sexual norms. One of the most difficult and neglected areas of socialist theory precisely concerns the complex relationship between the personal and the political. Socialist theory is based on the assumption that the personality is moulded by social forces, but it has assumed rather than explored this belief. The result is that socialist orthodoxies have concentrated on the external factors and underplayed ways in which these have affected the more individual aspects. Within socialist orthodoxies until recently, as in bourgeois ideology as a whole, certain factors were taken as given – such as the 'natural' basis of the sexual drives, of motherhood, of masculinity and femininity. Under the impact of the women's and gay movements, these beliefs have been questioned but not fundamentally abandoned. The result was that, at best, a liberal, civil-rights approach inevitably filled the gap.[5]

The gay liberation movement on the other hand had stressed from the beginning that the 'personal' *was* 'political'. Its stress on consciousness-raising, and on 'new styles of living', had been an attempt to express this belief and to articulate a new approach to political change. The discussions in small groups of wide issues, such as sexism, as well as more personal questions, such as sexual hang-ups, could be personally valuable, and liberating, but their political significance was severely constrained: a thousand acorns do not make an oak tree. But the absence of any stress on the personal could be devastating. What many of the left groups ignored was that to be homosexual in a heterosexual society is to be divided, to have your consciousness torn and undermined. To be effective in any political grouping, a gay person needs not only a political commitment but also a belief that the personal is entirely compatible with the broader political outlook. A gay support group is the minimal necessary base.

What homosexuals lack above all is a natural community to which they feel they belong. Traditionally, given the atomistic nature of the homosexual sub-culture, this community had to be constructed bit by bit, atom by atom. The gay movement offered an alternative approach, creating the conditions for a better, more open and satisfying gay community. But as we have seen, it is itself riven by divisions – sexual, social, political and cultural – reflecting increasingly the divisions in the wider society. To build relationships is thus still a political act for homosexuals: to establish links and ties – on various levels – which transcend the yawning chasms between people. It is my belief that properly fulfilled lives will only be possible in a new type of society based on socialist principles. In the meantime, the politically committed homosexual has a difficult task. He or she must '. . . look two ways: to the movement itself, which is fragmented, generally civil-rights oriented, and often apolitical . . . and to the labour and socialist movements, which have, over the past fifty years or so, almost completely ignored sexual matters'.[6]

The only way to succeed is by combining an unremitting struggle for personal relationships with an active and open commitment as a homosexual to socialist ideals. It will not prove an easy task.

Part of the strength will come from the solidarity offered by the gay movement. As a gay liberation song put it:

All you gay women,
All you gay men,
Come together,
Stand together,
And each other's rights defend.[7]

But the days of a euphoric rally to arms is over, and it is more likely that the most creative work of gay liberation in the immediate future will come from a multiplicity of relatively small groups burrowing through their specialized concerns rather than from a massive new national initiative. A strong national organization is indeed necessary, both to press for minimal but essential changes (for example, in the law) and to act as a line of defence against potential attacks on the gains already registered. These became more, not less, likely as the 1970s staggered along their downhill path. But the various regional and local problems, the multiplicity of particular employment pr^n^iems, the specific problem of lesbians and gay men will most effectively be confronted in specialist groupings. A real homosexual solidarity is more likely to spring from dialogue, and a recognition of a common antipathy to sexism in the midst of political diversity, than from any crude attempt at organizational unity.

A number of trends already suggest that much can be achieved. Several local gay centres are attempting to base themselves in their communities, establish contacts with local residents and involve themselves in local labour-movement activities. Much can be done by raising issues of sexism and sexuality at the work place and in trade-union meetings. Important links can be, and have been, established by homosexuals working in local anti-fascist campaigns and participating in such working-class events as the 'Right to Work' campaign. These are small steps, but they are steps being taken by homosexuals, for themselves. In so doing they are helping to transform not only their own consciousness, but the awareness of those with whom they work.

It has been a long and painful evolution to develop the present homosexual identity. From the nineteenth-century struggle to articulate a self-consciousness in a hostile environment to the present large-scale movement has been a significant change. Homosexuals can now begin to see the further possibilities of transforming the social environment itself. This could be the most significant change of all.

# Bibliographical Sources

INTRODUCTION: My general approach has been influenced by the following: Mary McIntosh, 'The Homosexual Role', *Social Problems*, vol. 16, No. 2, Fall 1968; Kenneth Plummer, *Sexual Stigma*, London, 1975; J. H. Gagnon and William Simon, *Sexual Conduct: the Social Sources of Human Sexuality*, London, 1973. For details on medieval attitudes, see Arno Karlen, *Sexuality and Homosexuality*, London, 1971, and C. A. Tripp, *The Homosexual Matrix*, London, 1977. F. E. Frenkel, 'Sex Crime and its Socio-Historical Background', *Journal of the History of Ideas*, vol. xxv, No. 3, July–September 1964, discusses attitudes to lesbianism. Other relevant works include Wainwright Churchill, *Homosexual Behaviour Among Males*, Englewood Cliffs, N.J. 1967; C. S. Ford and F. A. Beach, *Patterns of Sexual Behaviour*, London, 1952 (paperback, 1975); and articles in H. M. Ruitenbeek, *The Problem of Homosexuality in Modern Society*, New York, 1963.

CHAPTER 1: The standard work on the law is still H. Montgomery Hyde, *The Other Love*, London, 1972, despite its conceptual weaknesses. Hyde has gone a long way to cornering the market on the nineteenth century. See also his *Trials of Oscar Wilde*, London, 1948; *Oscar Wilde*, London, 1976; *The Cleveland Street Scandal*, London, 1976. François Lafitte discusses the law in his article mentioned in the text (see Ch. 1, n. 1, p. 247). The chief academic work is Sir L. Radzinowitz, *A History of English Criminal Law*, vol. 4: *Grappling for Control*, London, 1968. Jeremy Bentham discusses homosexuality in *The Theory of Legislation* (London, 1931 edition, p. xxiii). A. N. Gilbert has described naval attitudes in 'The Africaine Court Martial', *Journal of Homosexuality*, vol. 1, No. 1, Fall 1974; and 'Buggery and the British Navy, 1700–1861', *Journal of Social History*, vol. 10, No. 1, Fall 1976. On this, see also Colin J. Williams and Martin S. Weinberg, *Homosexuals and the Military*, New York, 1971. For information on the Boulton and Park case, I am indebted to the so far unpublished work of Peter Wells. For attitudes in the 1880s, I used the pamphlets of the Social Purity Alliance and similar bodies, and the columns of *The Sentinel*. Hyde, in *The Cleveland Street Scandal*, discusses the passing of the Labouchère Amendment, but the best careful discussion is F. B. Smith, 'Labouchère's Amendment to the Criminal Law Amendment Bill', *Historical Studies* (University of Melbourne), vol. 17, No. 67, October 1976, which takes issue with Hyde on several points. I tend to agree with Smith's view of Labouchère. The central theme of Hyde's book is, of course, the 'scandal'; on this, see also Lewis Chester, David Leitch and Colin Simpson, *The Cleveland Street Affair*, London, 1977. For changes in other attitudes to sex and gender during the period, see Ann Oakley, *Housewife*, London, 1976, and *Oral History*, vol. 3, No. 2, 'Family History Issue'. Sources on international changes are detailed in the notes (e.g. Ch. 1, n. 10, p. 248).

CHAPTER 2: Karlen, in *Sexuality and Homosexuality*, gives much detail on medical attitudes. For details of attitudes to masturbation, see E. H. Hare, 'Masturbatory Insanity: The History of an Idea', *Journal of Mental Science*, vol. 108, No. 452, January 1962; and Robert H. MacDonald, 'The Frightful Consequences of Onanism: Notes on the History of a Delusion', *Journal of the History of Ideas*, vol. xxviii, No. 3, July–September 1967. V. L. Bullough and M. Voght discuss the implications of these attitudes on homosexuality in 'Homosexuality and its Confusion with the "Secret Sin" in Pre-Freudian America', *Journal of the History of Medicine*, vol. xxvii, No. 2, April 1973, though they overstate the case. Similar 'confusions' abound in the British social-purity and other literature directed at schoolboys and their parents. Thomas S. Szasz talks of masturbation and its consequence in *The Manufacture of Madness*, London, 1971. Vern L. Bullough has a useful essay on 'Homosexuality and the Medical Model' in *Journal of Homosexuality*, vol. 1, No. 1, Fall 1974. J. Bancroft, though himself a good symptom of the medical ideologues, also has some useful information in his *Deviant Sexual Behaviour*, Oxford, 1974, especially on Morison of Bedlam, on 'cures', on the British Medical Association's attitudes, and on public-opinion polls in the 1960s. Havelock Ellis in *Sexual Inversion* (see notes below on Ch. 4, p. 254) sums up the current views of the early twentieth century. For those hardy enough, there are always the medical treatises themselves. The successive editions of Krafft-Ebing's *Psychopathia Sexualis* are the most entertaining.

CHAPTER 3: Plummer, *Sexual Stigma*, offers the best guide to the literature on the formation and structure of homosexual sub-cultures. I have also been influenced by the essays in Stuart Hall and Tony Jefferson, *Resistance through Rituals: Youth Subcultures in Post-war Britain*, London, 1976. Karlen, *Sexuality and Homosexuality*, and Hyde, *The Other Love*, provide some useful information on the sub-culture, but wherever possible I have tried to use contemporary or near-contemporary sources. In particular, I found the following very illuminating: pamphlets such as *Yokel's Preceptor* and *Sins of the Cities of the Plains;* the unpublished Memoirs of J. A. Symonds; the private papers of Edward Carpenter; early twentieth-century books, such as Ellis's *Sexual Inversion*, 'Xavier Mayne's' *The Intersexes*, Florence, 1910, A. Flexner's *Prostitution in Europe*, New York, 1914. Various memoirs, novels and biographies are revealing of the class-bound and often guilt-ridden attitudes of upper middle-class men from the 1890s to the 1930s and beyond, including *The Autobiography of G. Lowes Dickinson and Other Unpublished Writings*, ed. by Dennis Proctor, London, 1973; J. R. Ackerley, *My Father and Myself*, London, 1968; Christopher Isherwood, *Christopher and His Kind, 1929–1939*, London, 1977; John Lehmann, *In the Purely Pagan Sense*, London, 1976; Brian Inglis, *Roger Casement*, London, 1973. Timothy d'Arch Smith, in *Love in Earnest*, London, 1970, discusses the homo-erotic literary milieu of the period 1890–1930. For a discussion of the homosexual argot, see Mary McIntosh, 'Gayspeak', *Lunch*, No. 16, January 1973; Plummer, *Sexual Stigma*; and Karlen, *Sexuality and Homosexuality*. The most comprehensive guide to the actual words is Bruce Rodgers, *The Queen's Vernacular: A Gay Lexicon*, San Francisco, 1972; London, 1975.

CHAPTER 4: The standard work on Symonds is Phyllis Grosskurth, *John Addington Symonds*, London, 1964, which is the source for most of the biographical detail in this chapter. In most ways it is a very useful book, but is marred, like most in this tradition of biography, by the need to explain Symonds's homosexuality as a pathology. Hyde's biography of Oscar Wilde suffers from the same distorted problematic. The other major source is Symonds's manuscript Memoirs, which are held by the London Library and were closed for publication until 1976. I was fortunately allowed access, but not allowed to quote. Apart from this, the works where Symonds discusses homosexuality are *A Problem in Greek Ethics*, London, 1883; *A Problem in Modern Ethics*, London, 1891; *Walt Whitman: A Study*, London, 1893; and the first edition of *Sexual Inversion*, with Havelock Ellis. H. M. Schueller and R. L. Peters (eds.), *The Letters of John Addington Symonds*, 3 vols., Detroit, 1969, is a very revealing and important source.

CHAPTER 5: Sheila Rowbotham and Jeffrey Weeks, *Socialism and the New Life*, London, 1977, contains a longer essay, by myself, on Ellis as a sex reformer. There is an interesting essay on Ellis in Paul A. Robinson, *The Modernization of Sex*, London, 1976; and E. M. Brecher, in *The Sex Researchers*, London, 1971, also discusses Ellis. Ellis's autobiography, *My Life*, London, 1940, is very revealing. Phyllis Grosskurth is preparing the authorized biography. In the meantime we can make do with Arthur Calder-Marshall, *Havelock Ellis*, London, 1959. Of Ellis's own work, the most relevant to our purpose is *Sexual Inversion*, whose chequered history is described in the text (pp. 57ff.). The final version forms vol. 2 of *Studies in the Psychology of Sex*, I have used the 4-volume edition published in 1936. Ellis's *Psychology of Sex* (first published in 1933, and frequently reissued thereafter) is a useful summary of his ideas.

CHAPTER 6: The chief sources for this chapter have been the large collection of Carpenter papers and correspondence in Sheffield City Libraries, and Carpenter's own published works. Of these, the most relevant are his autobiography, *My Days and Dreams*, London, 1916; *Towards Democracy*, first published 1883; various revised editions; *Civilisation: Its Cause and Cure*, London, 1889; *Love's Coming of Age*, Manchester, 1896; *The Intermediate Sex*, London, 1908; and *Intermediate Types among Primitive Folk*, London, 1912. For an essay which extends some of the themes of this chapter, see 'Edward Carpenter, Prophet of the New Life', which forms Part 1 of Sheila Rowbotham and Jeffrey Weeks, *Socialism and the New Life*. A good summary of his career is Keith Nield, 'Edward Carpenter', in J. Bellamy and J. Saville, *Dictionary of Labour Biography*, vol. II, London, 1974, which also contains a bibliography. Gilbert Beith (ed.), *Edward Carpenter: In Appreciation*, London, 1931, has some interesting observations on Carpenter and his influence. For his influence on D. H. Lawrence, see E. Delavenay, *D. H. Lawrence and Edward Carpenter: a Study in Edwardian Transition*, London, 1971; and Jeffrey Meyers, 'D. H. Lawrence and Homosexuality', in Stephen Spender (ed.), *D. H. Lawrence: Novelist, Poet, Prophet*, London, 1973. Jeffrey Meyers, *Homosexuality and Literature 1890–1930*, London, 1977, has further observations.

CHAPTER 7: There is, unfortunately, still a dearth of sources on lesbianism. Contemporary medical or would-be scientific accounts are the most interesting. Havelock Ellis, in *Sexual Inversion*, summarizes many of these, despite the final inadequacy of his own book on the subject. Other volumes in his *Studies in the Psychology of Sex* are also very revealing for his attitude to female sexuality, as are his books *Man and Woman*, London, 1894; *Psychology of Sex*, London, 1933; and *The Task of Social Hygiene*, London, 1912. As I place attitudes to lesbianism firmly in the context of general attitudes to female sexuality, I found various works on this theme very valuable. I found very stimulating Jill Conway's 'Stereotypes of Femininity in a Theory of Sexual Evolution', in Martha Vicinus (ed.), *Suffer and Be Still*, Bloomington, Ind., 1972; and also the articles by Carl N. Degler and Carroll Smith-Rosenberg cited in the text notes (see p. 256). Helen Rugen provided me with a copy of her unpublished paper, 'Women on the Borderline of Pathology: Dominant concepts of female sexuality in health and illness, 1900–1920'. Specifically on lesbianism, the most helpful secondary sources are Jeanette H. Foster, *Sex Variant Women in Literature*, London, 1958; and Dolores Klaich, *Woman plus Woman: Attitudes towards Lesbianism*, New York, 1974. Karlen, as usual, has various references in *Sexuality and Homosexuality* which are helpful if used carefully.

CHAPTER 8: Most of the standard works on feminism and the early suffrage movement ignore lesbianism. Constance Rover, *Love, Morals and the Feminists*, London, 1970, discusses the prospect as if it were the worst imaginable slur; George Dangerfield, in *The Strange Death of Liberal England*, London, 1935, raises it to sneer at the feminists. Andrew Rosen, *Rise up Women!*, London, 1974, has some tangential comments on the social-purity element. F. W. Stella Browne was a feminist who *did* discuss the issue: see Sheila Rowbotham, *A New World for Women: Stella Browne, Socialist Feminist*, London, 1977. Stella Browne's pamphlet on *The Sexual Variety and Variability Among Women*, London, 1916, is revealing, as is her paper, 'Studies in Feminine Inversion', delivered to a meeting of the British Society for the Study of Sex Psychology, and reproduced in Jonathan Katz, *Gay American History*, New York, 1976. This latter book also reprints an article by Emma Goldman on 'The Unjust Treatment of Homosexuals'. The Goldman papers in the International Institute of Social History, Amsterdam, have several other references.

CHAPTER 9: H. Montgomery Hyde, *The Other Love*, has a detailed summary of the proposed legal changes after the First World War. On Edith Ellis there is little. Arthur Calder-Marshall's *Havelock Ellis* has relevant information, but Edith Ellis's own books are also important, especially *Three Modern Seers*, London, 1910, and *The New Horizon in Love and Life*, London, 1921. There is a biography of Vernon Lee: Peter Gunn, *Vernon Lee: Violet Paget, 1856–1935*, London, 1964; and I also used Vernon Lee's *Gospels of Anarchy*, London, 1908. Her private papers in this country are not available. More has been published on Radclyffe Hall and her circle. Vera Brittain, *Radclyffe Hall: A Case of Obscenity?*, London, 1968, deals with the actual trial quite well. Lovat Dickson, *Radclyffe Hall at the Well of Loneliness*, London, 1976, uses all the available papers and offers incidental insights. An indispensable source is, of course, Radclyffe Hall's *The Well of Loneliness* itself, in various editions. George Wicks, *The Amazon of Letters: The Life and Loves of Natalie Barney*, London, 1977, examines the career of a lesbian who much influenced Hall, and played a major part in the early twentieth-century articulation of a lesbian identity. Gayle Rubin's introduction to the reprint of Renée Vivian's *A Woman Appeared To Me*, New York, 1976, has a helpful overview of the Vivien–Barney milieu.

CHAPTER 10: Almost nothing has been written on this area. Hyde, *The Other Love*, does not even mention it; d'Arch Smith, in *Love in Earnest*, hints at but does not describe the existence of a secret homosexual reform grouping. I have relied on several unpublished collections of material: the Ashbee Journals in King's College, Cambridge; the Carpenter papers with Sheffield City Libraries; and the Ives archive with Mr Anthony Reid. The latter is the most revealing of all. The Diary, in particular, is a very valuable and hitherto unused source. Ives gives his views on Carpenter in Beith (ed.), *Edward Carpenter: In Appreciation*. Apart from the references in d'Arch Smith, there is no secondary source for Ives. Laurence Housman wrote an unrevealing autobiography, *The Unexpected Years*, London, 1931. D'Arch Smith's *Love in Earnest* is a useful source for the background to the literary outpouring. Anthony Reid has written a pamphlet on *Ralph Chubb, The Unknown*, The Private Library, 1970.

CHAPTER 11: For information on the German movement I have relied on the following: John Lauritsen and David Thorstad, *The Early Homosexual Rights Movement (1864–1935)*, New York, 1974; J. Steakly's articles in Toronto's *Body Politic*, Nos. 9, 10, 11, reprinted in book form in 1976; and an unpublished paper by Barry Davis, 'Sex and Social Change in Germany' (for which I am very grateful). Katz, in *Gay American History*, uses relevant documents, and his references reveal further links between the BSSP and American reform groupings; Havelock Ellis offered his views on Hirschfeld's work in 'The Institute of Sexual Science', *Medical Review of Reviews*, March 1920; Christopher Isherwood describes his personal reaction to the Institute in *Christopher and His Kind*. On the British reform organizations there is little in the way of secondary sources, but see Robert Wood, 'Sex Reform Movements', in A. Ellis and A. Abarbanel, *The Encyclopaedia of Sexual Behaviour*, vol. II, London, 1961. The pamphlets of the British Society for the Study of Sex Psychology are an invaluable source, as are the published books of members such as Ives and Norman Haire. Interesting comments on the BSSP appear in Cecil Reddie, *Edward Carpenter*, London, 1932; and Laurence Housman's article in Beith (ed.), *Edward Carpenter: In Appreciation*. For the British section of the World League for Sexual Reform, Dora Russell's comments in *The Tamarisk Tree*, London, 1975; paperback, 1977, are revealing. The Proceedings of the 1929 World Congress (ed. Norman Haire) illustrate the British contribution.

CHAPTER 12: A fuller discussion of the attitudes of the orthodox left can be found in Jeffrey Weeks, 'Where Engels Feared to Tread', *Gay Left*,

No. 1, Autumn 1975; and in Rosalind Delmar, 'Looking Again at Engels's "Origins of the Family, Private Property and the State",' in Juliet Mitchell and Ann Oakley (eds.), *The Rights and Wrongs of Women*, Harmondsworth, 1976. There are important insights in Eli Zaretsky, *Capitalism, the Family and Personal Life*, London, 1976. For the retreat in the USSR, and its impact on the communist movement, see E. Zaretsky; J. Lauritsen and D. Thorstad; Wilhelm Reich, *The Sexual Revolution*, New York, 1969; and Kate Millett, *Sexual Politics*, London, 1971. Sheila Rowbotham, *Hidden from History*, London, 1973, comments on the sexual conservatism of many of the early socialists. See also the Introduction to Rowbotham and Weeks, *Socialism and the New Life*.


CHAPTER 13: There is little on Haire and the Sex Education Society, apart from the article by Robert Wood, cited *supra*, 'Sex Reform Movements'. The chief source for this chapter has been the *Journal of Sex Education*, but I have also found valuable the comments of Dr Frank Forster, who is preparing a study of Haire.


CHAPTER 14: Elizabeth Wilson, *Women and the Welfare State*, London, 1977, is very good on the social climate of the 1950s. Also interesting is F. Pearce and A. Roberts, 'The Social Regulation of Sexual Behaviour and the Development of Industrial Capitalism', in R. Bailey and J. Young, *Contemporary Social Problems in Britain*, London, 1973. Hyde, *The Other Love*, and Peter Wildeblood, *Against the Law*, Harmondsworth, 1957, give details of the court trials of the period. Wildeblood's book is also an excellent impression of what it was like to be persecuted; see also his *A Way of Life*, London, 1956. Ian Harvey tells us what it was like *To Fall Like Lucifer*, London, 1974. Gordon Westwood's *Society and the Homosexual*, London, 1952, is a representative book for liberal opinion at the time; see also his *A Minority*, London, 1960. D. S. Bailey's *Christianity and the Western Christian Tradition*, London, 1954, is very interesting for both liberal church attitudes and illustrating the philosophical attitudes of the earliest reformers, especially in the careful (and ultimately pointless) distinction it makes between 'inversion', which is inborn and therefore has to be accepted (even though restraint should be exercised in its expression), and 'perversion', or wilful indulgence, which must be condemned. Frank Pearce's article in Stanley Cohen and Jock Young (eds.), *The Manufacture of News*, London, 1973, is very good on press attitudes. The Report of the Committee on Homosexual Offences and Prostitution ('Wolfenden Report'), Cmnd 247, HMSO, London, 1957, is, of course, the central document of the period. Sir John Wolfenden gives his views on it in 'Evolution of British Attitudes towards Homosexuality', *American Journal of Psychiatry*, vol. 125, December 1968; and in his memoirs, *Turning Points*, London, 1976.


CHAPTER 15: Antony Grey gives a description of his work for law reform in 'Homosexual Law Reform' in Brian Frost (ed.), *The Tactics of Pressure*, London, 1975; and there is an analysis of the campaign in Peter G. Richards, *Parliament and Conscience*, London, 1970. Christie Davies, *Permissive Britain*, London, 1975, has a chapter on 'Buggery and the Decline of the British Empire'. For the simultaneous campaign to reform the law on abortion, with which the pressure-group tactics of the Homosexual Law Reform Society had many similarities, see Victoria Greenwood and Jock Young, *Abortion on Demand*, London, 1976. Charlotte Wolff, *Love Between Women*, London, 1971; 2nd edition 1975, is useful for the development of lesbian groupings. On this, see also Diana Chapman's article on *Arena Three*, 'Mummy of Them All', in *Out*, No. 3, February–March 1977. For the campaigns during the 1960s and the workings of the Homosexual Law Reform Society, I used *Man and Society* and copies of *Spectrum*. An antique pleasure can also be obtained from exploring the columns of *Spartacus*, *TIMM* and *Jeremy*.

CHAPTER 16: There is little published so far on the British gay liberation movement. The best outline is David Fernbach, *The Rise and Fall of GLF*, LSE Gay Culture Society pamphlet, 1973. Parts of this were reproduced in *Lunch*, No. 22. Jack Babuscio distils some gay-liberation attitudes in *We Speak for Ourselves*, London, 1976. There are useful references to the British experience in Plummer, *Sexual Stigma*. The American movement, not surprisingly, is much better documented. See Dennis Altman, *Homosexual: Oppression and Liberation*, New York, 1971; London, 1973; Laud Humphreys, *Out of the Closets: The Sociology of Homosexual Liberation*, New Jersey, 1972; Karla Jay and Allen Young (eds.), *Out of the Closets: Voices of Gay Liberation*, New York, 1972; Len Richmond and Gary Noguera (eds.), *The Gay Liberation Book*, San Francisco, 1973; and Donna Teal, *The Gay Militants*, New York, 1971. For the American precursors, see Jonathan Katz, *Gay American History*. On the general political climate in Britain in the 1960s, the best book is David Widgery, *The Left in Britain*, Harmondsworth, 1975. However, the chief sources for this chapter have been twofold: my own memories of involvement in the movement since 1970; and the large collection of hand-outs, leaflets, pamphlets, magazines that I have collected. The spirit of the London GLF is captured in its ephemera, and in the hand-outs and newsletters of GLF offshoots, especially Camden GLF. See also the runs of *Come Together* and *Gay International News* (*GIN*), and, for the later stages, *Gay News*. There are also relevant articles in the underground press, especially *7 Days* and *Ink*. The most important GLF-orientated pamphlets are the *Manifesto*, 1971; *Psychiatry and the Homosexual*, Gay Liberation pamphlet No. 1, 1973; and Andrew Hodges and David Hutter, *With Downcast Gays*, London, 1974. For an experience of consciousness-raising in the women's movement, see Sue Bruley, *Women Awake*, London, 1976.

CHAPTER 17: This chapter is almost entirely based on the leaflets, hand-outs and magazines of the gay movement and the women's movement. Of particular use were *Gay News* (above all), the *Leeds Broadsheet*, *Lunch*, *Gay Marxist*, *Gay Left*, the *Newsletters* and *Bulletins* and other publications of the Campaign for Homosexual Equality, including, latterly, *Out*. For lesbianism and the women's movement the columns of the following have been invaluable: *Sappho*, *Red Rag*, *Spare Rib*. *Psychiatry and the Homosexual* (written collectively by Andrew Hodges, David Hutter, Randal Kincaid and Jeffrey Weeks) gives the background to the ideas of

Icebreakers. For Icebreakers I have used papers in my possession, and the advice of Micky Burbidge. The Albany Trust's views can be found in its new journal, *AT Work*. For a Christian view, see David Blamires's *Homosexuality from the Inside* (published by the Social Responsibility Council of the Religious Society of Friends), London, 1973; other references are in the notes (p. 268). The campaign for gay rights in the National Union of Students can be traced in *Come Together*, No. 12, and in *Gay News*, No. 21 and No. 39 (which discusses the first NUS Gay Rights Conference, 20 October 1973). Roger Baker discusses the growth of Gay Sweatshop in *After Lunch*, No. 1, Summer 1976, in an article suggestively called 'Cult into Establishment'. The genesis of *Gay News* can be traced in an article by Glenys Parry and Andrew Lumsden, 'A National Newspaper for Homosexuals', in the CHE *Bulletin*, March/April 1972. For gays and trade unions, see *Gay Left*, Nos. 1–3, 1975–6. For PIE, I have relied on information generously supplied by Keith Hose. For the foundation of PAL, see *Gay News*, No. 60, 5–18 December, 1974. For changing attitudes in the cinema, see Richard Dyer, 'Gays in Film', *Gay Left*, No. 2, Spring 1976; and J. Babuscio, R. Dyer and C. Sheldon, *Gays and Films*, British Film Institute, 1977.

CHAPTER 18: Jeremy Seabrook, *A Lasting Relationship*, London, 1976, has given the fullest account of a gay man's feeling of despair at the assimilative power of capitalism. For a brief criticism, see Jeffrey Weeks, 'A Permanent Divorce', *Gay Left*, No. 3, Autumn 1976. The debate on the left of the gay movement can be traced in *Gay Marxist*, 5 issues, 1973–4, *Gay Left* and *Red Rag*. The debate on the attitude of the Communist Party of Great Britain to gay liberation can be traced in the *Morning Star* and its fortnightly review *Comment*: particularly vol. 14, No. 21. See also the interview with two feminists who are party members in *Gay Left*, No. 4, Spring 1977. The International Marxist Group's Personal/Political Grouping produced a collection of documents on sexuality, 'News from the Gyroscope', March 1977.

# Notes and References

*Introduction*

1. François Lafitte, 'Homosexuality and the Law', in *British Journal of Delinquency*, vol. IX, 1958–9, p. 8.
2. For cross-cultural evidence, see Ann Oakley, *Sex, Gender and Society*, London, 1972; the quote is from J. H. Gagnon and W. Simon, *Sexual Conduct*, London, 1974, p. 261.
3. Christopher Caudwell, *Studies and Further Studies in a Dying Culture*, New York and London, 1971, p. 129.
4. Mary McIntosh, 'The Homosexual Role', *Social Problems*, vol. 16, No. 2, Fall 1968, p. 184.
5. See, for example, the Pope's condemnation of homosexuality and masturbation early in 1976 ('Pope Reaffirms Ethics of Sex', *Guardian*, 16 January 1976). The surprise is not in the fact that the condemnation was made, but that so many felt the need to justify it.
6. Mike Brake makes this point, 'I May Be a Queer, But At Least I Am a Man', in D. L. Barker and S. Allen, *Sexual Divisions and Society: Process and Change*, London, 1976.

## Part One: Definitions and Self-Definitions

*Chapter 1*

1. See François Lafitte, 'Homosexuality and the Law', *British Journal of Delinquency*, vol. IX, 1958–9. In Scotland, sodomy was a common-law crime and cases are cited from *c.* 1570. 'Lewd, indecent and libidinous practices' were also crimes, but not specifically homosexual ones. Statute law has only applied to homosexual acts in Scotland from 1885.
2. See Peter Fryer, *Mrs Grundy*, London, 1963, p. 103. The Societies for the Reformation of Manners claimed they were responsible in forty-four years for prosecuting 101,683 persons in London alone at the turn of the seventeenth century, mostly for sabbath-breaking, brothel-keeping and sodomy; the figure is presumably exaggerated. For the emergence of a homosexual sub-culture, see Chapter 3.
3. A. N. Gilbert, 'Buggery and the British Navy, 1700–1861', *Journal of Social History*, vol. 10, No. 1, Fall 1976. The army seems to have been even more severe with lashes, but less so with the death penalty. (ibid., p. 95, n. 74).
4. Sir L. Radzinowitz, *A History of English Criminal Law*, vol. 4: *Grappling for Control*, London, 1968, pp. 329–31. In 1846 there were more death sentences for sodomy than for murder (ibid., p. 330).
5. See Gilbert, 'Buggery and the British Navy', p. 73; and, for Rickards's comments, see J. A. Banks, *Prosperity and Parenthood*, London, 1954, pp. 24, 145.

6. See *Reynolds' News*, 22 May 1870. I am grateful to Peter Wells for providing me with information from his own researches on this case.

7. Radzinowitz, *Grappling for Control*, p. 432.

8. The 1898 Act enacted that any person who knowingly lived wholly or in part on the earnings of prostitutes or in any public place persistently *solicited or importuned for immoral purposes* was to be deemed a 'rogue and vagabond' under the terms of the 1824 Vagrancy Act. The 1912 Criminal Law Amendment Act made clearer the implications of this for homosexuals: *Parliamentary Debates*, 1912, vol. 43, col. 1858, 12 November 1912. The Scottish equivalent of the 1898 Vagrancy Act was the 1902 Immoral Traffic (Scotland) Act, but this did *not* apply to homosexual offences. See also H. Montgomery Hyde, *The Other Love*, London, 1972, pp. 325ff.

9. Hyde, *The Other Love*, p. 155; Lafitte, 'Homosexuality and the Law', p. 19.

10. For Germany, see John Lauritsen and David Thorstad, *The Early Homosexual Rights Movement (1864–1934)*, New York, 1974. For France, see comments in Guy Hocquenghem, *Le désir homosexuel*, Paris, 1972. In Holland, the Penal Code of 1886 imposed an age of consent, ostensibly to keep up with France and Belgium, though there was no specific mention of homosexuality until 1911. See Dr E. Brongersma, 'Sexuality and the Law', *Journal of the American Institute of Hypnosis*, vol. 14, No. 5, September 1973. I am grateful to Keith Hose for directing my attention to this. 'Xavier Mayne', *The Intersexes*, Florence, 1910, details the legal situation in Germany, France, Scandinavia, Greece, Italy and elsewhere, pp. 67ff.

11. Quoted in P. Dwyer, 'The Repeal Movement against the Contagious Diseases Act 1866' (unpublished thesis for history diploma, Ruskin College, Oxford, 1971), p. 2. The succeeding quote is from the 'Objects' of the Social Purity Alliance, founded in 1873.

12. Rev. J. M. Wilson, *Social Purity*, London, 1884; and *Sins of the Flesh* (Social Purity Alliance publication), London, 1885, p. 7.

13. Ronald Hyam, *Britain's Imperial Century*, London, 1976, pp. 84ff. I am grateful to Dr Hyam for drawing my attention to this information.

14. *The Sentinel*, June 1885, p. 427.

15. *The Sentinel*, April 1885, p. 411; Wilson, *Sins of the Flesh*, p. 7.

16. Rev. W. Arthur, 'The Political Value of Social Purity', *The Sentinel*, September 1885, p. 480; the Socialist League Manifesto is quoted in E. P. Thompson, *William Morris*, London, 1954, p. 455.

17. Beatrice Webb's Diaries, vol. 30, 6 November 1911; quoted in J. M. Winter, *Socialism and the Challenge of War*, London, 1974, p. 43.

18. Quoted in H. Montgomery Hyde, *Oscar Wilde*, London, 1976, p. 271. It is worth noting the other scandals involving sex which preceded the Wilde trials: 1886, the Dilke divorce case; 1890, the Parnell scandal; 1891, the Tranby Croft scandal, involving the Prince of Wales. In all, the Social Purity lobby made its voice heard.

19. Gareth Stedman-Jones, *Outcast London*, Oxford, 1971, pp. 490ff. See also Henry Broadhurst's comments at the 1877 Trades Union Congress: 'It was their duty as men and husbands to use their utmost efforts to bring about a condition of things, where their wives would be

in their proper sphere at home.' For the reaction to a drag ball in London's East End in 1879, see *East London Observer*, 3 May 1879, quoted in Chaim Bermant, *Point of Arrival*, London, 1975, p. 5. I am grateful to Anna Davin for drawing my attention to this.

20. Hyam, *Britain's Imperial Century*, p. 134. *Oral History*, vol. 3, No. 2, has various relevant articles on childhood.

21. Judith R. Walkowitz and Daniel J. Walkowitz, ' "We are not beasts of the field" : Prostitution and the Poor in Plymouth and Southampton under the Contagious Diseases Acts', in *Feminist Studies*, vol. I, Nos 3–4, 1973. Banks, *Prosperity and Parenthood*, pp. 162ff. also speculates on the impact of the Social Purity crusades.

22. Hyde, *Oscar Wilde*, p. 309; E. M. Forster, *Maurice*, Harmondsworth, 1975, pp. 138–9 (Peter Wells drew my attention to the relevance of this quote); W. T. Stead to Edward Carpenter, a letter in the Edward Carpenter Collection, Sheffield City Libraries, June 1895, MS. 386–54 (1–2).

23. Edward Carpenter, *The Intermediate Sex*, first published London, 1908; 9th impression, 1952, p. 79. There is evidence that Wilde was being blackmailed from *c.* 1893 (Hyde, *Oscar Wilde*, p. 156). For examples dating back to the 1760s, see Arno Karlen, *Sexuality and Homosexuality*, London, 1971, p. 143. This was an international phenomenon. Magnus Hirschfeld, the German sexologist, reported that out of the 10,000 homosexuals he had studied, 3,000 had been blackmailed (Karlen, op. cit., p. 248). No exact figures for convictions can easily be ascertained. For instance, homosexual men arrested for importuning were classified in the figures along with pimps for prostitutes under the Vagrancy Acts. Michael Schofield believed that even more people suffered under these than under the 1885 Act (quoted in Hyde, *The Other Love*, p. 326). R. Sindall, 'Aspects of Middle Class Crime in the Nineteenth Century': (unpublished M.Phil. thesis, Leicester University), p. 215, notes that the 1885 Act caused a sharp increase in the number of recorded indictable crimes against the person.

24. Havelock Ellis, *Studies in the Psychology of Sex* (4 vols.), vol. 2: *Sexual Inversion*, New York, 1936, p. 352.

*Chapter 2*

1. The quotations are from Caroline Bingham, 'Seventeenth Century Attitudes towards Deviant Sex', *Journal of Interdisciplinary History*, Spring 1971, p. 455; Arno Karlen, *Sexuality and Homosexuality*, London, 1971, p. 149; *Gloucester Journal*, 29 July 1967.

2. J. H. Plumb, 'The New World of Children in Eighteenth Century England', *Past and Present*, No. 67, May 1975, p. 93. This article traces the changes taking place in the eighteenth century. For earlier attitudes, see Philippe Aries, *Centuries of Childhood*, Harmondsworth, 1973: 'In Medieval society the idea of childhood did not exist' (p. 125).

3. Rev. Richard A. Armstrong, *Our Duty in the Matters of Social Purity* (Social Purity Alliance publication), London, 1885, p. 4.

4. I am grateful to Colin Buckle for information on this. He estimates that some six hundred clitoridectomies were performed in 1860–66,

and a few more afterwards. See also Charles E. Rosenberg, 'Sexuality, Class and Role in Nineteenth Century America', *American Quarterly*, May 1973, p. 147, n. 39.

5. Edward Lyttelton, *The Causes and Prevention of Immorality in Schools*, privately published, 1883, p. 29. V. L. Bullough and M. Voght, 'Homosexuality and its Confusion with the "Secret Sin" in Pre-Freudian America', *Journal of the History of Medicine*, vol. xxvII, No. 2, April 1973.
6. R. Krafft-Ebing, *Psychopathia Sexualis*, London, 1892, p. 13.
7. Karlen, *Sexuality and Homosexuality*, p. 185.
8. William Lee Howard, 'Sexual Perversion', *Alienist and Neurologist*, vol. xvII, No. 1, January 1896, p. 1.
9. Krafft-Ebing, *Psychopathia Sexualis*, p. 288. For Havelock Ellis's comments on (and claims to have influenced) Krafft-Ebing, see *Sexual Inversion*, New York, 1936, p. 70.
10. Phyllis Grosskurth, *John Addington Symonds*, London, 1964, p. 283.
11. Quoted in J. Bancroft, *Deviant Sexual Behaviour*, Oxford, 1974, p. 10.
12. *Penny Illustrated Paper*, 7 May 1870. (I owe this reference to Peter Wells.) One of the friends of Lord Arthur Somerset (who fled abroad to escape trial in the Cleveland Street case) made similar connections: 'For the man, in his defence, I can only trust that he is mad' (H. Montgomery Hyde, *The Cleveland Street Scandal*, London, 1976, p. 96).
13. Patrick Geddes and J. A. Thompson, *Sex*, London, 1914, pp. 143, 146.
14. Thus echoing an actual event, when a compositor refused to set one of J. A. Symonds's writings on homosexuality.
15. Quoted in Bancroft, *Deviant Sexual Behaviour*, p. 16.
16. F. E. Kenyon, *Homosexuality*, London, 1972. According to Kenyon, in this BMA publication, homosexuals 'indulge' their practices, are natural 'outsiders', are 'improved' by treatment, after which one poor girl 'made very good progress, lost all her lesbian inclinations'. Greeted at the time by many activists as a breakthrough, it was in its way, but also showed how far attitudes have to go. See my review in *Lunch*, November 1973, p. 18.
17. Thomas Szasz, *The Manufacture of Madness*, London, 1971, p. 173.
18. For example, in *Sexual Inversion*, p. 331. An interesting example of 'correctional zeal' involves circumcision. By the 1890s circumcision was routine for boys among the upper and professional classes of Britain and the United States. Dr Remondino in his *History of Circumcision*, Philadelphia and London, 1891, attacked the 'debatable appendage', and compared circumcision (shades of the political-economy model) to a 'well-secured life annuity', 'a better saving investment' making for a greater capacity for labour, a longer life, less nervousness, fewer doctors' bills. By the 1930s at least two thirds of public schoolboys had been circumcised (compared to a tenth of working-class boys), and some one third of the total male population – all for the sake of a medical myth. (See Ronald Hyam, *Britain's Imperial Century*, London, 1976. I am grateful to Dr Hyam for drawing my attention to this phenomenon.)
19. Karlen, *Sexuality and Homosexuality*, p. 332.

20. Bancroft's *Deviant Sex Behaviour* is a modern defence of the significance of behaviour modification through drugs and aversion therapy.
For an example of the effects of an early attempt (1964) at aversion
therapy for homosexuality, see Jim Scott's account of his treatment in
*Seven Days*, No. 18, 1–7 March 1972, p. 20.

21. *The Autobiography of G. Lowes Dickinson and Other Unpublished
Writings*, ed. by Dennis Proctor, London, 1973, pp. 10, 11; Brian
Inglis, *Roger Casement*, London, 1971, pp. 67–8. For a discussion of
the personal impact of all this, see Don Milligan, 'Homosexuality:
Sexual Needs and Social Problems', in R. Bailey and M. Brake (eds.)
*Radical Social Work*, London, 1975.

*Chapter 3*

1. In the categorization that follows I have freely adapted the divisions
that Kenneth Plummer suggests in *Sexual Stigma*, London, 1975,
pp. 98–100: (1) casual homosexuality; (2) personalized homosexuality;
(3) homosexuality as a situated activity; (4) homosexuality as a way of
life.

2. Quoted in Steven Marcus, *The Other Victorians*, London, 1966,
pp. 174ff.

3. *The Times*, 28 November 1851.

4. Ronald Hyam, *Britain's Imperial Century*, London, 1976, p. 137.

5. J. A. Symonds, Memoirs; *The Autobiography of G. Lowes Dickinson
and Other Unpublished Writings*, London, 1973, p. 8. I am grateful to
the Librarian of the London Library for allowing me to read the
manuscript Memoirs of Symonds, which were embargoed until 1976.

6. *The Sins of the Cities of the Plain: or the Recollections of a Mary-Ann*,
2 vols., London, 1881, vol. I, p. 84. These are the supposed memoirs of
a male prostitute of the period. For a view from the 1950s, see Simon
Raven, 'Boys will be Boys: The Male Prostitute in London', originally
printed in *Encounter*, November 1960, and reproduced in H. M.
Ruitenbeek (ed.), *The Problem of Homosexuality in Modern Society*,
New York, 1963. Even in the 1970s the issue could still be kicked alive,
e.g. 'Soldiers and Sex Report for DPP', *Evening Standard*, 28 January
1976.

7. See Arno Karlen, *Sexuality and Homosexuality*, London, 1971,
p. 104. As regards Britain, I am here following through suggestions
made in Mary McIntosh, 'The Homosexual Role', *Social Problems*,
vol. 16, No. 2, Fall 1968.

8. Karlen, *Sexuality and Homosexuality*, pp. 140ff. See also Mary
McIntosh, 'The Homosexual Role', and H. Montgomery Hyde, *The
Other Love*, London, 1976.

9. J. A. Symonds, quoted in Brian Reade, *Sexual Heretics*, London, 1970,
p. 251. Dennis Altman, in an unpublished paper on 'The State,
Repression and Sexuality', draws attention to a similar stereotyping,
the polarizing around butch/femme behaviour, and the furtiveness
in the homosexual sub-cultures of Mexico and Brazil and other
developing countries today. There is also a striking difference in
Britain today between the openness of the homosexual sub-culture in
London and the residual furtiveness of that in most provincial towns.

10. Rupert Croft-Cooke, *Feasting with Panthers*, London, 1967, p. 265.
11. 'Xavier Mayne', *The Intersexes*, Florence, 1910, pp. 427–8.
12. 'George Merrill', a biographical sketch by Edward Carpenter, in the Carpenter collection, Sheffield City Libraries.
13. Evelyn Hooker, 'The Homosexual Community', in J. H. Gagnon and W. Simon, *Sexual Deviance*, London, 1967, p. 174.
14. A. Flexner, *Prostitution in Europe*, New York, 1914, p. 30, where he estimates there were forty homosexual resorts tolerated by the police; Karlen, *Sexuality and Homosexuality*, p. 220.
15. 'Mayne', *The Intersexes*, p. 220.
16. H. Montgomery Hyde, *Oscar Wilde*, London, 1976, p. 217.
17. Havelock Ellis, *Sexual Inversion*, New York, 1936, p. 22.
18. *The Autobiography of G. Lowes Dickinson*, p. 64.
19. Symonds to Edmund Gosse, quoted in H. Montgomery Hyde, *The Cleveland Street Scandal*, London, 1976, p. 241.
20. On Forster, see the introduction by Oliver Stallybrass to E. M. Forster, *The Life to Come and Other Stories*, Harmondsworth, 1975, p. 16. Carpenter is quoted in Timothy d'Arch Smith, *Love in Earnest*, 1970, p. 192.
21. H. M. Schueller and R. L. Peters (eds.), *The Letters of John Addington Symonds*, vol. III: *1885–93*, Detroit, 1969, L2079, 21 January 1893, p. 808. See also William Paine, *New Aristocracy of Comradeship*, London, 1920, which sees cross-class relations as bridging the class divide. Further examples are given in Chapter 7 below.
22. Ronald Hyam, *Britain's Imperial Century*, London, 1976, p. 137.
23. Timothy d'Arch Smith, in *Jeremy*, vol. 1, No. 9, cites various familiar slang words apparently common *c.* 1910: 'drag', 'camp', 'chicken', 'cottage', 'on the game'. Others, now extinct, include 'BM', 'Tip the Velvet', 'to bottle', 'to buck' (i.e. 'to troll'). For further references, see bibliography, p. 240.
24. Quoted in Hyde, *Oscar Wilde*, p.152.
25. Symonds, Memoirs.
26. Quoted in Thomas Szasz, *The Manufacture of Madness*, London, 1971, p. 169. Gide's own behaviour was scarcely more liberated. During Wilde's Paris exile after his release from prison, Wilde saw Gide passing and beckoned him over to his boulevard table. Gide deliberately sat with his back to the street, so that passers-by would not recognize him (Hyde, *Oscar Wilde*, pp. 346, 363). Nor was he more noble in later life. Though telling the world of his interest in boys, he never talked about it with his wife.

## Part Two: Pioneers

### Chapter 4

1. Edward Carpenter, *The Intermediate Sex*, 1st published, London, 1908; 9th impression, 1952, p. 9.
2. For Burton, see the 'Terminal Essay' to his *Arabian Nights*, Vol. 10, London, 1885, pp. 205ff. There are several very thorough studies of the Uranian poets: Timothy d'Arch Smith, *Love in Earnest*, London,

1970; Brian Reade, *Sexual Heretics: Male Homosexuality in English Literature*, London, 1970. Brian Taylor, 'Motives for Guilt-Free Pederasty: Some Literary Considerations', *Sociological Review*, vol. 24, No. 1, February 1976, pp. 101ff., challenged d'Arch Smith's view that the poetry of the Uranians represents a sublimation of paederastic sexual desires: 'I want to consider the possibility that they were written to justify and to motivate the enactment of that love.' See Chapter 7 below for discussion of the activities of some of the Uranian poets.

3. Quoted in Phyllis Grosskurth, *John Addington Symonds*, London, 1964, p. 283. The following quote on Whitman comes from J. A. Symonds, *A Problem in Modern Ethics*, London, 1892, p. 125.
4. Grosskurth, *John Addington Symonds*, p. 217.
5. Havelock Ellis and J. A. Symonds, *Sexual Inversion*, 1st edition, London, 1897, p. 165. G. Lowes Dickinson's *The Greek View of Life*, published in 1896, was still, according to Noel Annan, 'part of the working library of liberation' for public schoolboys of the 1930s.
6. Grosskurth, *John Addington Symonds*, pp. 269, 271.
7. J. A. Symonds, *Walt Whitman: A Study*, London, 1893, p. v.
8. Grosskurth, *John Addington Symonds*, p. 267.
9. ibid., pp. 273ff.
10. Symonds, *Walt Whitman*, p. 72.
11. Symonds to Carpenter, 29 December 1892, *The Letters of John Addington Symonds*, London, 1969, p. 799.
12. See *Sexual Inversion*, (1897 edition), p. 263 n.
13. Grosskurth, *John Addington Symonds*, p. 281.
14. ibid., p. 275.
15. Symonds to Carpenter, 21 January 1893, *The Letters*, p. 808. The next quote is from Grosskurth, *John Addington Symonds*, p. 281.
16. Horatio Brown to Edward Carpenter, MSS. 386–76, 21 November 1897, Edward Carpenter Collection, Sheffield City Libraries.
17. Edward Carpenter, *Some Friends of Walt Whitman*, London, 1924, p. 12.

*Chapter 5*
1. For a fuller discussion of the importance of Havelock Ellis as a sex reformer, see Jeffrey Weeks, 'Havelock Ellis and the Politics of Sex Reform', in Sheila Rowbotham and Jeffrey Weeks, *Socialism and the New Life*, London, 1977. This book also contains a long essay on Edward Carpenter by Sheila Rowbotham, which amplifies several points made in Chapter 8 below.
2. Phyllis Grosskurth, *John Addington Symonds*, London, 1964, p. 285.
3. On 12 February 1893, J. A. Symonds sent Havelock Ellis sixteen biographical cases of 'inversion' and commented, 'If you have only met with one recorded case in English sources these may be interesting and may be used with profit perhaps in your part of the work.' (*The Letters of John Addington Symonds*, London, 1969, p. 816.)
4. Havelock Ellis, *The New Spirit*, 4th edition, London, 1926, p. viii.
5. Grosskurth, *John Addington Symonds*, p. 285; Symonds to Edward Carpenter, 29 December 1892, *Letters*, p. 797.

6. The fullest account of this episode is in Arthur Calder-Marshall, *Lewd, Blasphemous and Obscene*, London, 1972.
7. Quoted in ibid., p. 218.
8. See, for example, D. S. Bailey, *Homosexuality and the Western Christian Tradition*, London, 1955, p. ix. Canon Bailey's book was very influential among the reformers of the 1950s. See Chapter 14 below for details of the period.
9. Symonds to Ellis, L2039, 28 September 1892; to Carpenter, L2070, 29 December 1892; Symonds to Ellis, L1996, 7 July 1892: *Letters*. Havelock Ellis, *Sexual Inversion*, New York, 1936, pp. 317ff.
10. *Sexual Inversion*, pp. 325ff., 338.
11. Havelock Ellis, *The Psychology of Sex*, London, 1946, p. 217.
12. *Sexual Inversion*, pp. 203–4, 251, 257, 258, 261. For a fuller discussion of attitudes to lesbianism, see Chapter 8 below.
13. *Sexual Inversion*, p. 304. For an examination of the relationship between Ellis and Freud, see Vincent Brome, 'Sigmund Freud and Havelock Ellis', *Encounter*, No. 66, March 1959.

*Chapter 6*

1. Ellis to Carpenter, MSS. 357–82, Edward Carpenter collection, Sheffield City Libraries. Despite their friendship, a formal element remained. In correspondence they never became closer than 'My dear Carpenter' or 'Dear Havelock Ellis'.
2. Edward Carpenter, *My Days and Dreams*, London, 1916, p. 30. The biographic details come from this and Sheila Rowbotham's essay in Sheila Rowbotham and Jeffrey Weeks, *Socialism and the New Life*, London, 1977.
3. *My Days and Dreams*, p. 97; Carpenter to Walt Whitman, quoted in Traubel, *With Walt Whitman at Camden*, New York, 1908.
4. *My Days and Dreams*, p. 104.
5. Edward Carpenter, *Civilisation: Its Cause and Cure*, 15th edition, London, 1921, p. 46.
6. ibid., p. 53.
7. Edward Carpenter, *Towards Democracy*, London, 1883, section xi.
8. Carpenter, *Civilisation: Its Cause and Cure*, p. 192.
9. *My Days and Dreams*, pp. 60ff.
10. I owe this reference to Sheila Rowbotham.
11. Carpenter to George Hukin, MS. 361–21, 31 July 1895, Edward Carpenter collection, Sheffield City Libraries.
12. Edward Carpenter, *Intermediate Types Among Primitive Folk: a Study in Social Evolution*, London, 1914, p. 111; *The Intermediate Sex*, 9th edition, London, 1952, p. 77.
13. Edward Carpenter, *Love's Coming of Age*, Manchester, 1896, pp. 68–9.
14. *The Intermediate Sex*, p. 17. See also 'Birth Control and Bisexuality', MS. 248; a typescript in the Edward Carpenter collection.
15. *The Intermediate Sex*, pp. 93 and 131.
16. Carpenter, *Intermediate Types*, p. 60.
17. For a discussion of Noyes and the Oneida experiment, see Raymond Lee Muncy, *Sex and Marriage in Utopian Communities*, Baltimore, Md., 1973, pp. 160ff.

18. MSS. 352, Edward Carpenter collection. *The Adult*, February 1893; Kate Joynes to Carpenter, MS. 354–31, Edward Carpenter collection.
19. Carpenter to Oates, 18 December 1887, Edward Carpenter collection.
20. Hukin to Carpenter, MS. 362–10 (1–2), October 1887; MS. 362–16 (1), 21 November 1887, Edward Carpenter collection.
21. Edward Carpenter to James Brown, 2 March 1890.
22. 'George Merrill'; biographical sketch by Edward Carpenter, in the Edward Carpenter collection.
23. MS. 363–5, 11 November 1896.
24. *My Days and Dreams*, p. 164.
25. George Merrill to Carpenter, MS. 363–7, 12 February 1897.
26. *My Days and Dreams*, p. 34.
27. Hukin to Carpenter, 28 November 1906; Hukin to Carpenter, 10 August 1904, Edward Carpenter collection.
28. Robert Graves to Carpenter, MS. 386–234 (1–2), 30 May 1914.
29. *Socialism and Infamy*, Sheffield, 1909; copy in Edward Carpenter collection. See Carpenter to Kate Joynes, MS. 354–98 (1), 9 September 1909 Edward Carpenter collection.
30. MS. 184–20, 6 July 1909, Edward Carpenter collection. Carpenter, as he fully realized, was skating on thin ice. Certainly friends and acquaintances knew of his tastes: e.g. G. Lowes Dickinson; 'he believes in and practises the physical relation very frankly', *Autobiography of G. Lowes Dickinson*, London, 1973, p. 157.
31. Gilbert Beith (ed.), *Edward Carpenter: In Appreciation*, London, 1931, p. 67. *Love's Coming of Age* was published in Italian, 1908–9.
32. MS. 271–14, Edward Carpenter collection. For John and Katharine Bruce Glasier, see L. V. Thompson, *The Enthusiasts*, London, 1971.

## Part Three: Invisible Women

### Chapter 7

1. Jeanette H. Foster, *Sex Variant Women in Literature*, London, 1958, p. 116.
2. Arno Karlen, *Sexuality and Homosexuality*, London, 1971, p. 251; Radclyffe Hall, *The Well of Loneliness*, paperback edition, London, 1974; Lovat Dickson, *Radclyffe Hall at the Well of Loneliness*, London, 1976.
3. ibid., p. 14.
4. J. H. Gagnon and William Simon, *Sexual Conduct: the Social Sources of Human Sexuality*, London, 1973, p. 176, n. 1.
5. Karlen, *Sexuality and Homosexuality*, p. 25.
6. Quoted in Edward M. Brecher, *The Sex Researchers*, London, 1970, pp. 134–5.
7. Gagnon and Simon, *Sexual Conduct*, p. 180.
8. Jill Conway, 'Stereotypes of Femininity in a Theory of Sexual Evolution', in Martha Vicinus (ed.), *Suffer and Be Still*, Bloomington, Ind., 1972, p. 14.
9. Havelock Ellis, *Man and Woman*, London, 1894, p. 440.
10. ibid., p. 448.

11. Quoted in Havelock Ellis, *Studies in the Psychology of Sex*, vol. 4: *Sex in Relation to Society*, New York, 1936, p. 587.
12. Brecher, *The Sex Researchers*, p.151.
13. Ellis, *Studies in the Psychology of Sex*, vol. 1, Part 2, New York, 1936, pp. 24, 69.
14. Brecher, *The Sex Researchers*, pp. 154, 161.
15. Carl N. Degler, 'What Ought to Be and What Was: Woman's Sexuality in the Nineteenth Century', *American Historical Review*, vol. 79, No. 5, December 1974, p. 1486.
16. *British Medical Journal*, 28 July 1900, cited in Helen Rugen, 'Women on the Borderline of Pathology: Dominant conceptions of female sexuality in health and illlness, 1900–1920', unpublished paper. I am very grateful to Helen Rugen for showing me a copy of this paper.
17. Peter Fryer, *Mrs Grundy*, London, 1963, p. 54.
18. Dolores Klaich, *Woman plus Woman: Attitudes towards Lesbianism*, New York, 1974.
19. Quoted in Karlen, *Sexuality and Homosexuality*, p. 294. Marie Bonaparte, in *Female Sexuality*, New York, 1962, sees three types of women: (1) 'true woman': normal, vaginal, maternal; (2) those who abandon all competition with men, and are completely passive, (3) those who cling desperately to the psychical and organic male elements in all women, and are dominated by the masculinity complex and the clitoris.
20. Carroll Smith-Rosenberg, 'The Female World of Love and Ritual: Relations between Women in Nineteenth Century America', *Signs: Journal of Women in Culture and Society*, vol. i, No. 1, Autumn 1975.
21. ibid.
22. Quoted in Foster, *Sex Variant Women in Literature*, p. 130.

*Chapter 8*

1. See Lee Holcombe, *Victorian Ladies at Work*, Hamden, Conn., 1973. The 1851 Census showed that 42 per cent of women aged twenty to forty were spinsters.
2. George Dangerfield, *The Strange Death of Liberal England*, London, 1935. Edward Carpenter had his own stereotypes of women: either as earth-mother types, all bosoms and warmth, or militant and masculine minded, even 'homogenic' in temperament. See Sheila Rowbotham, 'Edward Carpenter', in Sheila Rowbotham and Jeffrey Weeks, *Socialism and the New Life*, London, 1977, p. 92ff.
3. Arno Karlen, *Sexuality and Homosexuality*, London, 1971, p. 256; Jeanette H. Foster, *Sex Variant Women in Literature*, London, 1958, p. 219. In late 1910 a new draft penal code was introduced in Germany, proposing to extend the law to include sex acts between women. Many women's groups took this up, and the League for the Protection of Mothers adopted a resolution condemning the proposed law. The German Scientific-Humanitarian Committee made conscious efforts to attract lesbian members (John Lauritsen and David Thorstad, *The Early Homosexual Rights Movement*, New York, 1974, pp. 15, 18). Stereotypes of lesbians and the 'new women' can be seen in cartoons published in the German satirical magazine *Simplicissimus* (see

selection by Stanley Appelbaum, New York, 1975, e.g. pp. 30, 31, 75).
4. Quoted in Constance Rover, *Love, Morals and the Feminists*, London, 1970, p. 53. Mrs Fawcett at one point refused to speak to Carpenter because of his views on homosexuality.
5. Christabel Pankhurst, *The Great Scourge*, London, 1913, p. vi.
6. ibid., p. 138.
7. David Mitchell, *Women on the Warpath*, London, 1966, p. 56. The WSPU launched a Moral Crusade, whose logic was that women should not marry till men's sex morality improved. The implications were that women's morals had to be of the very highest standards. See Andrew Rosen's *Rise Up, Women!*, London, 1974, pp. 206–7.
8. I have relied here on A. R. Cunningham, 'The "New Women" Fiction of the 1890s', *Victorian Studies*, vol. XVII, No. 2, December 1973.
9. Quoted ibid., p. 181.
10. ibid., p. 183.
11. I am very grateful to Helen Rugen for information about the debate in *The Freewoman* and for showing me a copy of an unpublished note by her on this topic.
12. F. W. Stella Browne, *The Sexual Variety and Variability Among Women* (BSSP pamphlet), London, 1916.
13. ibid., p. 12.
14. Emma Goldman to Havelock Ellis, 27 December 1924, in Emma Goldman collection, International Institute of Social History, Amsterdam.

*Chapter* 9
1. Introduction to Edith Ellis, *The New Horizon in Love and Life*, London, 1921.
2. A. Calder-Marshall, *Havelock Ellis*, London, 1959, p. 126.
3. Edith Ellis, *A Noviciate for Marriage*, London, 1892, p. 4.
4. Edith Ellis, *Three Modern Seers*, London, 1910, p. 201.
5. Republished in *The New Horizon*; see pp. 47, 62.
6. Peter Gunn, *Vernon Lee (Violet Paget) 1856–1935*, London, 1964, p. 98.
7. Vernon Lee, *Gospels of Anarchy*, London, 1908, pp. 269–70.
8. Lovat Dickson, *Radclyffe Hall at the Well of Loneliness*, London, 1976, pp. 40, 42, 48.
9. Jeanette H. Foster, *Sex Variant Women in Literature*, London, 1958, p. 261.
10. H. Montgomery Hyde, *The Other Love*, London, 1972, p. 195.
11. Arabella Kennealy, *Feminism and Sex Extinction*, London, 1920, p. 225.
12. Hyde, *The Other Love*, pp. 200ff.
13. Vera Brittain, *Radclyffe Hall: A Case of Obscenity?* London, 1968, p. 85.
14. Calder-Marshall, *Havelock Ellis*, p. 265.
15. Dickson, *Radclyffe Hall*, p. 124.
16. Brittain, *Radclyffe Hall*, p. 55.
17. Quoted in ibid., p. 154.
18. Dickson, *Radclyffe Hall*, p. 158; Brittain, *Radclyffe Hall*, p. 112.

19. *Time and Tide*, 10 August 1928, quoted in ibid., p. 50.
20. Radclyffe Hall, *The Well of Loneliness*, p. 509.
21. Dickson, *Radclyffe Hall*, p. 230.
22. Brittain, *Radclyffe Hall*, p. 50.
23. ibid., p. 154.
24. Quoted by Dickson, *Radclyffe Hall*, p. 208.

## Part Four: Approaches to Reform

*Chapter 10*
1. H. Montgomery Hyde, *Oscar Wilde*, London, 1976, p. 345.
2. The Moltke–Harden–Eulenberg affair is described briefly in John Lauritsen and David Thorstad, *The Early Homosexual Rights Movement*, New York, 1974, p. 19. For Orage, see Wallace Martin, '*The New Age*' *under Orage: Chapters in English Cultural History*, Manchester, 1968.
3. MS. 184–1, 21 June 1912; MS. 184–2, 22 June 1912, MS. 184–3, 29 June 1912; MSS. 184–8, 12 July 1912. Carpenter simultaneously widened his campaign, consulting friends and allies. Havelock Ellis replied with his experiences: MSS. 184–15, 25 July 1912, Ellis to Carpenter. Edward Carpenter collection, Sheffield City Libraries.
4. T. K. Fortescue, Keeper of Printed Books, to Carpenter, MSS. 184–13, 24 July 1912, Edward Carpenter collection.
5. MSS. 184–27, Edward Carpenter collection.
6. I am deeply indebted to Mr Anthony Reid for granting me access to the George Ives archives in his library (including a three million word unpublished diary, correspondence and records of the Order of Chaeronea), and for permission to quote from them. Without his assistance it would not have been possible to complete this chapter. I should like to record here my warm gratitude to Mr Reid and his wife for their help, courtesy and hospitality when I visited them. Further Ives material, including correspondence with Laurence Housman, is with the University of Texas, Austin. I have not been able to study these records, but a helpful summary of their scope was provided by the Humanities Research Center, Texas, for which I am very grateful.
7. C. R. Ashbee, Journals, 1 November 1899, p. 82, King's College, Cambridge. Gilbert Beith (ed.), *Edward Carpenter: In Appreciation*, London, 1931, p. 122. Ashbee Journals, p. 84.
8. Ives, Diaries, vol. XIV, 1892, p. 1395 (a postscript added in 1918). In the library of Anthony Reid.
9. The comments are from Beith (ed.), *Edward Carpenter*, pp. 122, 124 and 128.
10. Ives, Diaries, vol. XIII, 1892, p. 1322.
11. Timothy d'Arch Smith, *Love in Earnest*, London, 1970, pp. 110ff.
12. Quoted in ibid., p. 112. The Wilde quote below comes from the same source. Ives had suggested a rendezvous in a cabman's shelter, where they would not be recognized or overheard.
13. G. C. Ives, 'It May Be . . .', *Eros' Throne*, London, 1900, p. 45.
14. G. Lowes Dickinson, *The Greek View of Life*, 13th edition, London,

1920, p. 178. The Theban Band marched and fought hand in hand. When the three hundred lay dead together, their killer, Philip of Macedon, shed tears and said, 'Perish any man who suspects that these men either did or suffered anything that was base.' See also Arno Karlen, *Sexuality and Homosexuality*, London, 1971, p. 27.

15. In *Love in Earnest*, pp. 84–5, d'Arch Smith cites a 'puzzling letter', with a 'meaningless date', which is unsigned but which he attributes to Ives. The letter is to Samuel Elsworth Cottam, and has the date 24 December 2273. Clearly, in the fashion of the order, this is Christmas Eve 1935. This letter mentions one 'Backhouse', whom d'Arch Smith is unable to identify firmly. It seems likely this is Sir Edmund Trelawney Backhouse, the central character in Hugh Trevor-Roper's *A Hidden Life – The Enigma of Sir Edmund Backhouse*, London, 1976. Trevor-Roper is disposed to consider Backhouse's memoirs, in which he relates his sexual exploits, as pure fantasy. But there seems little doubt that Backhouse knew Wilde and his circle (see Hyde, *Oscar Wilde*, where there are several references), and he collected money for Wilde's defence. It is very likely that Ives knew the same Backhouse.

16. All the information on the ritual of the Order comes from papers in the possession of Anthony Reid.

17. H. Montgomery Hyde, *The Other Love*, London, 1972, p. 13.

18. Housman described himself as 'unmarried, a rabid pacifist and internationalist'. He gives his own account of his early life in *The Unexpected Years*, London, 1937. Significantly he mentions neither Ives, nor the BSSP though he does talk of his feminist work. The Rev. Alphonsus Joseph-Mary Augustus Montague Summers wrote various works on witchcraft, mysticism and the occult, as well as poetry. He founded the Phoenix Society for the Production of Old Plays in 1919. Nicholson was the author of the eponymous poem, 'Love in Earnest'. The fullest description of the role of both men is in d'Arch Smith, *Love in Earnest*.

19. It is possible that Ashbee's death was linked with worry about the pressures on his homosexual life. For Charles Kains Jackson and Cottam, again see d'Arch Smith, *Love in Earnest*, who also discusses *The Quorum*, and the work of the Rev. Edwin Emmanuel Bradford (1860–1944) and Captain Leonard Henry Green. With regards to age, Kains Jackson was born in 1857; Cottam in 1863; Nicholson in 1886. An artist of a younger generation who was influenced by Ives was Ralph Nicholas Chubb (1892–1960), who devoted his life to the production of privately printed books extolling boy-love, lavishly illustrated with drawings of naked boys, and with outspoken texts.

20. Housman to Ashbee, 10 February 1914.

21. Ives to Janet Ashbee, 15 February 1904: letters in Ashbee, Journals, King's College, Cambridge.

22. At the heart of the grouping's activities was, of course, a search for a sexual identity, and there is a strong suggestion that most of those involved had pedophile leanings. Brian Taylor ('Motives for Guilt-free Pederasty: Some Litary Considerations', *Sociological Review*, vol. 24, No. 1, Feb. 1976) examines the Uranian literary tendency to which many of them belonged and discovers certain unifying themes:

'the transcience of boyhood', 'lost youth', 'the divine sanction', 'the
class sanction' and 'misogyny and the erotic superiority of pederasty'
(p. 102). I have suggested that in the case of Housman at least there
was a strong political identity also. The 'misogynist' tendencies have
also probably been over-stressed. As we have seen, many of the sex-
reformers from Carpenter on supported feminist aspirations. But we
can agree with Taylor's argument that the Uranian poetry which
Nicholson, Ives and others wrote seemed to 'confirm and reassure them
of the acceptability of the erotic preferences expressed in them'
(p. 101). In this sense the verse, though usually published anonymously
or privately, can be seen as an affirmative act of identity. The fullest
account of this literary tradition is, of course, d'Arch Smith's *Love in
Earnest*. It would be instructive to compare this type of literature to
the homosexual flavour of the Bloomsbury group. I have not felt it
appropriate in this book to try to compete with the Bloomsbury
industry, but as a homosexual coterie it does provide elements of
comparison.

## Chapter 11

1. Cecil Reddie, *Edward Carpenter* (British Sexological Society publication), London, 1932.
2. Laurence Housman in Gilbert Beith (ed.), *Edward Carpenter: In
   Appreciation*, London, 1931, p. 110.
3. Magnus Hirschfeld, *Sexual Anomalies and Perversions*, London,
   1946, p. 23.
4. ibid., p. 19. The Wilde trial seems to have stirred him on to write his
   first work on homosexuality.
5. Magnus Hirschfeld, 'Presidential Address', in Norman Haire (ed.),
   World League for Sexual Reform: Proceedings of the Third Congress,
   London, 1930, p. xiv.
6. Housman's comments are in Beith (ed.), *Edward Carpenter*, p. 100;
   for Carpenter's invitation see MS. 271–145, Edward Carpenter collection, Sheffield City Libraries; for Hirschfeld's comments on the 1913
   conference, see his 'Presidential Address', p. xi.
7. British Society for the Study of Sex Psychology, *Policy and Principles;
   General Aims*, London, 1915, pp. 3, 9.
8. Housman to Janet Ashbee, 22 February 1917, in Ashbee Journals,
   King's College, Cambridge. (The talk was published as BSSP pamphlet No. 4.) *Policy and Principles; General Aims*, p. 14.
9. Stella Browne to Margaret Sanger, 18 April 1917. I am indebted to
   Sheila Rowbotham for this reference.
10. E. Delavenay, *D. H. Lawrence and Edward Carpenter*, London, 1971,
    pp. 28ff., cites evidence for a closer state interest in Carpenter's work.
11. The catalogue is in the Anthony Reid archive of Ives material.
    Additional information is from the University of Texas, which has a
    collection of BSSP material in *its* Ives collection.
12. *The Social Problem of Sexual Inversion*, BSSP pamphlet No. 2,
    London, 1915, p. 3. For the German version, see John Lauritsen and
    David Thorstad, *The Early Homosexual Rights Movement*, New York,
    1974, p. 14.

13. Timothy d'Arch Smith, *Love in Earnest*, London, 1970, p. 137. See Montague Summers, *The Marquis de Sade: A Study in Algolagnia*, BSSP pamphlet No. 6, London, 1920.
14. G. C. Ives, *The Graeco-Roman View of Youth*, London, 1926, p. 66.
15. G. C. Ives, *The Sexes, Structure and 'Extra-Organic' Habits of Certain Animals: An Address to a Study Group*, Woking and London, 1918, p. 26. A copy of 'The Plight of the Adolescent' is in the care of Anthony Reid.
16. Batkis is quoted in Lauritsen and Thorstad, *The Early Homosexual Rights Movement*, p. 64; Haire in *W.L.S.R. Proceedings 1929*, p. 110.
17. Robert Wood, 'Sex Reform Movements', in A. Ellis and A. Abarbanel, *The Encyclopaedia of Sexual Behaviour*, vol. ii, London, 1961, p. 961.
18. Dora Russell, *The Tamarisk Tree*, London, 1975, p. 210. I am grateful to Dora Russell for so fully answering my inquiries in personal correspondence. Further information on Haire has also been given to me by Dr Frank Forster, who is preparing a study of Haire, and I am greatly indebted to him.
19. *Journal of Sex Education*, vol. 3, No. 2, October–November 1950; vol. 4, No. 2, October–November 1951.
20. Russell, *The Tamarisk Tree*, p. 206.
21. John Van Druten, 'Sex Censorship in the Theatre', *W.L.S.R. Proceedings 1929*, p. 319; Ives is quoted in *W.L.S.R. Proceedings 1929*, pp. 341, 342.
22. Cecil Reddie comments in *Edward Carpenter*, p. 6; the Hiller speech, translated by John Lauritsen, was republished in *Gay News*, 98, London, 1976, pp. 15–16.
23. *Journal of Sex Education*, Vol. 1, No. 1, August 1948.
24. Russell, *The Tamarisk Tree*, p. 218.

## Chapter 12

1. F. Engels, *The Origin of the Family, Private Property and the State*, ed. by Eleanor Burke Leacock, London, 1972, p. 140. For an explicit view of homosexuality ('the abominable practice of sodomy'), see ibid., p. 128.
2. John Lauritsen and David Thorstad, *The Early Homosexual Rights Movement*, New York, 1974, pp. 59, 22.
3. See Blatchford's letter to Edward Carpenter, 11 January 1894, Edward Carpenter collection, Sheffield City Libraries. For Blatchford's views on the family, see Sheila Rowbotham, *Hidden from History*, London, 1973, p. 73.
4. E. Belfort Bax, *Ethics of Socialism*, London, 1893, p. 126.
5. There is no doubt that many communists, especially in Germany but also in Britain (e.g. in London's East End), were prepared to use homosexuality as a weapon to discredit the fascists. In personal matters the party generally preferred not to know: 'Once, a friend of mine . . . went to Harry [Pollitt, general secretary of the British party] after a bout of self-criticism and said: "Harry, I think it's my duty to tell you: I'm a homosexual." Pollitt snapped sharply in his brisk on-duty way: "Cut it out, 'Erbie, cut it out!" And that was the end of it. The party

directive was: Cut it Out – as if changing one's nature were an act of will like giving up smoking' (Michael Davidson, *The World, The Flesh and Myself*, London, 1966, p. 151).
6. Juliet Mitchell, *Psychoanalysis and Feminism*, London, 1974, p. 141.
7. Alec Craig, *Sex and Revolution*, London, 1934, p. 129.
8. *Journal of Sex Education*, vol. 2, No. 1, August–September 1949, pp. 32–3.

*Chapter 13*
1. *Journal of Sex Education*, vol. 1, No. 1, August 1948, p. 22. For information on the society see Robert Wood, op cit.
2. See *Journal of Sex Education*, vol. 1, No. 4, February 1949, p. 162.
3. For a discussion of Kinsey's work, see Edward M. Brecher, *The Sex Researchers*, London, 1970; and Paul A. Robinson, *The Modernization of Sex*, London, 1976. As Robinson puts it (p. 43), Kinsey 'is important because he has been influential'. Kinsey sought to put human sexuality on a firm quantitative foundation. He carried to their logical conclusion the speculations about the varieties of sexual experience that Ellis's generation indulged in, and put them on a taxonomic foundation. He was critical of Ellis for his looseness over statistics, his reliance on submitted case-histories and his refusal to go and seek out evidence. Kinsey's work has been very influential in modifying the popular and theoretical views of homosexuality. Popularly, by demonstrating at least to his satisfaction that 37 per cent of American males had homosexual experiences to orgasm and thus demystifying the subject; and by his matter-of-factness about sex. Theoretically, by his 'naturalism', by his assumption that the experience of lower animals was a useful guide to human behaviour (this can be traced in the cross-species evidence often adduced to prove that homosexuality is 'natural'), and by his argument that a man is what he does with the consequent undermining of the belief that homosexuality is a fixed condition. For a use of his work in this latter context, see Mary McIntosh, 'The Homosexual Role', *Social Problems*, vol. 16, No. 2, Fall 1968.
4. *Journal of Sex Education*, vol. 4, No. 3, December 1951–January 1952, pp. 134–6.
5. *Journal of Sex Education*, vol. 3, No. 4, February–March 1951, p. 145. Could this be Ives he is referring to? Ives died in 1950.
6. *Journal of Sex Education*, vol. 2, No. 6, June–July 1950, p. 269.
7. *Journal of Sex Education*, vol. 4, No. 3, December 1951–January 1952, p. 105.
8. *Journal of Sex Education*, vol. 2, No. 2, October–November 1949.
9. Charlotte Wolff, *Love Between Women*, London, 1971, p. 157, briefly discusses this grouping. According to information supplied to me by Haire's executor, the records of the Sex Education Society, which had about six hundred members, were destroyed after his death, 'since a number of names were well known' (letter in my possession).

*Chapter 14*
1. Elizabeth Wilson, *Women and the Welfare State*, London, 1977, p. 60. This was prefigured in the Labour Party Manifesto for the 1945 elec-

tion, *Let Us Face the Future*, which endorsed the Beveridge Report: 'Labour will work especially for the care of British mothers and their children – children's allowances and school medical and feeding services, better maternity and child welfare services. A healthy family life must be fully ensured and parenthood must not be penalised if the population is to be preserved from dwindling.'

2. Gordon Westwood, *Society and the Homosexual*, London, 1952, p. 42.

3. The stress on 'petting' in the sex literature of the 1940s and 1950s underlines better than anything the ambivalence of the period: the recognition of the need for some sort of sexual outlet, and the fear of unmarrieds going 'too far'. For an excellent brief discussion of this, see Paul Robinson, *The Modernization of Sex*, London, 1976, p. 63.

4. Figures are given in H. Montgomery Hyde, *The Other Love*, London, 1972, p. 221; and in the 'Wolfenden Report': Report of the Committee on Homosexual Offences and Prostitution, Cmnd 247, HMSO, London, 1957, pp. 130–1.

5. Hyde, *The Other Love*, p. 240. Hyde gives the fullest account of the situation in the early 1950s. The reference to the correspondent of the *Sydney Morning Telegraph* comes from Peter Wildeblood, *Against the Law*, Harmondsworth, 1957, p. 50.

6. Donald Webster Cory, *The Homosexual Outlook: A Subjective Approach*, New York and London, 1953, p. 275.

7. A. J. P. Taylor, 'London Diary', *New Statesman*, 20 August 1976, p. 238. The episode is referred to in Tom Driberg, *Ruling Passions*, London, 1977.

8. Wildeblood, *Against the Law*, p. 80. This gives the fullest account of the case with the special insight of the victim.

9. ibid., p. 36. Details of press attitudes to homosexuality come from Frank Pearce, 'How to be immoral and ill, pathetic and dangerous, all at the same time: mass media and the homosexual', in Stanley Cohen and Jock Young (eds.), *The Manufacture of News*, London, 1973.

10. Cory, *The Homosexual Outlook*, p. 39; Westwood, *A Minority*, London, 1960, p. 139. Cory's comment has a singular irony in it. In the 1960s and 1970s, Cory (pseudonym of the American sociologist Edward Sagarin) was to become increasingly embittered with the American gay movement because of its unwillingness to envisage a 'cure' for homosexuality: see *Fag Rag/Gay Sunshine*, Stonewall 5th Anniversary Issue, Summer 1974.

11. Wildeblood, *Against the Law*, p. 188. The representative mood was well put by the character Michael in the 1960s play, *Boys in the Band*: 'Show me a happy homosexual and I'll show you a gay corpse'.

12. Report of the Committee on Homosexual Offences and Prostitution, p. 87. Engels made a pointed comment on this double standard in the 1880s. Prostitution and the exploitation of women is condemned, but this hits only the women: 'They are ostracized and cast out in order to proclaim once again the absolute domination of the male over the female sex as the fundamental law of society!'

13. Report of the Committee on Homosexual Offences and Prostitution, p. 44.

14. *Man and Society*, vol. 1, No. 1, Spring 1961, p. 3.

Chapter 15

1. Antony Grey, 'Homosexual Law Reform', in Brian Frost (ed.), *The Tactics of Pressure*, London, 1975, and H. Montgomery Hyde, *The Other Love*, London, 1972, pp. 262ff., give descriptions of the origins of the society.

2. Grey, 'Homosexual Law Reform', p. 38.

3. *Man and Society*, vol. 1, Spring 1961, p. 38.

4. *Man and Society*, No. 5, Spring 1963, p. 23. The book was pro-homosexual, but not in such a way as to undermine the moral consensus: 'It is a condition, like having a hare lip, or small ankles, or thick lips, or bad eyesight, or large ears' – all harmless, but not particularly desirable characteristics (Douglas Plummer, *Queer People: The Truth about Homosexuals*, London, 1963). The book caused some controversy because it named famous homosexuals, such as Gilbert Harding and Ivor Novello. 'Douglas Plummer' was the pseudonym of John Montgomery, author of *The World of Cats* and various novels and social histories (see *Gay News*, No. 10).

5. See *Spectrum*, No. 5.

6. Grey, 'Homosexual Law Reform', p. 45.

7. Alastair Heron (ed.), *Towards a Quaker View of Sex: An Essay by a group of Friends*, London, 1963, stated that, 'We see no reason why the physical nature of a sexual act should be the criterion by which the question whether or not it is moral should be decided' (p. 36). D. J. West wrote that no one in their right mind would want to be homosexual as it meant ridicule, contempt and the absence of an ordinary family life. In 1974 he was confronted about this book in a meeting of militant homosexual students in the University of London. He was apparently preparing to modify his views for a revised edition. Bryan Magee's *One in Twenty*, London, 1968, developed from two television programmes he prepared on homosexuality in 1964 and 1965.

8. Peter G. Richards, *Parliament and Conscience*, London, 1970, p. 82.

9. Grey, 'Homosexual Law Reform', p. 45.

10. Richards, *Parliament and Conscience*, p. 84.

11. Quoted in Hyde, *The Other Love*, p. 303. For a discussion of the limitations of the Act, see Jack Babuscio, *We Speak for Ourselves*, London, 1976, pp. 46ff. Between 1967 and 1972, according to the annual volumes of Criminal Statistics, the number of offences of buggery and attempted buggery 'known to the police' and 'cleared up' declined, as did the number of those convicted. But offences of indecency between males increased, over the same period, from 444 convicted in 1967 to 1,137 in 1971, an increase of 160 per cent. See 'Tom Harper on the State of the Law' (an article reproduced from the *Listener*) in *Lunch*, No. 22, November 1973, p. 26.

12. Grey, 'Homosexual Law Reform', p. 50.

13. Quoted in Richards, *Parliament and Conscience*, p. 54.

14. Quoted in Arno Karlen, *Sexuality and Homosexuality*, London, 1971, p. 459.

15. Quoted in Charlotte Wolff, *Love Between Women*, London, 1971, p. 112. On the absence of literature, see Chapter 7 above; and see also

Dolores Klaich, *Woman plus Woman: Attitudes towards Lesbianism*, New York, 1974.

16. The two quotations are from Elizabeth Wilson's article, 'Gayness and Liberalism' in *Conditions of Illusion: Papers from the Women's Movement*, Leeds, 1974, p. 114.
17. Wolff, *Love Between Women*, pp. 78, 162, 19.
18. Peter Wildeblood, *Against the Law*, Harmondsworth, 1957, p. 39. Plummer, *Queer People*, pp. 51ff., describes the discreet 'membership only' gay club.
19. Kenneth Plummer makes this point in *Sexual Stigma*, London, 1975, p. 226, n. 18.
20. Roger Baker, in *Spartacus*, No. 23, p. 6.
21. See Hyde, *The Other Love*, p. 311.
22. Letter from Horsfall, *New Statesman*, 8 October 1976, p. 481; Minutes of the Committee, 15 June 1967.
23. Hyde, *The Other Love*, p. 37.
24. Hyde, *The Other Love*, p. 308. The Albany Trust conducted a postal survey of the social needs of homosexuals between Summer 1969 and February 1970: see Plummer, *Sexual Stigma*, p. 216, n. 15. For a polemical commentary on the findings, see *The Joke's Over*, a Gayprints and Ratstudies pamphlet, London, 1973.
25. Karlen, *Sexuality and Homosexuality*, p. 539.

## Part Five: The Gay Liberation Movement

*Chapter 16*
1. Ray Gosling in Trafalgar Square, 23 November 1975.
2. Dennis Altman, 'The Homosexual Movement in America and its Relationship to Other American Movements', *GLP* No. 5 (Sydney), November–December 1974, p. 5.
3. *Fag Rag/Gay Sunshine*, special joint edition, Summer 1974, p. 3.
4. Carl Wittman, *A Gay Manifesto*, San Francisco, 1970; Diggers, quoted in Aubrey Walter and David Fernbach, 'Sexism: Male Ego-tripping: Reactionary Left Politics', *7 Days*, No. 14, 2–8 February 1972, p. 22. They saw GLF as embodying all that was positive in the counter-culture.
5. Dennis Altman, *Homosexual: Oppression and Liberation*, London, 1973, pp. 105, 110.
6. Laurence Collinson, *Lunch*, No. 5, January 1972.
7. Andrew Hodges and David Hutter, *With Downcast Gays*, Pomegranate Press pamphlet, London, 1974, p. 37.
8. See *The Gay Liberation Front Demands*, London, GLF leaflet, 1970.
9. Alex Slater in *Come Together*, No. 14. For a representative 'coming-out' account, see Angus Suttie, 'From Latent to Blatant', *Gay Left*, No. 2, Spring 1976. Sometimes it became gay chauvinist: 'Gay is much better than straight and *not* just as good as' (Aubrey, in *Come Together*, 6).
10. 'We're Coming Out Proud', *Come Together*, 1.
11. *Come Together*, 6, p. 4.

266      *Notes and References*

12. GLF leaflet, February 1971.
13. Camden GLF News, 2 March 1972.
14. *Guardian*, 7 September 1971.
15. *People*, 27 December 1970.
16. *Come Together*, 4. The demo was on 4 February 1971; Aubrey, quoted in *7 Days*, 6, 1–7 December 1971, p. 14.
17. Camden GLF Newssheet, 24 May 1972; see also GLF Calendar, N.D. (August 1972).
18. *Come Together*, 2.
19. London GLF *Manifesto*, 1971, pp. 2, 7.
20. GLF handout, June 1972.
21. Personal information. The Counter-Psychiatry Group issued a number of printed handouts including 'Oh What a Lovely Lovely Book', with telling quotes from the book.
22. 'Towards a Revolutionary Gay Liberation Front' was submitted as an article to the Media Workshop in October 1971, and rejected on the grounds that it was élitist and pseudo-revolutionary; spurious grounds, considering the nature of the response from media workshop, which was moving rapidly towards a form of radical feminism. But it caused a furious row, which clearly prefigured the demise of GLF as a political unit in London.
23. There is a report of the split in *Ink*, 29, 25 February 1972, p. 5.
24. *Come Together*, 10, p. 6.
25. Jeffrey Weeks, 'Ideas of Gay Liberation', *Gay News*, No. 6, 1972, p. 6.
26. GLF *Manifesto*, p. 14. For articles on communes, see 'Gay Family', *Gay International News*, 5, November/December 1972, p. 6; also *7 Days*, 15–21 March 1972. The apotheosis of commune ideology can be seen in *Come Together*, 16, Notting Hill edition. For experiences of commune living, and the problems, see Keith Birch, 'A Commune Experiment', *Gay Left*, 2, Spring 1976, pp. 11–12.
27. See Elizabeth Wilson, 'Libertarianism: Ideas in the Void', *Red Rag*, 4, p. 7.
28. See 'Ideas of Gay Liberation', *Gay News*, No. 6. The debate in GLF can be followed in a number of handouts distributed at the time, of which I have copies. Of particular importance are 'Gay Activism and Gay Liberation; a message to Gay Brothers', 11 February 1972, by Aubrey Walter and David Fernbach, distributed at the Lancaster think-in, February 1972; and a rebuttal from a small socialist grouping, 'Radical Feminism and the Gay Movement', signed by Jeffrey Weeks, Mary McIntosh, Nettie Pollard and Paul Bunting.
29. See *The Times*, 10 September 1971: 'Uproar at Central Hall'; and *Guardian*, 10 September 1971: 'Demonstrations during Festival of Light'. The 'Underground' held an 'alternative Festival of Life' meeting in late September in Hyde Park. GLF was an enthusiastic supporter. 'Operation Rupert' was the cover-all name under which the counter-culture organized its opposition to the Festival of Light. See 'Darkness in our Light', *Guardian*, 11 September 1971. For an example of the demented 'liberalism' that equated gay liberation with psychopathology, see David Holbrook's letter to the *Guardian*, 28 September 1972.

*Chapter 17*

1. Letter from Paul Temperton, headed, aptly enough, 'Nothing queer about CHE', *Guardian*, 17 April 1971. For similar attitudes, see Ian Harvey, 'The Homosexual Plight', *New Statesman*, 9 April 1971, and a reply from members of GLF, *New Statesman*, 23 April 1971.
2. Most of the following information is drawn from the *Leeds Broadsheet*, 3 December 1971. The *Broadsheet* was an attempt between 1971 and 1974 to provide a monthly list of gay movement activities. Under-capitalized (though the Albany Trust once gave it a grant), a duplicated work, it became redundant as *Gay News* grew more successful. The Leeds GLF was one of the liveliest groups outside London.
3. For the situation in Ireland in 1975, see *Gay News*, 48, pp. 5, 6. *Gay News* throughout 1976 carried stories about police harassment of gays in the North of Ireland.
4. *Gay News*, 31, p. 6.
5. *Bulletin*, April–May 1973. By 1976, CHE's membership was *c.* 5,000.
6. For comments on 'The Lessons of Burnley', see CHE's *Bulletin*, July–August 1971.
7. *Lunch*, 3 November 1971.
8. See Liz Stanley's piece, *Bulletin*, July 1972.
9. The Malvern conference was held on 24–7 May 1974. For a full report, see *Gay News*, 48, pp. 1, 3–6. On the 1975 conference, see John Lindsay, 'Sheffield Incident', *Gay Left*, No. 2, Spring 1976; and his article on the Southampton Conference, 'All At Sea', *Out*, No. 1, September 1976. Glenys Parry, chairwoman at Southampton, echoed the disillusionment. CHE was afraid of 'debates, ideologies and principles' – *Guardian*, June 1976.
10. *Annual Report*, 1975, p. 1.
11. *Sappho*, vol. 4, No. 3, 1975. A National Women's Conference on Homosexuality was organized by Glenys Parry and Liz Stanley of CHE in Manchester, in January 1973 (see *Gay News*, 17). A pamphlet, *Women Together* (CHE Activist Paper No. 1), was produced, sum-marizing some of the discussion. Though this was important in itself, little seems to have flowed from it.
12. For early attitudes of the women's movement, see *Come Together*, 7, 'Women's Issue', and an article by Elizabeth Wilson in *Red Rag*, 6. *Spare Rib* carried regular news items and articles which illustrate the developing relationship. On *Sappho*, see *Gay Week*, 15, 18–24 November 1976, p. 4.
13. See *Spare Rib*, 50, September 1976, pp. 6–8.
14. *Gay News*, 90, has an account of the conference, as does *Spare Rib*, 46, May 1976.
15. For details on the August Trust, see *Gay News*, 100.
16. Jack Babuscio's book, *We Speak for Ourselves: Experiences in Homo-sexual Counselling*, London, 1976, gives an account of the kinds of issue that confronted helpers and the approach that organizations like Friend adopted. Babuscio was for a time London Organizer of Friend.
17. *AT Work*, 1, p. 2. Antony Grey always made clear his disagreement with the philosophy that only gays could help gays (see *Lunch*, 18,

March 1973, pp. 6–7). Icebreakers responded: 'Icebreakers Reply to Attack by Albany Trust', press statement issued October 1976.

18. *Come Together*, 12 reports on the conference.
19. Jack Babuscio discusses some of the problems of gay Christians, in *We Speak for Ourselves*, pp. 74–92. See also Sara Coggin, *Sexual Expression and Moral Chaos*, first pamphlet of the Gay Christian Movement, 1976. For Crockford's see 'Control Urged on Gay Clergy', *Guardian*, 17 November 1976.
20. David Seligman describes its evolution in *After Lunch*, 1, Summer 1976, p. 34.
21. *Gay News*, 1. The original collective, already changed by No. 1, consisted of Martin R. Corbett, David Seligman, Peter Reed, Denis Lemon, Gerald Wheatley, Sylvia Room, Glenys Parry, Andrew Lumsden, Suki Pitcher.
22. *Gay News*, 25, p. 12.
23. *Gay News*, 25, which dates this change from issue 16.
24. David Fernbach, 'Gay Liberation: Capitalist Style', *Gay Marxist*, 3, October 1973, p. 37.
25. 'Within These Walls', *Gay Left*, No. 2, Spring 1976.
26. See *Ink*, 23, 3 December 1971, for a feature on Rachel and Edith. See also *Gay Sunshine*, 21 (San Francisco), Spring 1974.
27. *Transvestism and Transsexualism in Modern Society*, Conference Report of the First National TV/TS Conference, held at Leeds, 15–17 March 1974. For some of the problems of coming out as a transsexual, see *Come Together*, 14, 1972. See also Mike Brake, 'I May Be a Queer, But At Least I am a Man', in D. L. Barker and Sheila Allen (eds.), *Sexual Division and Society: Process and Change*, London, 1976.
28. Sven Hansen and Jasper Jensen, *The Little Red School-book*, Stage 1, 1971, p. 103. See the 'Appeal to Youth' in *Come Together*, 8, published for the GLF Youth Rally, 28 August 1971.
29. See her speech to the CHE Morecambe Conference, quoted in *Gay News*, 21.
30. *Sunday People*, 25 May 1975. For the inevitable consequences of this type of unprincipled witchhunt, see *South London Press*, 30 May 1975: 'Bricks hurled at "sex-ring" centre house', describing an attack on one of the addresses named in the *Sunday People* article.
31. There is a brief note on PIE's questionnaire in *New Society*, vol. 38, No. 736, 11 November 1976, p. 292 ('Taboo Tabled').
32. So far as jobs are concerned, one could cite cases at random for 1976: Tony Whitehead, sacked by British Home Stores after appearing briefly on a Southern Television programme on homosexuality (*Gay News*, 89); Ian Davies, refused permission by Tower Hamlets Council to return to his own job after a minor offence (*Gay News*, 92); or Louise Boychuk, sacked for wearing a 'Lesbians ignite' badge at work (*Gay News*, 107, p. 1). Louise also had to endure the moralizing of the Chairman of the Industrial Tribunal examining her case, who quoted from Genesis. For custody cases, see *Gay News*, 107.

*Chapter 18*
1. *Gay News*, 99.

2. I have to declare an interest here: I was a founder member of the *Gay Left* collective in 1975, and a frequent contributor.
3. The Communist Party's paper, *Morning Star*, gave frequent coverage to homosexuality. For the fullest discussion, see Brian Allbutt, 'The Politics of Personal Liberation', *Morning Star*, 11 October 1976. *Socialist Worker* published a few short articles in 1974–6, and a number of letters, together with its regular statement in 'What We Stand For' in *Socialist Worker*, from Autumn 1976. See also Rosalind Davis, 'Gay Liberation and the Left', *Red Mole*, 20 January 1973, for earlier International Marxist Group views.
4. *Socialist Review*, December 1957, republished in a collection of articles. *A Socialist Review* (*International Socialism, 1965*), London, 1965. Bob Cant has given the fullest account of the gay group in 'A Grim Tale: The I.S. Gay Group 1972–75', in *Gay Left*, 3, Autumn 1976. The quotations are from this article.
5. The fullest debates seem to have taken place in socialist groups in the United States, especially in the International Socialists and the Socialist Workers' Party. The Socialist Workers' debate is the best recorded, and shows a similar pattern of an initial reluctance to accept the issue as relevant, followed by a debate encouraged by the enthusiasm of gay comrades, followed by the formal adoption by the leadership of liberal, minimal positions which effectively stilled further debate. For an account of this, see David Thorstad, 'Gays vs SWP', *Gay Liberator* (Detroit), December 1974–January 1975; and *Gay Liberation and Socialism. Documents from the Discussion on Gay Liberation inside the Socialist Workers' Party (1970–1973)*, selected, introduced, and with commentary by David Thorstad, New York, 1976.
6. Jeffrey Weeks, 'Where Engels Feared to Tread', *Gay Left*, 1, Autumn 1975, p. 3.
7. 'Stand Together' by Bradford GLF, on Chebel Records.

# Index

Charlotte Wolff
BISEXUALITY
A Study

'It's worth noting the pioneer status of Charlotte Wolff's latest book: it is, quite simply, the first extensive study of bisexuality . . . undeniably a major work, and, as an exercise in applied humanism as well as perceptive and forcefully argued sexual psychology, it fully deserves the seminal influence it should quickly accumulate. Not least of its achievements is a style that bridges the layman and professional approach' Mike Sanderson, *Psychology Today*

'Wolff's study is an important follow-up to her *Love Between Women* and makes a valuable contribution to the study of sexuality . . . it indicates the possibility of a sane, non-sexist future' Trevor Jones, *Tribune*

£1.95
ISBN 0 7043 3253 1

Tom Driberg
RULING PASSIONS

The original William Hickey of the *Daily Express,* Labour Cabinet Minister, *Ruling Passions* is Tom Driberg's posthumous autobiography.

'What is now printed is what Tom wrote . . . What had bothered his friends, and what Tom was determined not to modify, was the defiant – you could call it crusading – exposition and defence of homosexuality: its pleasures, its dangers, its right to be practised, its case against discrimination' David Higham, Tom Driberg's literary executor.

'But there's no doubt how seriously to take the homosexuality. This was *the* ruling passion of Driberg's life . . . Everything relating to this is brilliantly and, I would judge, honestly written . . . He recollects best what is most personal' Paul Barker, *The Times*

'There is no great bitterness in what Tom Driberg has written. The story is unfolded in that scalding prose style for which he was renowned, with wit, with much dramatic incident, and with a strange dignity' Michael Mason, *Gay News*

'A classic of its kind' Alan Watkins, *Spectator*

£2.95
ISBN 0 7043 3223 X